THE DEAL
CHURCHILL, TRUMAN, AND STALIN REMAKE THE WORLD

Charles L. Mee Jr.

ACKNOWLEDGMENTS

I must acknowledge great debts to the late Charles Bohlen, Robert Murphy, W. Averell Harriman, Eugene List, James Tuthill, Lord Avon, Joan Bright Astley, Lord Gladwyn, and Sir William Hayter for their help in clarifying both the issues and particular moments at Potsdam; to my editor Herb Katz, who had the original inspiration for this book, and on whom I relied throughout its writing; to Kaethe Ellis for her help with research in the United States; to Sarah Waters for her work in the British archives and the lively reports of her conversations with members of the British delegation and their friends and with English journalists; to the staffs of the British Foreign Office archives, the Nalional Archives in Washington, and the Truman Library in Missouri;

to J. Muriel Vrotsos for her unstinting assistance both in research and in the organization of the research and for her help in arranging all my travels to Moscow, London, Washington, and Potsdam; to Suzi Mee, who helped to guide me, chapter by chapter, in the earliest stages of the conception of the book; to Lounsbury Bates, the Librarian of the Harvard Club of New York City, where much of the book was written; to Professor Harold Poor of Rutgers University and E. M. Halliday of American Heritage magazine for their painstaking criticisms of the original draft of the manuscript; to Priscilla Flood, whose sensitivity to nuance saved me from many mistakes; and to Audre Proctor, who refined a typescript from scribblings.

—C.L.M.

IN MEMORIAM

Allie Pratt Lowe, who liked a good story

PROLOGUE

For two weeks in the summer of 1945, from July 17 to August 2, Harry Truman, Winston Churchill, and Joseph Stalin gathered to reconstruct the world out of the ruins left by the Second World War. They met "only a few miles," as President Truman noted, "from the war-shattered seat of Nazi power" — around a baize-covered table in the Cecilienhof Palace at Potsdam, a suburb of Berlin, a place they later remembered vividly for its hardy mosquitoes and muggy heat.

The Big Three emerged from the war with naturally divergent interests, inherently conflicting ambitions, and fundamentally different political systems and beliefs. Most nations, most of the time, have naturally — perhaps even inevitably — divergent interests that have been shaped by their histories, their economic needs, their military power, their political ideals, and their fears. It is the business of diplomacy to ease or to exacerbate those differences — depending on whether the goal is cooperation or hostility.

During the war, the Big Three had held two major conferences, at Teheran in November 1943 and at Yalta in February 1945. Both of those conferences are usually regarded as successful meetings: Roosevelt, Churchill, and Stalin engaged in cordial horse trading and kept their military alliance together in order to prosecute the war against Germany. Roosevelt has since been criticized for being too generous to Stalin at Yalta, but the Yalta meeting nonetheless succeeded in its principal purpose. It seemed, moreover, that the harmony developed among the Allies during the wartime conferences might endure in the postwar world and so act as a good influence for world peace. At the conclusion of the Yalta conference, *Time* magazine reported, "All doubts about the Big Three's ability to cooperate in peace as well as in war seem to have been swept away."

At Potsdam, however, the doubts returned quite forcibly. Most of the issues were the same as they had been at the previous conferences — questions of how to treat Germany, conflicts of aims in eastern Europe, disputes over territorial claims — but most of the diplomacy was different. In the course of this last of the Big Three conferences, conflicts were not resolved but were rather intensified; customary diplomatic suppleness vanished; rhetoric was inflamed; and stubbornness and aggressiveness were elevated to a level of national policy.

Because Allied harmony ended at Potsdam, because the conference did not ensure a generation of peace, it is commonly considered a "failure," and so a minor episode in international diplomacy. We imagine, most of us, that victorious leaders gather at the end of a war to guarantee future peace. And so we cannot imagine, most of us, why our postwar political architects left us with a struggle over a divided Germany and over eastern Europe, with Russian-American conflict extended over most of the earth, with threats and fears amidst a nuclear arms race, and with occasional "minor" wars with major casualties. Somehow, it would seem, Potsdam failed.

To explain how the Big Three took the world so unerringly into new hostilities, some historians have pointed to worldwide Russian aggressiveness; leftist revisionists have divined an aggressive imperialism inherent in American capitalism; economists have perceived a natural competition for trade and raw materials; military strategists have written of the power vacuum left by the devastation of western Europe and of the inevitable tendency of powerful nations to fill such vacuums; others have discovered a naïveté in the American character, an inability to cope with the nasty power politics of the Old World and a wish to find security by projecting a provincial American image of democratic liberalism around the globe.

None of these explanations is entirely satisfactory, and each is flawed by the assumption that men sought peace only to be overwhelmed by forces beyond their control. Unhappily, the story of the Potsdam conference will not support that comforting view of good intentions thwarted by irresistible forces.

Instead, the conference exhibits three men who were intent upon increasing the power of their countries and of themselves and who perceived that they could enhance their power more certainly in a world of discord than of tranquility. Thus, in the transcripts of the formal meetings of the conference, in the notes of the informal chats, in the recollections of dinner parties, in the jokes and the laughter, in the reports of Churchill's dreams and nightmares, the offhand remarks of Harry Truman, and in Stalin's cool dissembling, we see three men who took the stuff of historical forces, of natural international conflict, of differing political and economic needs, and shaped them into the stuff of casus belli. At the end of the conference they did not write the peace agreement that the press anticipated; rather, they signed what amounted to a tripartite declaration of the Cold War. How they rescued discord from the threatened outbreak of peace is the story of this book.

Meeting at Potsdam

1
TRUMAN

"I am getting ready to go see Stalin and Churchill," President Truman wrote to his mother on July 3, "and it is a chore. I have to take my tuxedo, tails... high hat, top hat, and hard hat as well as sundry other things. I have a briefcase all filled up with information on past conferences and suggestions on what I'm to do and say. Wish I didn't have to go but I do and it can't be stopped now."

At six in the morning on July 7, Truman stepped briskly off a special train onto pier number 6 at Newport News, Virginia, and was piped aboard the cruiser S.S. Augusta. The President was surrounded by an entourage of advisers, old friends, and Secret Service men. They headed first for the mess, for breakfast. Afterward, the President — wearing a jaunty cap, a polka-dotted bow tie, and two-toned brown-and-white summer shoes — clambered up to the flag bridge with his party following after. At 6:55 the President ordered the *Augusta* to get under way, and the ship set out for Antwerp under a clear sky, on a smooth sea, with a balmy 79-degree breeze at 23 knots.

"The first impression that one gets of a ruler and of his brains," Machiavelli wrote, "is from seeing the men that he has about him. When they are competent and faithful one can always consider him wise, as he has been able to recognize their ability and keep them faithful. But when they are the reverse, one can always form an unfavorable opinion of him, because the first mistake that he makes is in making this choice." Standing closest to Truman on the bridge were his new Secretary of State, James F. Byrnes, and his military adviser, Admiral William D. Leahy.

Jimmy Byrnes was regarded, according to *Time* magazine, as "the politicians' politician." Joseph Alsop and Robert Kintner described him as "a small, wiry, neatly made man, with an odd, sharply angular face from which his sharp eyes peer out with an expression of quizzical geniality." He was considered sly by his enemies, "able" by his friends. Born in 1879, he had made his way up from a poor childhood in a "little, sagginggalleried frame house in King Street" in old Charleston, South Carolina. By 1910 he was in Congress. "I campaigned on nothing but gall," he said, "and gall won by 57 votes." His first accomplishment in Congress was to force the formation of the House Committee on Roads, one of the greatest patronage dispensaries of our century. By the time of World War I, he was a member of the House Appropriations Committee, one of a select few who held the nation's purse strings. He was elected to the Senate in 1930, and *Time* observed that Roosevelt never "lost in the Senate on an important bill when Senator Byrnes was with him; almost never has he won when Senator Byrnes was against him." As Alsop and Kintner said, "To see him at his best, he must be watched getting McNary's promise not to object, conciliating the prideful House leaders and craftily waiting his chance on the Senate floor to drive one of the great defense [spending] bills to immediate passage."

"A vigorous extrovert, accustomed to the lusty exchanges of South Carolina politics," Dean Acheson said, "Mr. Byrnes is not sensitive or lacking in confidence." To this insensitive overconfidence, Byrnes added a broad ignorance of foreign countries. The result was that the career men in the State Department scorned him for his lack of cultivation — and quite forgot his formidable powers as a fixer.

Byrnes and Truman had been passably good friends until the recent summer of 1944. That summer, President Roosevelt had permitted rumors to circulate that he might favor dumping Vice President Henry Wallace from the coming reelection campaign. Byrnes pushed forward as a Vice Presidential candidate and, shortly before the convention in Chicago, telephoned to ask Truman to put his name up for nomination. Truman agreed — and later insisted he had no idea his own friends were pressing Roosevelt to endorse Truman himself. Byrnes arrived in Chicago convinced the nomination was his. Truman arrived and was called into a meeting with Robert Hannegan, a political manager from Truman's home state of Missouri, who that year — with Truman's backing — had been made National Chairman of the Democratic party. With Hannegan were Frank Walker, "tight-lipped as an earthworm," who was Postmaster General and Hannegan's predecessor as Democratic National Chairman, and three of the party's "big bosses" — Hague of Jersey City, Kelly of Chicago, and Flynn of the Bronx. At the end of the meeting, so the story goes, Hannegan got President Roosevelt on the phone to persuade the reluctant Truman to take the nomination. "Tell him if he wants to break up the Democratic party in the middle of a war," Roosevelt is said to have said to the bosses, and, by implication, to the convention, Jimmy Byrnes, and history, "that's his responsibility."

Byrnes fled Chicago, bewildered, humiliated, and enraged. When Roosevelt died on April 12, 1945, and Truman called Byrnes to Washington to serve as Secretary of State, the new President thought this favor would somehow balance things out. Perhaps Byrnes did not quite see it that way. Some thought Byrnes felt he had been cheated of the Presidency; Acheson said that Byrnes treated Truman — or that Truman thought Byrnes treated him — with "the attitude of the leader of the Senate to a freshman senator." But Byrnes himself insisted he harbored no "ill feelings toward Mr. Truman, whose position I fully understood." Whatever their feelings for one another, Byrnes and Truman spoke the same language and had much the same understanding of the workings of politics.

Admiral William D. Leahy was born in Iowa in 1875 and graduated from the United States Naval Academy in 1897. His career sounds oddly like that of a British imperial admiral. He first saw service in the Spanish-American War during the Philippine insurrection. He was chief of staff of the occupation of Nicaragua in 1912 and of the Haitian campaign in 1916. He was in command of the *U.S.S.* Dolphin in the Mexican Punitive Expedition of 1916, and when he retired from the Navy in 1939 he was appointed governor of Puerto Rico by President Roosevelt.

He was a tall, erect man, balding and with bushy eyebrows, a strict disciplinarian who was easygoing off duty. He called his memoirs *I Was There*, as indeed he was, standing just behind President Roosevelt and President Truman at conferences, receptions, dinners, in map rooms and airplanes, on shipboard, and in ceremonial photographs. And yet, despite his ubiquitousness, Leahy never quite seemed to perceive all that was going on around him. He was the last man around the White House to get the message about Byrnes. At the time of the Democratic convention, Leahy was sitting, as usual, next to Roosevelt — this time on a Presidential train journey — when Roosevelt mentioned that Truman was to be his Vice Presidential running mate. "Who the hell is Harry Truman?" the Admiral asked.

If Leahy was not always the first to get the word, he was the last to forget it, and he served throughout the war years as the clearinghouse for military information. Although Leahy might sometimes appear the buffoon, his command of mundane facts was dependable and serviceable, and his predilection for straightforward military solutions was, by virtue of its predictability, easy for Truman to evaluate. The Admiral possessed, too, the quality that politicians prize above all others: Leahy was unfailingly loyal to his commander in chief. Others — more sophisticated, more daring, or merely flashier — might come and go; Leahy never left Truman's side.

Not far away on the bridge stood Brigadier General Harry Vaughan, the President's personal rascal. A bluff, five-foot-eleven-inch, 216-pound, backslapping, poker-playing practical joker, Vaughan never got over Missouri politics. In the White House he indulged a style of petty, bargain-basement influence peddling that was, finally, so naïve as to be charming. While billion-dollar contracts were let on all sides, Vaughan courted perfume manufacturers. Whenever a minor embarrassment was exposed in the newspapers, the word went around the White House, "Cherchez le Vaughan."

At the moment, Vaughan had two deals working. On May 1, he had written — on White House stationery — a letter of introduction for David A. Bennett, owner of Albert Verley and Company, perfume manufacturers, noting that Mr. Bennett was "entitled to the courtesies of American officials abroad." Mr. Bennett brought back forty-one kilos of perfume essence from abroad — by way of a free ride from Air Transport Command.

A friend of a friend of Bennett's looked to the future and thought he might build a bit of goodwill toward his fruit freezer business. In June, he sent freezers worth 390 dollars each to Harry Vaughan and to Truman's wife in Independence, Missouri. While Vaughan and the President stood on the bridge of the S.S. *Augusta,* freezers were on their way to Presidential aides James K. Vardaman and Matthew Connelly. Several days later, as the *Augusta* approached the end of its voyage, overhead the Air Transport Command would be flying a few more of the boys from Albert Verley and Company to Europe to make a deal on "essence of orange" for the perfume factory.

Truman met Vaughan when they served together in World War I, and in 1940 then Colonel Vaughan joined Truman's campaign for reelection to the Senate. "We wanted somebody for treasurer and somebody with a name or a title," one of the campaign managers said, "so we hit on Harry Vaughan, who had the title of colonel and was then selling loose-leaf book equipment in Illinois...." From then on, Vaughan and Truman were inseparable pals. Vaughan was the first to see the President in the morning, he attended the daily staff conferences, often had lunch with the President, swam with him in the afternoon, and, as court jester, kept the President amused. When inspiration flagged, Vaughan would bring out the cards for poker and regale the inner circle with reminiscences of the early days, such as the time he let loose a steer in the lobby of the Baltimore Hotel back in Kansas City, or stopped traffic at the corner of Twelfth and Baltimore Streets by staging a huge crap game in the intersection. Old Harry Vaughan, he was a hell of a good fellow. As Vaughan said of one of his own chums and business associates (convicted of perjury several years later), "Maragon is a lovable sort of chap. You can't get mad at him."

Of the other close friends of the President aboard the *Augusta*, Matthew J. Connelly (who was about to be the recipient of a fruit freezer) had been the chief of the investigating staff of a Truman committee set up to look into war contracts; James K. Vardaman (another on the fruit freezer list) went back to Missouri political days; Fred Canfil, a Secret Service man, was another Missouri operative and later a congressional investigator; Charlie Ross, the President's press secretary, was a childhood friend from Independence — a gray-haired, stoop-shouldered man with a dignified bearing, whom Truman lured away from an editorial job at the St. Louis *Post-Dispatch*. They all, evidently, played poker.

It is a rare prince who, like Shakespeare's Hal, can bear to rid himself of his Falstaffs, Bardolphs, Pistols, Shallows, and Snares. And, to be sure, not all of Truman's intimates were comic characters. How much influence they exercised over Presidential decisions is a moot question. "I don't suppose anyone gives him more advice than I do," Vaughan said, "or has less of it used." The President had his experts — career State Department men, economists, area specialists — and he studied their advice avidly. He was a voracious reader. He could read, he said, when he was four years old, and he went straight through the family Bible twice. It was said that he had read all 3, 000 volumes in the Independence public library "including the encyclopedias." According to Leahy, "he was amazingly well informed on military history, from the campaigns of the ancients such as Hannibal and Caesar down to the great global conflict into which he suddenly had been thrust in virtual supreme command. He absorbed very quickly the gist of the dispatches brought to his attention in our daily conferences and frequently he would go to the Map Room to discuss some particular development."

Still, to get some notion how close the President felt to the experts available to him, one need only scan the memoirs of a career man such as Charles Bohlen. Bohlen, too, was on board the *Augusta*. Born in New York, the handsome, suave son of a well-known sportsman, Bohlen graduated from St. Paul's School, and then Harvard, where he was a member of the Porcellian Club. He played tennis, wondered about his future, joined the State Department, and, in 1929, was assigned by the Department to Prague. In 1934, he was sent to Moscow, where he learned to speak Russian "like a Muscovite." Roosevelt took Bohlen to the wartime Big Three conferences to serve as his interpreter. Aboard the *Augusta*, Bohlen was doubtless the best-informed man on Russia and eastern Europe. Yet Bohlen rarely sat in on conferences with the President. Bohlen's most exciting moment on the voyage was the time he watched the *Augusta's* crew hold target practice. "Truman and Secretary Byrnes were standing on a three-gun turret when it fired a salvo. Two of the guns went off properly. The third gave a sort of belch, and a shell eased out of the muzzle and fell into the water a hundred yards or so from the ship. Actually, there was no danger, because the shells carried no warheads."

On important matters, for gut reactions, for political advice of the sort he wanted, Truman turned to men like Byrnes, Connelly, Ross, Vardaman, Canfil — and even Vaughan. Bohlen didn't play poker. Nor, presumably, did H. Freeman Matthews, chief of the European division of the State Department. Matthews, age forty-six, was a graduate of the Gilman Country School, Princeton, and l'École Libre des Sciences Politiques in Paris; his presence aboard the *Augusta* was so unnoticeable that some accounts say he went separately to Potsdam by plane.

Truman himself had grown up in the land of Huck Finn and Jesse James where questions of honor and integrity, of promises kept and broken, of political power and influence, were not abstractions but matters of his family's farm mortgage being foreclosed, of his eighty-eight-year-old mother moved out with the furniture, of the feel of roads laid out by the Ready-Mixed Concrete Company, of the look on the face of an ex-partner in the savings and loan business whom Truman helped send to the penitentiary, of the cash take of a slot machine under the protection of Tom Pendergast, the Kansas City boss who, as Jonathan Daniels said, "knocked out the only man who ever knocked out Jack Dempsey."

No one has ever turned up evidence that Truman was personally involved in the assorted crimes of the Kansas City machine. But, as a Missouri politician, as "the senator from Pendergast," he certainly observed Pendergast's full repertoire. We should not be distracted by all the tales of gambling, graft, rackets, bootleg liquor, brothels, and shakedowns. All of that is the sideshow of politics; the point of politics is the acquiring, the holding, and the disposing of power. As Pendergast practiced it, politics is the art of trading nothing — money, liquor, or whores — in return for something in the way of power.

By tradition, Missouri was divided into two turfs, or spheres of influence — an eastern sphere, run from St. Louis by Mayor Bernard Dickmann, and a western sphere, run from Kansas City by Tom Pendergast. In 1934 Dickmann put up a candidate for the Senate in Pendergast's territory. Pendergast's machine had recently been subjected to a bad press. During the previous summer gangster Frank Nash and three federal men who were taking Nash off to Leavenworth were machine-gunned to death in the

Union Station Massacre. In the midst of the 1934 primaries Big Tom's head "enforcer," Johnny Lazia, king of the Kansas City rackets, was murdered by shotgun as he was getting out of his car. No one quite knows what all the fuss was about or just what it settled; but, in any case, Big Tom survived the strife and the attendant bad press and got his man elected to the Senate — Harry Truman.

No one called Big Tom Pendergast an idealist, or an ideologue, or an altruist. No one thought he ever did anything for anyone's interest but his very own. No one thought he had any sense of scruples, or that he intended to honor his word a moment longer than it suited his needs. No one ever thought you could make a dime with Big Tom through personal diplomacy, or that there was anything much to "cooperating" with Big Tom. Nor did anyone imagine that Tom Pendergast preferred peace to the ceaseless jostling, deal-making, and discord through which he increased his political power. On the other hand, no one thought Big Tom was an evil or godless man. A sphere of influence was only that; it was not a moral crusade, or a conspiracy against the world. It was simply the assumed base of power politics, to be preserved at all costs — and enlarged if possible. Big Tom kept his word after a fashion. He went to church. He drove a hard bargain, and then, if it did him any good, he kept it.

Josef Stalin, Truman said after he met the Generalissimo at Potsdam, "was as near like Tom Pendergast as any man I know."

Truman played poker almost every night with his friends aboard the *Augusta*. Every night, after dinner, the Navy men and bureaucrats sat down to watch movies in the wardroom: *The Princess and the Pirate, The Corn Is Green,* A *Song to Remember, To the Shores of Iwo Jima.* And, as the official logbook discreetly put it, the President "was called out early and did not return to see the entire feature," or "the President did not attend, as he stated he planned to turn in early."

During the days, Truman briskly walked the decks, inspecting the ship, as Admiral Leahy said, "from the bridge to the bilges." Truman had not traveled abroad since he had been posted to France in World War I, and the occasional photographs taken of the President on the deck of the *Augusta* show the broad grin of a man who was having a wonderful time. His political habits called him to dinner in the officers' mess, the warrant officers' mess, the petty officers' mess, and the crew's mess, and in the remaining hours, Leahy said, the President "squeezed facts and opinions out of us all day long. " As his starting point, Truman used a briefing book that was composed of papers prepared by the State Department. The daily conferences, sometimes twice-daily conferences, were usually restricted to Truman, Leahy, and

Byrnes. Byrnes might consult Bohlen or Matthews on his own time; Truman might spend his evenings at poker with Harry Vaughan and James Vardaman; but the conferences themselves were tight little meetings. They reviewed, among other things, thoughts like these:

"The foreign policy of any country," as Roosevelt's old counselor Joseph Davies wrote in a memo to James Byrnes, "is nothing more or less than setting rules to govern its relations with nations and people outside of its own borders. The purpose of these rules... is to protect its people from the outside, and then to promote the general welfare of the world and the administration of justice, consistent with its own well-being. The primary concern is to prevent physical invasion, attack, or enslavement. ... The next purpose is to preserve the standard of living and the way of life of its own people." Davies's memo seems modest enough; it advocated mere self-protection, though it is not clear just why self-protection requires a nation "to promote the general welfare of the world." The memo went on to say that "we should declare that the United States will not attempt to impose its political, religious, or social ideologies upon other peoples." Davies read the memo over and realized that this last sentiment was a potent limitation on American involvement in the rest of the world. He picked up his pen and added in a longhand addition to the typescript that American policy "however demands that no aggressor shall impose by internal or external aggression its ideologies upon other nations." Davies's afterthought encapsulated the rationale for American foreign policy for the next several decades.

Americans have traditionally understood themselves to be well-intentioned people, dwelling in a new nation, conceived according to a set of principles of liberty and justice for all that admit of no sacrifice of blood or treasure for venal reasons. We have regarded ourselves as a special people, motivated by ideals that, more than distance or the great oceans, have held us apart from the sordid politics of the Old World from which we fled. We have not believed in wars of conquest; we have not believed that human beings should spill their blood for the sake of good trade agreements or access to raw materials; we have not believed it was good for our liberties or our character to enter entangling foreign alliances or to participate in the dirty expediencies of balance-of-power politics and spheres of influence.

And so, when we took on the postwar mantle of a global power, we designed the United Nations, a liberal democratic gathering of all the great and small nations of the world, dedicated to the peaceful resolution of differences, with liberty and justice for all. The United Nations was the perfect vehicle for us to ride into the world as a global power. The only trouble with the UN was that its professed ideals immediately had to confront some lamentable realities. We wanted, for instance, to do away with the old rivalries for spheres of influence; yet, of course, our State Department recognized that we had a "special relationship" with South America. But, on the other hand, we did not want our own "hemispherical solidarity" to provide Russia with a pretext to claim any "special relationship" with her bordering countries in eastern Europe. At the same time — for Americans focused their attentions on the British as well as on the Russians — it was essential to undermine British attempts to create a western European bloc. The American delegation resolved the dilemma first by outlining a structure that forbade any political or economic blocs and then by drafting Article 51 of the UN Charter, which permitted "collective self-defense" treaties. And thus, over the years, the major powers constructed their spheres of influence by espying threats all over the world and arranging a proliferating series of "collective self-defense" treaties. The campaign for a United Nations organization was begun by Roosevelt; its charter was ratified by the Senate while Truman was at Potsdam; it was conceived with a charter that would in no way interfere with the conduct of power politics; it was, by design, born dead.

Truman viewed history, as indeed most politicians view history, as the actions of men, not as an abstract play of ideas or forces or institutions. He understood Tom Pendergast; he understood political turf; he understood what a fine thing it is to dispose of greater rather than lesser power; and he tended to choose and abandon men as he chose and abandoned their plans. It is interesting that Byrnes and Leahy were always present at the *Augusta* briefing sessions; it is even more interesting that other advisers were entirely absent from the *Augusta's* passenger list.

In addition to the advisers the President ignored, others he positively excluded — or tried to exclude — from Potsdam. To keep Henry Morgenthau away, the President "accepted his resignation" a few days before the *Augusta* sailed. James Forrestal, Secretary of the Navy, was kept out of the delegation, and so he took a European "vacation" and turned up one morning to crash the party. Both Henry Stimson, the Secretary of War, and W. Averell Harriman, who was at the time — the point cannot be too sharply emphasized — ambassador to Moscow, had to invite themselves. Each of these men, by the treatment Truman gave them, provides a clue to the President's developing notions of foreign policy. Each of the men advocated a policy that Truman had decided to reject.

"Henry the Morgue," as Roosevelt called him, had suggested that, in order to prevent Germany from making war ever again, the country should be completely dismembered, "deindustrialized," and converted into a weak, if not prostrate, agricultural nation. The proposal appealed to many people's sense, at the time, of rage and vengefulness. The catch to a permanently prostrate Germany, however, was that it would be a breeding ground for discontent — and an invitation for the Russians to drive into the center of Europe. In the simplest terms, the trick to Germany was to find a way to keep the country sufficiently weak so that it could not cause trouble for any of the other powers — and sufficiently strong to serve as a buffer against the Russians, and, from the Russian point of view, as a buffer against the West. To achieve this delicate balance, each of the Big Three had its own extraordinarily complex combination of plans for reparations, spoils, permissible levels of industry, number of zones to be established, zonal authority, and other devices.

Revenge against Germany was not a practical policy. In some form, the defeated Germans had to be useful to the postwar goals of the Big Three. As Truman said disingenuously, "We intended to make it possible for Germany to develop into a decent nation and to take her place in the civilized world." Morgenthau, still lighting World War II as late as July 1945, was allowed to resign.

It is a remarkable coincidence that all the men President Truman chose to ignore had a common prep school, Ivy League background. Yet the President ignored James V. Forrestal, too; and, although Forrestal had attended Princeton, he'd worked his way through, and before he went to Princeton he had been a public school boy. Forrestal was alarmed by what he took to be Roosevelt's trust in Stalin, and he had a profound fear of making "concessions" to Russia. Suspicious of New Dealers, contemptuous of intellectual "meddlers," Forrestal's nightmare was that capitalism itself was under siege all over the world. During the war his personal files fattened alarmingly — filled with the names of journals and organizations and individuals who were "under Communist influence." Forrestal was a committed, if not over-committed, anti-Communist ideologue and economic imperialist. If Truman would later become a spokesman for an ideology, and a leader of economic imperialism, it is worth remembering that, at the time of Potsdam, the President left Forrestal behind.

W. Averell Harriman was impeccable in most respects. Madeleine Carroll, a movie star of considerable charm, put him on her list of America's ten most handsome men; he had an eight-total rating as a polo player, and he collected French art. He was given a start in business by inheriting 100,000,000 dollars from his father, a railroad man who "feared neither God nor Morgan," and he assumed his father's business interests with apparent skill. He became chairman of the board of

Union Pacific Railroad in 1932, the same year that he became Roosevelt's adviser on railroad policy. He paid his first official visit to Russia in 1941, just after the Germans attacked the Soviet Union, to confer about American aid to Russia.

After meeting with Stalin, Harriman wrote to Roosevelt, "I left feeling that he had been frank with us and if we came through as had been promised and if personal relations were retained with Stalin, the suspicion that had existed between the Soviet Government and our two governments [Britain and America] might well be eradicated." It was on the basis, then, of personal diplomacy and economic assistance — and the promise to open a second military front — that an alliance was built between the United States and Russia. Then, in 1945, with the war in Europe finished, that second military front ceased to be a help to Russia.

As for economic aid, four days after Germany surrendered Truman canceled Lend-Lease aid to Russia without advance warning; ships that had been loaded were unloaded; ships that were steaming toward Russia were called back. As for personal diplomacy, when Roosevelt died, Stalin had made a point of reassuring Harriman that Russia wished "to continue on a cooperative basis" with the United States. If that were the case, Harriman said, Stalin should reconsider a previous decision not to send his foreign minister

Vyacheslav Molotov to a United Nations conference in San Francisco. Stalin reconsidered and sent Molotov to San Francisco. On his way to the west coast, Molotov stopped in Washington to pay his respects to the new President. The President spoke to Molotov, as Truman recalled it, "bluntly," and complained about the way the Polish government was being formed. "I have never been talked to like that in my life," Molotov told Truman. "Carry out your agreements," said the President, "and you won't get talked to like that." Harriman was slow to grasp Truman's intent; and so the ambassador to Moscow had to invite himself to Potsdam.

Harriman was under no illusions that Stalin was America's good friend, and all of his proposals for cooperating with Russia included tough-minded plans for Russian concessions in return, but his policy of cooperation with the Soviet Union was now based only on the two remaining slender supports of economic aid and personal diplomacy.

The difficulty with Henry Stimson was that he couldn't make up his mind. It may be that he perceived that a new policy was in the making, and that he recognized that he did not know what it was. Stimson was by this time very much an elder statesman. He was seventy-seven years old, another of those east coast prep school and Ivy League men (specializing in fox hunting), and was known as "the original anti-appeaser" — an interventionist before most Americans knew there was any place in which to intervene. He served as Secretary of State to Herbert Hoover (he was the first Secretary of State to have a military aide) and was named Secretary of War in 1940 after calling for aid to Britain — to be delivered "in our own ships and under convoy if necessary." In the course of his long career Stimson was characterized as a liberal and a conservative, as a militarist and a pacifist, and sometimes all of these simultaneously. He first advised Roosevelt to take a relaxed attitude toward Russia on central Europe, then he advised Truman to pursue a firm policy, and he no sooner proposed firmness than he began to think, like Harriman, about cooperation.

Stimson was not invited to Potsdam. He invited himself and sailed, full of thoughts and doubts, at the same time the President did, aboard another ship. He no sooner arrived at the conference than he began to pursue the President with yet more second and third thoughts. Stimson is a sympathetic and touching figure at Potsdam. Surrounded by men who were, or seemed, so sure of how to dispose the fates of nations great and small, which lives to spare, which to sacrifice, which men and women to surrender to tyranny, which to use as pawns and counters, Stimson wandered, full of doubt — as most of us would have done. He took no great stand, played no heroic part, made no policies, saved no lives. Perhaps, at last, he was simply overwhelmed by the awesomeness of it all.

When Roosevelt died, his advisers and the career people in the State Department were so busy briefing the new President on what the options had been that they had no time, perhaps no desire, to listen to the neophyte President tell them what the policies would be in the future. It seems never to have occurred to them that Truman would have any ideas of his own. Whether Truman simply did not bother to share his thoughts with the Ivy Leaguers, or whether they could not, or would not, understand when he did, is not clear. It may be that, like Roosevelt, he preferred to string along men such as Forrestal so that he could trot them out later, if and when he found them useful. Some of the men at Potsdam simply did not understand what the President hoped to achieve.

There is always the danger in international relationships — however remote it may seem — that the opposing negotiators will cave in and submit to all demands. In such cases, all problems are resolved, and a conference does indeed guarantee a generation or so of peace. A more likely possibility, though still remote, is that all sides will decide that they have managed to get all they can expect; each side gives a little, bargaining counters are traded as they were at Teheran and Yalta, compromises are reached, all sides agree to abide by the outcome — and, again, a generation or so of peace is secured and everyone goes home.

If, however, you have a strong nation, and you have every expectation that it will grow even stronger in the future, you are very reluctant to solve problems and feel obligated by the agreements you have reached. The strategy then calls for the making of more problems than you have solutions. This, it might be said, is in the realm of the "grand strategy" of foreign affairs. Truman's key tactic in pursuing this grand strategy was so obvious as to be utterly unobserved. All three of the participants at the Potsdam conference spoke of their meeting as an essential preparation for the full peace conference that was to follow the end of World War II. Truman often reminded Stalin and Churchill of this assumption during the Potsdam sessions, and, especially when it came to discussions of determining the permanent boundaries of nations after the war, Truman would say that he thought the question should be postponed, as it properly belonged on the agenda of the "full peace conference." What Stalin and Churchill did not know was that in Truman's briefing book it said, "It seems clear that it would be desirable to avoid the convocation of a full-fledged peace conference to deal with the major political problems that have arisen as a result of the termination of the war in Europe." In short,

Truman put off problems to a peace conference that would never be held.

The twentieth century, Henry Luce declared in 1941, was to he the "American Century," and the men aboard the *Augusta* went to Potsdam conscious of the historic occasion of an "American Century," of the opportunities to be made or lost in these grandiloquent terms, and of the great strength of their country. The Russians, it was true, had a vast and certainly a hardened army. The English had their Commonwealth. But the Americans had suffered none of the horrible physical damage of war. The American economy was very strong, and, given the proper nurturing, it had the promise of growing even stronger. America dominated the oceans and the air. At the beginning of an age that would be shaped to a great extent by technology, America had the technology. Indeed, the momentous and unpredictable fact underlying these days of conversation on the high seas was the countdown at Alamogordo, New Mexico, on the atomic bomb. "Admiral Leahy and I talked quite a bit about the Manhattan Project," Charles Bohlen recalled. "He felt that the 'longhairs' were gypping the American government out of some $5 billion because the bomb would turn out to be no better than cordite, a simple smokeless powder." "This is the biggest fool thing we have ever done," Leahy told Truman. "The bomb will never go off, and I speak as an expert in explosives."

Truman and most military men had more sanguine hopes about the bomb. The strange riddle, however, was what use to make of the bomb. It was not at all clear that the bomb was needed any longer to defeat Japan. Some hoped it could be used quickly and effectively enough to defeat Japan before the Russians joined the war in the Far East and earned the spoils of war in the Orient as they had in Europe. But, according to Leo Szilard, one of the scientists who tried vainly to get the President's attention to argue against using the bomb at all, Jimmy Byrnes said the bomb's biggest benefit was not for its effect on Japan; the bomb would be used, Byrnes said, for another purpose, to "make Russia more manageable in Europe."

In Japan, hawks and doves argued and plotted around the clock. The Japanese government was torn apart on the issue of whether to fight to the end or seek some form of peace, a form, they hoped then, short of the unconditional surrender that had been demanded of them.

The Americans had been sensible for some time that the "unconditional surrender" formula might cause the Japanese to resist far beyond the point at which they would otherwise accept surrender under negotiated terms. Many said that the demand for Germany's unconditional surrender had needlessly prolonged the European war. Henry Stimson was especially anxious to give the Japanese a chance to surrender before the atomic bomb was used. Before the *Augusta* sailed, Stimson's aides worked on a draft of a proclamation — to be issued to Japan by the United States and England from Potsdam — calling one last time for Japanese surrender and otherwise threatening "the utter devastation of the Japanese homeland."

The sticking point for the Japanese, as Stimson and others saw it, was the emperor. If allowed merely to retain their emperor, the Japanese, they thought, could "honorably" surrender. Thus they wrote in the Potsdam Proclamation that the Allied forces would withdraw from Japan after surrender as soon as a "peacefully inclined and responsible government" had been established that accorded with the will of the people. "This may include a constitutional monarchy under the present dynasty...." It was, Stimson felt, a clear enough statement that the Allies would allow Japan to keep its emperor. Aboard the *Augusta,* Truman and Byrnes reviewed the Proclamation — and cut out the provision for the emperor.

On July 12 in Tokyo, the emperor of Japan summoned Prince Fuminaro Konoye, the former prime minister of Japan, from his summer home to a private meeting. In a remarkable violation of protocol, the emperor was alone. He looked exhausted and pale. He asked Konoye for his opinion on the course of the war. Konoye replied, "It is necessary to end the war as soon as possible," and the emperor told him to prepare for a trip to Moscow.

Shigenori Togo, Japan's foreign minister, sent a radio message to Ambassador Naotaki Sato in Moscow: "His Majesty is extremely anxious to terminate the war as soon as possible, being deeply concerned that any further continuation of hostilities will only aggravate the untold miseries of the millions upon millions of innocent men and women in the countries at war. Should, however, the United States and Great Britain insist on unconditional surrender, Japan would be forced to fight to the bitter end." The emperor wished to send a special envoy, Prince Konoye, to speak with the Soviet government. Sato was to convey this message to the Russian foreign minister, Molotov. The message was intercepted and decoded by American monitors and sent up the line to Truman.

Only July 12, in Alamogordo, the plutonium core for the atomic bomb was transported in the backseat of an Army car to the bomb site.

On July 12, the crew aboard the *Augusta* changed to blue uniforms to ward off the chill of the day. The President and Jimmy Byrnes took aluminum trays and went down the chow line in the crew's mess. Over a lunch of boiled ham, mashed potatoes, tomato soup, buttered carrots, string beans, and, for dessert, apple cobbler, the President chatted with Albert Rice Seale, of Independence,

Missouri, and Elmo Buck, Ph M2C, of Marceline, Missouri. That night, the President stayed to watch the full feature in Jimmy Byrnes's cabin. It was *Something for the Boys*, starring Carmen Miranda, Michael O'Shea, and Vivian Blaine, with Phil Silvers, and introducing Perry Como, "a sleek new singer." Bosley Crowther said in the *New York Times* that the movie had "much gay humor and a superabundance of beautiful girls. As a matter of fact, the latter element is so winsomely and generously revealed that the senses pulsate at such extravagance. If it's girls the boys want, that's what they'll get. Tall girls, small girls, fair girls, redheads and raven brunettes, all in lovely Technicolor — and all of them shapely."

Three days later, on Sunday, July 15, the *Augusta* moored to the municipal dock in Antwerp. The President went from Antwerp to Brussels by car, by Presidential plane *(The Sacred Cow)* to Berlin, and there piled into a car with his friends Byrnes, Vardaman, and Harry Vaughan for the short drive to Babelsberg, a Berlin suburb right next to Potsdam. After dinner, Truman and his traveling companions retired early. It was still light at midnight in that part of the world, but the President was sound asleep when, in Alamogordo, the technicians made a last check-out of the gadget at the top of the tower and then went to hunt for rabbits' feet and four-leaf clovers.

2
CHURCHILL

On July 12, at the chateau of Bordaberry in Hendaye, on the border between France and Spain, Prime Minister Winston Churchill, age seventy, awoke with indigestion — the result, he said, of his painting. He had been laboring for several days on a view of a house overlooking the Bidassoa River, and the house refused to yield to his assaults. He had a photograph taken of the view and compared it to his handiwork. His hostess at the chateau, Margaret Nairn, tried her hand at painting the same scene, and Churchill stood silently peering at the two canvases for a long while. The light on the house and on the water and in the treetops refused to correspond to the way Churchill wanted to paint it. Landscapes often declined to submit to

Churchill's will, but he was never daunted by that inconvenience.

Baroness Asquith once had the pleasure of seeing Churchill with palette in hand: "When we were both staying in a country house, set in a monochrome of dull, flat, uneventful country, I went out to watch him paint, half wondering what he would make of it. Looking over his shoulder, I saw depicted on his canvas range upon range of mountains, rising dramatically behind the actual foreground. I searched the skies for a mirage and then inquired where they had come from — and he replied: 'Well, I couldn't leave it quite as dull as all that.'"

Churchill learned early about canvases that "anyone could see that it could not hit back," and he assaulted one vista after another with gusto and audacity. "I cannot pretend to feel impartial about the colors," he said. "I rejoice with the brilliant ones, and am genuinely sorry for the poor browns. When I get to heaven I mean to spend a considerable portion of my first million years in painting, and so get to the bottom of the subject. But then I shall require a still gayer palette than I get here below."

As Churchill vacationed in Hendaye before the Potsdam conference, the canvas seemed to strike back from time to time. "I'm very depressed," he said one day before luncheon as he collapsed into an armchair. "I don't want to do anything. I have no energy. I wonder if it will come back." He sat musing, plunged in gloom.

With the end of the war in Europe, Churchill had dissolved his Cabinet and called for a new general election in Great Britain. He gave his last speech of the campaign on June 30, and, while the voters went to the polls and the politicians waited for the tally to be completed, Churchill went off to paint in the French countryside. The outcome of the election would not be known until midway through the Potsdam conference: the votes of the soldiers were a long time coming in from around the world. "I shall be only half a man until the results of the poll," Churchill said from the depths of the armchair. "I shall keep in the background at the conference."

After lunch, after his cocktails and his wine, the Prime Minister sprang up from the luncheon table and went in search of his paintbox. He marched through his wife Clemmie's room, rousing her from a nap, and out onto the small balcony where his paints had been put out for him. His personal physician, Sir Charles Wilson, Lord Moran — who had tagged along to watch — noticed that the Prime Minister's feet "brushed the floor as if he were too tired to lift them off the ground."

"Where are the other paints?" the Prime Minister boomed at his valet Sawyers. "I've no reserves here," he said, his voice rising as he prepared to go into battle — "you've left a lot behind. Why did you do that? Who told you to bring only these?"

Sawyers begged off any responsibility.

"Where is the cobalt? You ought not to have left everything at home. Ah, here it is" — the Prime Minister subsided — "get me a stool. I must sit."

And so he sat, quiet and contented, and he painted — absorbed by the task at hand, oblivious to all else, at peace with the world his paints and brushes were transforming.

"Mr. Churchill sees history — and life," Isaiah Berlin once wrote, "as a great Renaissance pageant.... He sees vivid historical images — something between Victorian illustrations in a child's book of history and the great procession painted by Benozzo Gozzoli in the Riccardi Palace." The "central, organizing principle of his moral and intellectual universe is an historical imagination so strong, so comprehensive, as to encase the whole of the present and the whole of the future in a framework of a rich and multi-colored past..."

What Isaiah Berlin did not say — but might have — was that the Prime Minister's sense of his own place in that pageant of history was complete: he was a part of Gozzoli's procession, inseparable from it. He had encased himself in the grand pageant of British history during the war years; when he spoke of the challenge to Britain, of its finest hours, of its triumphs and tragedies, many of his countrymen felt — and he felt with them — not only that he himself spoke, but that British history and the indomitable British people spoke through him. His life and the history of his country were fused in his mind. And, by the time of the Potsdam conference, whether by coincidence or because the destiny of Britain had become so much a part of his life and soul, Britain and Churchill could at last be described in the same words: both he and Britain were exhausted; both he and Britain were slowly coming apart; and both he and Britain were defeated — though neither yet knew it.

After his painting, Churchill went back into his bedroom, with Lord Moran tagging along behind. "I'm going to relax completely. I'm not going to look at any papers." And then the Prime Minister added, without apparent connection, "Only twice in my life have my knees shaken under me when speaking: at Edinburgh and on Richmond Common, when I was speaking for Harvie-Watt. I imagine one is nearly all in when that happens. Take my pulse, Charles."

Americans have never been great diarists. The English, at least since the time of Pepys, have known that a man might win more lasting fame for his diary than for his actions. And so, while Truman's digestion might go unremarked, we have a whole generation of would-be Pepyses and Boswells vying to record Churchill's every mood and whim. "He is thinking a lot these days of the election," Lord Moran carefully noted in his diary for July 9. "One moment he sees himself victorious; the next he pictures himself beaten.... He finds this state of suspense unpalatable, and turns for comfort to other thoughts."

Churchill sought refuge from his anxiety by grasping at any passing thought and practicing his rhetoric on any subject that presented itself. "Two things have disappeared in my lifetime," lie said one day at luncheon. "Men no longer study the classics. It was an advantage when there was one common discipline and every nation studied the doings of two states. Now they learn how to mend motor cars. The other thing is — can you guess what I am thinking of?" he asked one of his audience at the table. "No? Why, the horse. We have lost a good deal in these two things."

Like the thoughts, we are told, of a drowning man, odd recollections of his whole life flitted through his mind. "I think," he said, "I gained a lot by not overworking my brain when I was young. I never did anything I didn't like." The talk drifted to the Russian purges. Eduard Beneš, head of the Czechoslovakian government-in-exile, had warned Stalin "of the plot of high Russian officers to make an alliance with Germany. The plans passed through the Russian Embassy at Prague. So

Stalin acted, and four thousand or so officers in the Russian army... were liquidated."

"Stalin was thoroughly justified," Churchill said casually. "These officers were acting against their country."

He sat at the luncheon table talking, reminiscing without stop. One afternoon the local Basques put on a show of games and dancing, and one of the party was deputed to get Churchill away from the table early so that the house servants could attend the entertainment. At quarter to four, Churchill was led away from the table complaining that he had not finished his coffee.

The local dignitaries were introduced to the Prime Minister, and they presented him with flowers and Basque bowls. Finally the games began, and the Prime Minister abruptly rose from his front-row seat and clumped out — followed by Lord Moran and a personal aide Tommy Thompson. When they were away from the crowd, Churchill turned to Thompson and said, "I don't know why they arranged this, they know I hate all games."

An emissary was sent to fetch the petulant Prime Minister back to the festivities. "They were very much upset by your leaving," the messenger said.

"Go to hell."

Forty-five minutes later another emissary led

Churchill back to the dancing and games, and, when it was over, Churchill rose and made a pretty little speech in his "most Churchillian French."

As he returned to the house, he said to Lord Moran, "It would have killed me if I had stayed all the time." It was, Moran conceded, fairly stuffy. "Hot and boring," the Prime Minister pronounced.

He sang songs from The Mikado and played word games and talked some more. Britain had offered common citizenship to the French after the British Expeditionary Force fled Dunkirk: Churchill recalled the Sunday meeting of the Cabinet when the idea of common citizenship had been proposed. "That rough Cabinet to which men had come by so many different ways was carried off its feet. It was like a religious revival. It was a *cri de coeur* from the rough heart of Britain."

Tears came to the Prime Minister's eyes. The full range of emotions played through him, as they will through a thoroughly exhausted person, and he let all of his feelings flow out, orchestrating them to a greater or lesser extent now and then, building a bit here, pausing a moment there, relishing his own expressive powers. His expressiveness had become a phenomenon in itself — finely tuned, delicate, powerful — and it ranged over history, over past, present, and future, developing its own haunting and passionate airs and variations that were often, by now, as out of touch with the mundane world as the works of Puccini or Verdi.

"He marveled at America's disinterestedness. She had come into this war and 'cast away her wealth for an idea,'" Churchill said, forgetting that the United States was persistently nibbling away at the sterling bloc even at that moment. "If his father as well as his mother had been an American," he said, "he was not certain he would have advised [America] to come into the war."

"The P.M. had been speaking with great animation," Moran wrote. "The vast brow, which mounts straight above his eyes, was puckered, so that a deep line passed up vertically from his nose. The eyelids seemed pressed down on his eyes by the weight of his brow, the thin lips were pursed together, pouting. At the summit of his forehead two wisps of hair went their several ways, and gave an impression that he had more hair than was actually the case. He became silent and no one spoke. At last he looked up and laid bare where his thoughts were: 'I hear the women are for me, but that the men have turned against me.'"

When his mind strayed from thoughts of the election to the coming Potsdam conference and the future of Britain, Churchill found little solace. "I've just thrown the reins on the horse's neck and let things rip," the Prime Minister said. "I've never done it before." He had studied no briefs during his holiday of painting. He had dictated no letters.

What he did not already know, hardly seemed worth knowing, nor could he cope well with what he did know, and fear. "The maid brought coffee and we sat round the table listening to the P.M., who had some difficulty in keeping awake. He nursed his head in his hands, and for a time seemed oblivious of the company. Then he looked up.

"Tommy, could you get me some brandy?"

The facts were, as the revisionist historian Gabriel Kolko has written, that "between 1938 and 1945 Britain's exports declined from £471 million to £258 million, and its imports increased over the same period from £858 million to £1, 299 million. Its overseas debt increased nearly five times, to £3, 355 million.... By the following year its foreign indebtedness was far greater than that of all western Europe combined and, excluding debts to the United States, three times larger than that of France. The British virtually dissipated the legacy and power of nineteenth-century imperialism."

Britain was on the way to a long slide down, without the power to reverse or even halt its own decline, its only hopes pinned to Churchillian rhetoric about the natural union of the English-speaking peoples and pinned as well to whatever feelings of gratitude the Americans might have toward the nation that stood alone against Hitler "for the sake of service to mankind and for the honor that comes to those who faithfully serve great causes." Churchill had once offered common citizenship to the Americans as well as the French, and now that the war was over he tried to evoke a common fear of Russia and Communism to draw America closer to Britain. He played a desperate game — for he never saw a cause he embraced as a small cause — and he used every bit of cajolery and threat, and what few bargaining counters he had left, to wed the United States to the cause of propping up Great Britain, without letting Britain be absorbed into a new American empire.

Churchill had met Truman only in passing during wartime visits to Roosevelt in Washington, and did not know quite how to deal with the new President. In order to prepare for the Potsdam conference Truman had sent Joseph E. Davies to London at the end of May that year. Davies was the son of Welsh immigrants to the United States, a poor boy who worked his way into a lucrative political-law practice. He was a natural charmer, ebullient, and a naïve idealist who embraced Woodrow Wilson's and Josef Stalin's dreams with equal enthusiasm. Roosevelt had appointed Davies ambassador to Moscow, and the lawyer exulted after a short stint in Russia, "My wife and I thank God that Franklin gave us ringside seats at the greatest experiment in the history of man. ... [We and the Russians are] both pioneers, young, vigorous. We've both got the virtues of pioneers, the same concepts of peace, justice, and the brotherhood of man." That Truman chose to send Davies of all people to London must have struck Churchill as curious at least, and perhaps the Prime Minister saw it as a warning signal.

At his first meeting with Churchill, which lasted from eleven o'clock one Saturday night until four-thirty the next morning, Davies conveyed the President's concern "over the serious deterioration in the relations of the Soviets with both Britain and the United States. It was clear," Davies said, "that without continued unity of the Big Three there could be no reasonable prospect of peace. The causes of their dangerous situation were also clear. They were differences over what the agreements arrived at in Yalta actually were, conflict over new matters which the speed of military victory in Europe had developed, all induced by and fed by fears, distrusts, and suspicions, on both sides." These natural suspicions, Davies continued, were made worse by the Soviet belief that Britain and America were "ganging up" on Russia. Because of that mistaken belief, and because the President had never met Stalin, "the President, therefore, desired an opportunity to meet the Marshal immediately before the scheduled, forthcoming meeting."

Churchill readily agreed to Davies's general assessment and the notion of having Truman meet with Stalin before the conference, and then the Prime Minister began to review the situation in Europe as he saw it. He was bitter toward France and toward de Gaulle, who seemed to be acting arbitrarily and needed to be "brought up sharply"; he was bitter toward Tito, who seemed to be under the domination of Moscow; he was bitter about Soviet behavior in the Balkans. As the Prime Minister went on, his passion began to rise to the occasion. He feared the advance of the Communists across Europe "like locusts." He feared what would happen if the American armies were withdrawn from Europe. The lines of the American armies should be maintained as far forward in Germany as possible — and never mind about prior agreements to withdraw to occupation zones. The Russians, he said, had clamped down a "steel curtain" across eastern Europe, and they posed a great danger throughout western Europe. The Prime Minister had referred to an "iron curtain" in the past; he would pick up and abandon catch phrases in the months ahead — lapsing into the weak image of an "iron fence" on one occasion — until he finally settled on the chilling words "iron curtain" and repeated them until all his Western friends saw the world in his image.

Suddenly Churchill realized the strangeness of Truman's desire to meet Stalin first. After all, he had never had more than a quick introduction to Truman. He was "surprised and hurt" that he was to be "excluded" from the first post-victory meeting with Stalin. Had Churchill not supported the United States throughout the war? And was this to be the reward for his support? Had he not supported the American formula of unconditional surrender when he could have made a separate peace with Hitler? What was the meaning of this? Such a meeting, Churchill declared, smacked of a "deal." He would "never, never consent." The Prime Minister was profoundly alarmed. It appeared that the United States would not support its old ally after all. The withdrawal of troops, this cool attitude toward its old friend and ally, what did it all mean if not that America had decided to ditch Britain in its hour of vital need? "Are you trying to say for the President," Churchill asked Davies coldly, "that the United States is withdrawing from participation in European affairs?"

Davies replied noncommittally, and the Prime Minister declared with a bravado that had worn thin and tired — and was recorded by an unimpressed Davies with some casually placed "etceteras" — that if the Americans did not understand the threat Russia held to Europe, England would stand alone. England, the Prime Minister said plaintively, was not a "negligible factor" in world affairs. She could still protect herself. England could stand alone. "She had done it before," Davies quoted the Prime Minister, "etc."

With that, Davies took off his own gloves and tried, pathetically, to match the Prime Minister's eloquence. He reviewed the great Russian contribution to the war, the legacy of suspicion, and — as Churchill might have recorded it — "etc." In conclusion, Davies said, "there are many who believe that England, finding now no great rival power in Europe to offset the new rising power of Russia, would try to use American manpower and resources to support the classic British policy of 'leading' Europe."

The Prime Minister declined to reply to Davies's speech — perhaps because Davies had struck so closely to the truth. He would like, Churchill said, to be "heard" personally by the President and suggested that he and Davies exchange *aides-mémoire*. In the note Churchill wrote Truman, the bewildered and anguished Prime Minister said, "It must be remembered that Britain and the United States are united at this time upon the same ideologies, namely, freedom, and the principles set out in the American Constitution and humbly reproduced with modern variations in the Atlantic Charter. The Soviet government has a different philosophy, namely, Communism, and use to the full the methods of police government, which they are applying in every State which has fallen a victim to their liberating arms. The Prime Minister cannot readily bring himself to accept the idea that the position of the United States is that Britain and Soviet Russia are just two foreign powers, six of one and half a dozen of the other, with whom the troubles of the late war have to be adjusted.... The great causes and principles for which Britain and the United States have suffered and triumphed are not mere matters of the balance of power. They in fact involve the salvation of the world."

Churchill doubtless believed these sentiments, just as the Americans believed democratic principles were far more desirable than Russian tyranny. Churchill, as Davies concluded, "had convinced himself that by serving England, he was best serving peace." And Truman believed that by looking out for American interests, he was looking out for the good of the world. If there is a measure of self-deception in these views, it is only to be expected. The job of the President and the Prime Minister was to remain cold enough to see to it that their selfless sentiments for the good of the world did not interfere with the selfish aims they had for their countries and themselves.

At the time of Yalta, Field Marshal Alexander tried to plead over lunch — as Sir Alexander Cadogan recorded in his diary — "that we must do the best we can to help the Italians. P.M. resisted this, so that Alexander was stung into saying that, after all, that was more or less what we were fighting this war for — to secure the liberty and a decent existence for the peoples of Europe. P.M. said, 'Not a bit of it: we are fighting to secure the proper respect for the British people!'"

If the "grand strategy" for a nation on the way up

is to avoid commitments, the "grand strategy" for a declining nation is to grasp hold of as many commitments as possible to buttress its position. The slightest signal that a commitment might be withdrawn, or might not be forthcoming, or that the President wanted to mollify Russian "suspicion," took on the appearance of a mortal blow to Churchill. With Europe smashed, there was no power to balance on the continent. Churchill hoped to balance Russia against the United States and, with the blessing of its natural ally, seize for itself, as Davies had said, the leadership of Europe. It was a devilishly difficult strategy to pursue. Having exhausted England's powers, Churchill had to juggle the power of Russia and America while, by fine words and the few scraps of military and economic force left to him, he stole the prize of Europe. It was a plan for nothing less than a new British empire — but such, in Churchill's view, were England's rightful spoils of war.

The essence of Churchill's strategy, therefore, was disruptiveness — to bring the United States and Russia into conflict. "An iron curtain is drawn on their front," Churchill cabled Truman. "We do not know what is going on behind. There seems little doubt that the whole of the regions east of the line Lübeck-Trieste-Corfu will soon be completely in their hands." While the attentions of the English and Americans were elsewhere, it might be open to the Russians, the Prime Minister warned, "to advance if they chose to the waters of the North Sea and the Atlantic."

The point worth observing is not that Churchill invented a devil where none existed. By any standard Stalin was one of the supremely evil men of history, and Russian foreign policy was neither altruistic nor unaggressive. The point was that Churchill was eager to exaggerate the threat Stalin posed, to exacerbate the differences between Russia and America while he stole the prize of a western European bloc. He was playing most licentiously with fire.

In fact, Churchill not only used words to stir up trouble; he was prepared to use captured German troops to fight against the Russians. As Gabriel Kolko has written, "On May 17 Churchill ordered his officers not to destroy any German planes... and ten days later discussed the use of air power for 'striking at the communications of the Russian armies should they decide to advance farther than is agreed.' The British kept approximately 700, 000 German troops in essentially military formations in their zone at this time...."

If this all seems disingenuous on Churchill's part — toward both Russia and America — well, Machiavelli had said that a prince must "learn how not to be good, and to use this knowledge and not use it, according to the necessity of the case," since "the experience of our time shows those princes to have done great things who have had little regard for good faith, and have been able by astuteness to confuse men's brains, and who have ultimately overcome those who have made loyalty their foundation." It was well, Machiavelli said, "to *seem* merciful, faithful, humane, sincere, religious, and also to be so; but you must have the mind so disposed that when it is needful to be otherwise you may be able to change to the opposite qualities."

While Churchill painted in the south of France, Miss Joan Bright, an Englishwoman with deep reserves of chipperness, led the British civilian hospitality corps to Potsdam to check out the setting the Russians had chosen for the conference. Potsdam squats a few miles to the southeast of Berlin, just beyond the edge of the narrow Lake Griebnitz. Relatively untouched by bombs, the town provided a good number of abandoned private homes — once the summer retreats of German movie producers and stars — to accommodate the diplomats, as well as a convenient palace for the conference sessions, and it had the additional virtue of being close to the Western zones of occupation while remaining within the Russian zone.

The formal sessions were to be held in the Cecilienhof, Europe's last grand palace, which had been finished in 1917, on the eve of Germany's crushing defeat in World War I. It was a 176-room ersatz Tudor country house, with swatches of stucco here and there interrupted by mock-Elizabethan windows and stone portals that appeared embarrassed by their lack of moats and drawbridges. Topping it all off was a collection of chimneys, one vaguely Islamic in inspiration, some reminiscent of the columns of the baldacchino in St. Peter's Cathedral, and all of them together resembling nothing so much as the rooftops of nineteenth-century Nottingham. Into this uneasy Tudor manqué palace that might have been designed by a mad illustrator of children's books, the Russians had brought a selection of furnishings that had been scavenged from all over Potsdam. Massive German armchairs enhanced with carved lions' heads were settled peremptorily on French carpets; Murano glasses for champagne toasts were jammed into glass cabinets, and the walls were defaced with odd paintings of seascapes and drab little village street scenes. Miss Bright flitted through the palace and, when she came upon the library, instinctively swiped two books.

The main conference room was on the ground floor, where windows opened onto a sloping lawn down to Lake Griebnitz — and let the mosquitoes in to vex the diplomats. The room was squarish and dark-paneled, and the solid round table in the center was only large enough to accommodate fifteen chairs — twelve small, straight-backed chairs and three large wooden armchairs upholstered in red plush. Each of the delegations had been assigned a suite of rooms to which they could retire for private consultations. Churchill's was upstairs, and Miss Bright noticed that the easiest way for the Prime Minister to reach the conference room would be to descend the main staircase and enter through the large double doors. The double doors were locked. Could the doors be unlocked? she asked the Russian commandant who was showing her around.

"Not possible. They use the three smaller doors, one each."

The three smaller doors were of equal size. Churchill might have to walk downstairs and then detour through a corridor to reach his door — but his door would be no bigger than the other two.

"The commandant looked at me and said something. 'He asks if you are pleased,' said the interpreter. 'Yes? No?' 'Yes,' I said. It was a hot day."

The houses in which the delegates lived during the conference were several miles down along Lake Griebnitz, in the neighboring suburb of Babelsberg. The houses were beefy suburban affairs of brick and stucco with massive dark molding around the doors and windows and solid front porches that were more imposing than welcoming; but they were set along tree-lined streets and were surrounded by pleasant, if somewhat neglected, lawns and gardens. The British were planning for a delegation of 260 people plus casual visitors, and they had been allotted fifty houses, each with a Steinway or Bechstein grand piano. "The general atmosphere at Babelsberg," Miss Bright cheerfully noted, "between the British and American sectors, was that of a community compound, where people lived in self-contained working units, invited each other to their houses, greeted each other in the street." It was a good party, with plenty to eat and drink and a lot of old friends to see. "Absolutely *everyone* was there," Miss Bright recalled later. "It was the last great beano of the war.

"Dear, bald General Karanadze was there, beaming, making it cozy again" — or, almost cozy. Russians popped in for visits at the American and British compounds, but permission was required to pass by the armed guards into the Russian compound. As another Britisher remarked, ungallantly, "The whole area was, of course, in the occupation of the Russian Army and the several miles of road which separated [the airport] from Babelsberg were lined by Russian soldiers, standing, it seemed, shoulder to shoulder, bucolic, inattentive, unsmart, but creating at once in my mind the impression of the limitless resources of Russian manpower. The traffic-control points seemed for the most part to be manned [sic] by women, strong, robust, Amazonian types, totally devoid of feminine charm."

Miss Bright and her civilian colleagues had tireless help from British Army men with the arrangements for the conference. The Army began issuing directives almost immediately. Number 53 advised: "Laundry for V.I.P.s will be located in Delegation Area." And the next day, number 87 said: "(see serial 53) Miss Bright will be asked to state who should be permitted to use the special laundry facilities." For a time it appeared that Miss Bright had the conference firmly in control — but eight days later Army Ordnance moved against her: "Number 253. (see serial 87). Ordnance has obtained agreement with Russians to use a German laundry for V.I.P.s. This laundry is able to accept laundry for all the troops of 4 L. of C. if materials (soap and coal) are provided."

Miss Bright fought back with all the bargaining counters she had. She cabled back to England for: "Bell transformers 230 volt, bells, bell wire, cotton-covered, five hundred yards. Wood screws one by six inches, wood screws one and a half by six inches, staples, insulated, four gross."

Having seized control of communications, she moved next on credentials, cabling for "Two thousand Conference Passes," and then on transportation, calling for "One hundred transfer Union Jacks for cars, size six inches by four."

The Army countered with more directives:

18. Furniture taken out of houses will be stacked reasonably and not thrown in heaps. Articles such as desks, tables, chairs, etc. which are likely to be required elsewhere will be placed alongside roads and on pavements and sorted at the time of removal from houses.

29. Russian policy will be adhered to, i.e., civilian labor will NOT be fed by us.

48. (see serial 29). Delete the word "NOT."

Perhaps the most severe blow was delivered to Miss Bright by directive number 59, which hit her directly in the decorations: "Although a certain amount of bunting has been flown over, it is not considered likely to be required. Decoration of the Central Conference Hall is the responsibility of the Russians."

Miss Bright cabled for "sixty dustpans, brushes and brooms, pails, scrubbing brushes. Two hundred house flannels. Sixty mops. Twenty-four saucepan brushes. One hundred cups and saucers white. Two gross dusters, thirty three-tier bunks with palliasses and pillows. One hundredweight soda and one hundred tins bath and sink cleaner. Two hundred cotton sheets" — and, at last, perhaps with an eye to strictly feminine ruses — "Could you ask Winnie to bring with her a precious pocket comb I left in my office?"

But doubtless Miss Bright's cleverest stroke of all

in her battle with the Army was to bring in Chief Petty Officer Pinfield of the Royal *Navy,* who "had supervised the construction of the Persian ice pudding" at Teheran, to take charge of the Prime Minister's kitchen.

After that, the Army, which had provided the fire brigade, the barbers, and the chiropodists, was reduced to nattering at its own troops: "336. New shirts are available for issue to the Prime Minister's guard if required. The standard of dress of troops in Delegation Area must be improved immediately."

When the preparations were finished, and the delegates had not yet arrived, Miss Bright and her friend Betty Gibbs went to "tea" with dear, bald General Karanadze and his helpers Nina Alexandrovna and Gala. They were entertained with "the usual vodka marathon" and left at last in an Army car. "We told the driver to drive anywhere, while we sat by open windows and tried to get the fumes of drink and cigarette smoke out of our system" — two young Englishwomen gliding breezily through a balmy summer evening, along the clear calm lake that reflected still in the light of dusk the green of the trees and the slowly drifting clouds. Potsdam, Miss Bright mused, was "an oasis of material comfort in a desert of devastation."

In Sussex, England, Foreign Minister Anthony Eden boarded a plane at Tangmere aerodrome; at Northolt aerodrome in Middlesex another airplane took on Clement R. Attlee, leader of the opposition; in France, Winston Churchill was driven from St. Jean-de-Luz to the Bordeaux airport.

"We flew over Antwerp and part of the Ruhr," Cadogan wrote home to his wife. "Flying rather high, one couldn't see very much detail on the ground. There certainly were some good patches of devastation, but there were some towns and even large factories that didn't seem to show any signs of damage. I hardly saw a train moving anywhere in Germany, and nothing on the roads except military convoys.

"... Here we are, in the midst of this devastated and denuded country, living in a little town of our own, consisting of villas set amidst trees (not unlike Le Touquet) with more or less every comfort of a rough and ready kind. My bedroom has a large balcony looking on to a garden which slopes down to a narrow lake — more like a wide river — with a bank opposite covered with pine-trees. My house, which I share with 5 or 6 others, is comfortable enough, though there's only one bathroom. However, I get my Marine to secure that for me when I want it. The house next door on one side is a mess where we have our meals, run by ATS and none too good, but not too bad.

"The house on the other side is a nice little modern house reserved for Anthony. The P.M. is the next one further on, really a charming house, though some of the decoration rather modern German. Then, several houses further on, is a drab and dreary little building destined to house Attlee! Very suitable — it's just like Attlee himself!

"... Masses of people have already arrived. Anthony and P.M. due today some time.

"I believe this particular lot of villas belonged to the German UFA (Film) people. All Germans have of course been turned out. Where they've gone, no one knows. Can you imagine what we should feel if Germans and Japanese were doing this in England, and if we had all been bundled out to make way for Hitler and Co. to squat in our homes and decide our fate while we lived in holes in the rubble heaps of London? ... It's beautiful country — sandy with pines and birches and a chain of lakes."

Sir Alexander Cadogan, age sixty-one, was the youngest son of the fifth Earl of Cadogan, whose family came to prominence in the eighteenth century. The fifth Earl, who had served as Under-Secretary in Disraeli's ministry, impressed upon his son the habits of reserve, devotion to duty, shyness of publicity, punctiliousness in work, and a certain modulation of aesthetic inclinations so that the arts would provide pleasure but not distraction from affairs of state. Although it was a Cadogan who had said, "Don't go abroad; it's a horrible place," the young Cadogan was expected from the earliest age to become Under-Secretary for Foreign Affairs and so steel himself to accept the privations an Englishman must endure when he travels off English soil. He attended, as a matter of course, Eton — where he was editor of the *Eton College Chronicle*, captain of the Oppidans, and president of the Eton Society. Upon passing out of Balliol College, Oxford, he prepared for two years for his examinations for the diplomatic service. As Permanent Under-Secretary for Foreign Affairs during World War II, Cadogan had the duty of running the whole of the Foreign Office and shaping its performance and advice to the wishes and characters of the Foreign Secretary and the Prime Minister. Or perhaps it would be more accurate to say that Cadogan perceived his duties to be to shape the wishes and characters of the Foreign Secretary and the Prime Minister to the performance and advice of the Foreign Office.

"How have we conducted this war," Cadogan once asked his diary, "with the P.M. spending *hours* of his own and other people's time simply drivelling, welcoming every red herring so as only to have the pleasure of more irrelevant, redundant talk?" Cadogan often felt that Churchill — as well as the other world leaders - tended to make a mess of what was otherwise very tidily under control by the Foreign Office and the bureaucrats of the American State Department. In general, however, he took the optimistic view that "we could clean up the mess afterwards."

Cadogan detested above all to see politics and the real world of power-seeking intrude on the smooth operations of the Foreign Office. Shortly before the Potsdam conference, he exploded in his diary, "How I *hate* Members of Parliament! They embody everything that my training has taught me to eschew — ambition, prejudice, dishonesty, self-seeking, light-hearted responsibility, black-hearted mendacity."

Traveling with Churchill and Eden, both of whom hungered for crowds and cheers and opportunities to make speeches, was, Cadogan said, "like travelling about with Melba and Tetrazzini in one company!" As Cadogan saw it, Anthony Eden — who was always eager to get out from under the shadow of the P.M. and go around on his own "collecting cheers from troops" — had one "V. dangerous" tendency: "the urge to *do* something, irrespective of the sense of it."

Anthony Eden, age forty-eight, had attended Eton, where he declined to make himself conspicuous "either by prowess or by misdeed." He graduated from Christ Church, Oxford, in 1922 and was elected to Parliament in 1923. He came from a good family, had the proper education, dressed well, had private means, was possessed of both tact and patience, and was, perhaps, too handsome. He was, finally, a conventional man, lacking brilliance, and flawed by an inner core of softness. He remained, impatiently, in Churchill's shadow for too long, and there he burned with frustrated ambition. Churchill nursed his career, and held it in check. "Anthony and I flew to Athens this morning," Cadogan recorded at the time of the Yalta conference. "Anthony of course delighted at the idea of a trip on his own and not as a member of the P.M.'s suite. But the P.M. evidently had second thoughts about allowing Anthony to go gathering laurels on his own, and announced that he would come with us tomorrow — to Anthony's rage and horror."

Nobody much liked Clement Attlee. He was a short, slight man, a year older than Cadogan, and he had the air, it was said, of a "safely berthed schoolmaster." The son of a London solicitor, he had attended University College, Oxford, and, after taking a degree in history, devoted himself to social work — and earned his keep in east London with jobs on the docks. He was not of the right class and—what was almost as bad — he was a Socialist, sincere if not eloquent, honest if not invigorating. When the war was over, Attlee insisted in his high-pitched, staccato voice, Britain would be a Socialist country, "with cake for none until all had bread." It was Attlee who had been one of the most outspoken critics of the Munich settlement, Attlee who had branded Chamberlain a failure in 1940, and Attlee who, by refusing to form a coalition Cabinet with Chamberlain, provoked the fall of the Chamberlain government. When Churchill was then asked to form a Cabinet, he created a coalition government, with Attlee as Lord privy Seal. This was the coalition government that was dissolved now that the European war had ended, and Attlee was the man who led the Labour party against Churchill's Conservatives in the general election. Few people — except Churchill — thought Attlee had a chance.

"His thought," Dean Acheson said of Attlee, "impressed me as a long withdrawing, melancholy sigh." He was, Churchill said, "a sheep in sheep's clothing." During the war, Attlee presided over Cabinet meetings when Churchill was off traveling. As Cadogan once noted: "Attlee presides — like a soured and argumentative mouse." Attlee once delivered a written protest to Churchill about the disorganized style of the Prime Minister's Cabinet meetings. It seemed that everyone objected to Churchill's rambling monologues. The Prime Minister brooded in bed about it until four o'clock one afternoon. Then, abruptly tossing off the covers, he said happily to a companion, "Let us think no more of Hitlee or Attler; let us go and see a film. " It seemed inconceivable that Attlee might become Prime Minister, but Churchill invited him to have a seat at the table at Potsdam, just in case Attlee would have to take over.

Next to Churchill, all the others in the British delegation seemed to recede with tact and good manners into the background. By the sheer force of his character, the Prime Minister drew his age and his country about him in such a way as to become himself an historical event. His ministers ministered to him as much as to Britain. And while one saw Foreign Office men and military men pressing him with advice and counsel, it was not possible to point to this statesman or that general, as one could with the men surrounding Truman, as an embodiment of Churchillian policy. For the Prime Minister was, as Cadogan complained, constantly making a mess of things.

Churchill and his party landed at Gatow airport outside Berlin on the afternoon of July 15. "The sun blazed down," Lord Moran said, "and members of the Conference, who had been waiting for a long time on the airfield outside Berlin, looked hot and uncomfortable buttoned up in their uniforms. There were Russian soldiers everywhere, lining the road, behind bushes, knee deep in the corn. We drove to where a substantial stone house, which was said to have belonged to Schacht, the banker, had been reserved for the Prime Minister. I followed him through two bleak rooms with great chandeliers to the opposite side of the empty house, where French windows that had not been cleaned for a long time opened upon a balcony, and there, without removing his hat, Winston flopped into a garden chair, flanked by two great tubs of hydrangeas, blue, pink and white. He appeared too weary to move. Presently he looked up:

"'Where is Sawyers?' He turned to Tommy Thompson. 'Get me a whisky.'"

"We sat in silence for a long time," Moran recalled, "looking at the lawn that sloped to a lake, into which, so it was said, the Russians had thrown some German soldiers who could not walk because of their wounds. Beyond the lake a field rose sharply to a wood. The only sign of life that we could see was a Russian sentry, who came out of the wood, looked round and disappeared again into the trees. When the light had gone a rifle shot, that seemed to come from the wood, broke the silence that had fallen on everything."

3
STALIN

J ust before Stalin was scheduled to leave for the Potsdam conference, he suffered a mild heart attack. The illness did not seem to affect him; no one noticed the least difference in his health or vigor; but the heart attack did delay his journey, and the start of the Big Three conference, by one day. The Man of Steel was afraid of flying, and so, for the trip to Potsdam, he and his entourage boarded a special train that consisted of eleven coaches, including four luxurious cars that were taken out of a museum and dusted off for the occasion. These four splendid carriages had once formed part of the imperial Czarist train. The train passed slowly through the war-ravaged landscape of western Russia and into Lithuania and East Prussia. The more direct route would have been through Poland to Berlin, but Stalin wished to travel only through countries that had been thoroughly subdued and secured. The train, and the route along which it traveled, bristled with armed guards. From the window of one of the comfortable imperial coaches, Russia's Communist czar surveyed his newly conquered territories.

Stalin was, according to the Yugoslav Communist Milovan Djilas, "of very small stature and ungainly build. His torso was short and narrow, while his legs and arms were too long. His left arm and shoulder seemed rather stiff. He had a quite large paunch, and his hair was sparse, though his scalp was not completely bald. His face was white, with ruddy cheeks. Later I learned that this coloration, so characteristic of those who sit long in offices, was known as the 'Kremlin complexion' in high Soviet circles. His teeth were black and irregular, turned inward. Not even his mustache was thick or firm. Still the head was not a bad one; it had something of the folk, the peasantry, the pater familias about it — with those yellow eyes and a mixture of sternness and roguishness."

He chain-smoked cigarettes, except when he wanted to make an impression — and then he affected a pipe bearing the small white dot that identified it as an English Dunhill. He had a curious admiration for Churchill, for the English, and for the British Empire. The British were abandoning uniforms for their diplomats, just as Stalin was ordering his diplomats to wear uniforms; and the British were losing their empire, just as Stalin appeared to be thinking what a nice thing it is to have an empire.

He was born in poverty, in harsh poverty, in 1879 in the province of Tiflis in Georgia. For all the pride he would later take in being the leader not just of the Soviet Union but especially of Russia, the language of his childhood was Georgian and he would always speak Russian with an accent. His father was a drunken, failed shoemaker, his mother a laundress. The stiffness that Djilas noticed in his left arm was the result of a childhood illness or accident. He was a small boy, an energetic, scrappy athlete, bright, sensitive, and deeply resentful when anyone picked on him. He answered practical jokes with his fists.

According to his biographer Adam Ulam, Stalin first began to take an interest in Marxist meetings at the age of sixteen or seventeen, while he was a student at Tiflis seminary. Marxism in Georgia was not quite the sophisticated intellectual pursuit it was in the European capitals. As the local Georgian theoretician put it, "Our life shows us two hostile classes, one the representatives of physical and mental labor, the other the bourgeois and capitalists." It hardly seemed fair; it seemed worth resenting; Stalin resented it. He was no theoretician; he was from the first an activist, and a regard for niceties never played a part in his career. Before he was twenty-two years old, his companions in the Tiflis underground "found him overbearing," as Adam Ulam writes, "and suggested he transfer to another locality."

As an adolescent and a young man, he was a revolutionary in a police state. He was surrounded by coconspirators, spies, counterspies, plots, and counterplots. He was arrested and jailed; he saw friends jailed and murdered; he was part of a movement that engaged in strikes, riots, beatings, stonings, torture, assassination, and civil war. It has been said that he was himself a double agent for the Czarist police; and, whether he was or not, some of his friends certainly were. He was surrounded on all sides by the threat of betrayal and murder, and he himself betrayed and murdered.

The crucial question about Stalin in 1945 was whether he was the dictator of a nation, with personal and national interests, or whether he was a Communist ideologue bent upon world revolution. Stalin had given the first hint of an answer to that question as early as 1906. The year before, he had written a pamphlet, *Briefly About Intra-Party Differences*, in which he savagely attacked the Mensheviks and copiously quoted Lenin. As it happened, Lenin had need of an educated — but genuine — peasant in his circle, and he nursed Stalin's career along. At the Party Congress in Stockholm in April 1906,

Stalin was presented as the leading spokesman for the Bolsheviks of the Caucasus.

The Congress was split over the issue of the peasants. According to Marx, peasants were petit bourgeois manque, who wanted nothing so much as to own the land they farmed. Individual ownership of farmland was, of course, anathema. Yet, it was all jolly well for it to be anathema to Marx, sitting in the reading room of the British Museum. For practitioners of revolution, however, for those who knew the revolution could not succeed without the support of the peasants, and that such support was not forthcoming without the promise of land, it was a very different matter. The Bolsheviks proposed a compromise, as Ulam has written, "nationalization: all land to be vested in the state. The peasants would understand, said Lenin, that their rights in the land would be undisturbed and only the large landowners' property would be confiscated. But, expostulated the Mensheviks, that would mean that the bourgeois democratic state would hold the land, and would not the bourgeoisie work to strengthen private property? They opted for *municipalization:* all land to be vested in the hands of local authorities. Ah, retorted the Bolsheviks, but would not local authorities be controlled by the peasants?..." and so forth. Stalin cut through the Gordian knot: if the revolution will fail without the peasants, *give the land to the peasants!* In 1917, Lenin worked the idea into a slogan, "All land to the peasants." Thus the pattern was established to abandon ideological Marxism whenever it interfered with the demands of power politics.

In retrospect, the successful career of a revolutionary always appears to have an air of inevitability about it. Given the character of the individual and the events of the time, no other outcome seems possible. Stalin could hardly have seen it in such comforting fashion. He was arrested, released, arrested; he escaped, was arrested, and exiled to Siberia where many Czarist political prisoners died when the temperature dropped below minus 40 degrees centigrade, or committed suicide in the long and lonely winter dark of the Arctic wastes, or died of disease and neglect, or went mad. From his early revolutionary days, Stalin acquired the lifelong habit of working through the night and lying low during the day. And from his four-year exile in Siberia, beginning in August 1913, he seems to have acquired a taste for austerity and reclusiveness.

Just before his exile, in April 1912, Stalin encountered Vyacheslav Molotov, the secretary of the editorial board of *Pravda*. Stalin had been appointed to the Bolshevik Central Committee that year and among his duties was the supervision of the editorial line of *Pravda*. One of Stalin's biggest chores, as it turned out, was to censor the articles of Lenin. Writing from his exile abroad, Lenin insisted on excoriating the Mensheviks—whom Stalin himself had been drubbing only a few years before. Times had changed; the Mensheviks were influential among the workers; the Bolsheviks had to work for accommodation; and so Stalin censored Lenin.

In 1917, Stalin was called out of exile to serve in the Czarist army. His career was short-lived. He was rejected because of his stiff arm. Early that year, however, the Czarist government, rocked by some minor strikes and riots, went into a spastic collapse. The revolutionaries, Stalin among them, hurried to Petrograd. There Stalin found his old colleagues, who for their part passed a resolution saying that "in view of certain personal characteristics of [Stalin's] the Bureau decided to invite him only in an advisory capacity."

It was Molotov, apparently, who was the source of this blackball — one of the greatest betrayals of Stalin's career — and it is ironic to think that, of the millions Stalin would suspect in his life, of all those he would purge, Molotov was never touched. Molotov was, in fact, the only member of Stalin's politburo whom the dictator addressed throughout his life with the Russian familiar pronoun *ty* rather than the formal *vy*.

Stalin's reaction was instantaneous. Within two days, he seized control of *Pravda*, fired all the editors, including Molotov, and, as Ulam writes, "not only became a full member of the Bureau, but also replaced Molotov on its presidium and became the Bolshevik representative in the executive committee of the Petrograd Soviet. And Molotov found his master. He would henceforth serve him — the worn-out simile is precisely right here — with doglike devotion, enduring kicks, taunts, injuries to those closest to him for over thirty years."

"Molotov is not a very talkative man," Djilas said of him years later. It may be that he kept silence, in part, because he stuttered badly when he spoke. "While he was with Stalin, when in a good mood, and with those who think like him, contact was easy and direct. Otherwise Molotov remained impassive, even in private conversation." When he laughed, he laughed soundlessly, and "not only his thoughts but also the process of their generation was impenetrable. Similarly his mentality remained sealed and inscrutable." Molotov seemed to look upon everything "as relative, as something to which he had to, rather than ought to, subordinate his own fate. It was as though for him there was nothing permanent, as though there was only a transitory and unideal reality which presented itself differently each day." He was "thorough, deliberate, composed, and tenacious. He drank more than Stalin, but his toasts were shorter and calculated to produce a particular political effect.... When... I met his wife, a modest and gracious woman, I had the impression that any other might have served his regular, necessary function." Churchill described Molotov succinctly as the complete modern robot. Broken at the very beginning of the Revolution in 1917, Molotov was the first of the new Stalinist men.

All the men with whom Stalin worked in the following years had disappeared by the time of the Potsdam conference: Leon Trotsky was deported in 1928; Sergei Kirov was assassinated in 1934; Lev Kamenev was tried and shot in 1936; Gregory Zinoviev, tried and shot in 1936; Maxim Gorky, died mysteriously, 1936; Karl Radek, purged, 1937; Nikolai Bukharin, purged, 1938; Michael Tomsky, committed suicide, 1938; Alexei Rykov, purged, 1938.

Those who survived Stalin's reign of terror long enough to accompany him to Potsdam were very careful men. In 1938, Nikolai Yezhov, the chief of the NKVD who had administered the most intensive phase of the Great Purge, was replaced by Lavrenti Beria. Yezhov was not himself purged, or convicted of any crime, or even put on trial. He simply disappeared without a trace. Beria, like Stalin, had been born in Georgia. In 1922, at age twenty-three, he was appointed head of the Secretive-Operative Division of the Cheka of Georgia. The *Cheka,* which had been charged after the Revolution with suppressing subversive and dissident elements, later became OGPU and even later the NKVD. Tall, heavy-set, bronze of complexion, and balding, Beria was, according to *Life* magazine, "precise, self-controlled, very calm in manner." He wore pince-nez, made few gestures when he spoke, and rarely had to refer to a note. Beria impressed Djilas as "somewhat plump, greenish pale, and with soft damp hands.... His expression [was] that of a certain self-satisfaction and irony mingled with a clerk's obsequiousness and solicitude." A Western journalist observed, with no intention of black humor, that not long after Beria took over as head of the Russian political police "the NKVD is almost certainly the largest single employer of labor in the world."

Molotov had survived to become Minister of Foreign Affairs. Working directly under him was Andrei Vishinsky, who was once called (also without humor) "one of the fathers of the Soviet judicial system." It was Vishinsky who gave the rallying cry to the Great Purge: "Shoot them like the mad dogs they are." Vishinsky served throughout the purge years as the leading state prosecutor. He believed that the courts have an "educational" as well as a "corrective" function, and the New York Sun pronounced him "one of those just men by whom impartial laws are written." Dean Acheson described him as "short and slim, with quick, abrupt gestures and rapid speech, he gave an impression of nervous tension.... I was braced for a dangerous and adroit antagonist, but... he proved to be a long-winded and boring speaker, as so many Russians are."

Georgi Malenkov, Djilas said, was "even smaller and plumper" than Beria, "but a typical Russian with a Mongol admixture — dark, with prominent cheekbones, and slightly pockmarked. He gave one the impression of being a withdrawn, cautious and not very personable man. It seemed as though under the layers and rolls of fat there moved about still another man, lively and adept, with intelligent and alert black eyes.... He was the one who had invented 'cadre lists' — detailed biographies and autobiographies of all members and candidates of a Party of many millions." As Beria was a student of terror and Vishinsky of argument, Malenkov was a student of people. At Potsdam, Stalin was unquestionably the best briefed of the Big Three. He, understood Western history, the Western democracies, and the personalities of his opponents across the conference table. It was probably Malenkov who provided the briefing on the personalities.

The chairman of State Planning was Nikolai Voznesensky, "an orderly, cultured, and above all withdrawn man," Djilas said, "who said little and always had a happy inward smile." The other chief economists were Anasthasias Mikoyan, from Soviet Armenia, in charge of foreign trade, and Lazar

Kaganovich, the only surviving Jew in the politburo, who was in charge of Russian heavy industry.

Andrei Zhdanov was the custodian of Communist propaganda. A buoyant, quick-witted, jolly raconteur, he was chock full of anecdotes from Russian history and folktales. He was the house "intellectual," and, as Djilas noted, "Although he had some knowledge of everything, even music, I would not say that there was a single field that he knew thoroughly." Djilas was not amused by Zhdanov's unsophisticated sense of humor, either, and summed up Stalin's public relations man as being "rather short, with a brownish clipped mustache, high forehead, pointed nose, and a sickly red face."

It will be noticed that nowhere in this group is a man who could be described as a Marxist theoretician, or as a bold adventurer.

At the end of the war, with Russia devastated and needing the hardest of work and sacrifice to rebuild, Stalin's needs were those of a tyrant in a very particular sort of trouble. He perceived a new and vital danger: millions of Russian soldiers had seen foreign lands, foreign wealth, foreign freedom. Thousands and thousands had traded everything they had with British and American troops for — wristwatches. Wristwatches, gold plated, silver plated, with seventeen-jewel movements: what unimaginable wealth they represented, and every single British and American soldier seemed to have one, and treat it *casually*, as though it were a mere convenience.

"They fear our friendship more than our enmity," Churchill said of the Russian leaders. Stalin did indeed fear that the Russian people would be infected by contact with the West, its wristwatches and its ideas. He had great need of the iron curtain, and he had great need of the time-tested monarchical forger of internal unity: an external enemy. He jailed thousands upon thousands of returning soldiers; he pushed the West further and further away with the buffer states of eastern Europe — not to expand Communism around the world, but to hold Stalinism together in Russia. That was how he used international Communism, and if ever Communism — French Communism or Italian Communism or British Socialism — interfered with Stalinism, he cut it dead.

Stalin's personal need corresponded, too, to Russia's historical experience and tendencies. "From the beginning of the ninth century," Louis Halle wrote in *The Cold War as History*, "and even today, the prime driving force in Russia has been fear. Fear, rather than ambition, is the principal reason for the organization and expansion of the Russian society. Fear, rather than ambition in itself, has been the great driving force. The Russians as we know them today have experienced ten centuries of constant, mortal fear. This has not been a disarming experience. It has not been an experience calculated to produce a simple, open, innocent, and guileless society." Splayed over a vast land, with no natural frontiers for protection, as Halle remarks, Russia has been overrun "generation after generation, by fresh waves of invaders," by the Huns, "the Bulgars, the Avars, the Khazars, the Magyars, the Pechenegs, and so on — up through the Tartars, the so-called 'Golden Horde,' which did not disappear from Europe until the end of the fifteenth century.... Lying defenseless on the plain, they were slaughtered and subjugated and humiliated by the invaders time and again." For any Russians who had faulty historical sensibilities, the Germans had recently reminded them of their open frontiers and their dreadful vulnerability.

The foreign policy that Stalin adopted was in no way novel. In a classic essay on the Cold War written by Walter Lippmann in 1947, Lippmann quoted Robert Strausz-Hupe, a professor at the University of Pennsylvania with a sense of *déjà vu:* "The Western frontiers of the Soviet Sphere of Influence coincide so closely with those Czarist Russia planned to draw after the defeat of the Central Powers, that Czarist and Soviet policies appear to differ as regards method only.... The aggregate of annexed territories, protectorates, alliances and Pan-Slav affiliations would have extended Russian influence to the Oder River, the Alps, the Adriatic and the Aegean. The Czarist project, cleansed of the dynastic and social preconceptions of Czardom, took shape in the system of annexed territories, occupation zones, friendly regimes and ideological affiliations which constitutes the Soviet sphere of influence in Europe. It is only at the Straits [the Dardanelles] that the Soviet government failed to attain the goals set by its predecessors."

Toward the end of May 1945, President Truman dispatched Harry Hopkins to the Kremlin to prepare the way for the Potsdam conference. *Fortune* magazine had once described Hopkins as giving off "a suggestion of quick cigarettes, thinning hair, brief sarcasm, fraying suits of clothes," but Hopkins's loose-limbed frame had begun to sag; the cigarettes were not as quick; he was exhausted from his wartime chores, and he was sick.

The choice of Hopkins for this preconference mission was meant to reassure Stalin. Hopkins was Roosevelt's old friend and a representative of the close cooperation of the war years. The message he bore, however, was not at all reassuring. Never mind the particulars, he told Stalin; there were a number of things he wanted to discuss; but the "real reason" he had come to Moscow was to tell Stalin that the American people were so seriously dis turbed about Russia "as to affect adversely the relations between our two countries." Just where Hopkins saw evidence of a dramatic change in American public opinion, so serious as to affect American foreign policy, is moot. The Hearst newspapers and the Chicago Tribune continued their long-standing complaints about Russia, but there was no evidence of a mounting chorus. Stalin knew what was in the American papers and doubtless drew the correct inference that when Hopkins spoke of public opinion it was simply a manner of speaking. The heart of the problem, Hopkins told Stalin, was "our inability to carry into effect the Yalta Agreement on Poland."

At Yalta, the Big Three had agreed that the government of Poland was to be "restructured." Russian troops had rolled right over Poland on their way to Germany, and the whole of Poland had come under Russian control. The Russians had overseen the establishment of a provisional government that was, naturally, "friendly" to the Soviets. At the same time, another group, the government-in-exile in London, claimed to be the rightful government of Poland. The Big Three had agreed at Yalta to combine the two governments, but inevitably the question was who was to have the greatest number of ministers, who was to have the predominant influence in the new government — who was to control Poland?

Charles Bohlen sat nearby taking careful notes of the conversation:

"Marshal Stalin replied that the reason for the failure on the Polish question was that the Soviet

Union desired to have a friendly Poland, but that Great Britain wanted to revive the system of *cordon sanitaire* on the Soviet borders.

"Mr. Hopkins replied that neither the government nor the people of the United States had any such intention.

"Marshal Stalin replied that... the British conservatives did not desire to see a Poland friendly to the Soviet Union.

"Mr. Hopkins stated that the United States would desire a Poland friendly to the Soviet Union and in fact desired to see friendly countries all along the Soviet borders.

"Marshal Stalin replied if that be so we can easily come to terms in regard to Poland."

There is no doubt that Hopkins wished to have America and Russia continue a cordial relationship, and he said again and again that the issue was very serious; he was personally concerned; he felt it was urgent, fundamental; and he wanted to clear up any doubts Stalin had about America's attitude toward Russia. The Americans wanted to cooperate with Russia; Poland had become the issue over which cooperation would flourish, or fail.

On the following day, Stalin said he did indeed feel "a certain alarm in regard to the attitude of the United States Government," and he would not "attempt to use Soviet public opinion as a screen" but would speak candidly about what troubled him. The way in which Lend-Lease had been canceled was "unfortunate and even brutal." If it had been meant to put "pressure on the Russians in order to soften them then it was a fundamental mistake." The way the United States had brought Argentina into the United Nations mocked the value of agreements of the Big Three "if their decisions could be overturned by the votes of such countries as Honduras or Puerto Rico." He did not think, he said, that it necessarily follows that "a country is virtuous because it is small." Stalin raised other questions. They were nettlesome, and Hopkins answered them, but both Stalin and Hopkins understood that Poland was the central issue. At Yalta, Stalin said, it had been agreed "that the existing government was to be reconstructed and that anyone with common sense could see that this meant that the present government was to form the basis of the new.... Despite the fact that they were simple people the Russians should not be regarded as fools... nor were they blind and could quite well see what was going on before their eyes.

"Mr. Hopkins said that he wished to state this position as clearly and as forcibly as he knew how. He said the question of Poland per se was not so important as the fact that it had become a symbol of our ability to work out problems with the Soviet Union.... We would accept any government in Poland which was desired by the Polish people and was at the same time friendly to the Soviet government.... Poland... bore a direct relation to the willingness of the United States to participate in international affairs.... Our people must believe that they are joining their power with that of the Soviet Union and Great Britain in the promotion of international peace and the well-being of humanity.

"Mr. Stalin replied that... in the course of twenty-five years the Germans had twice invaded Russia via Poland. Neither the British nor American people had experienced such German invasions which were a horrible thing to endure and the results of which were not easily forgotten. He said these German invasions were not warfare but were like the incursions of the Huns.... Germany had been able to do this because Poland had been regarded as part of the *cordon sanitaire* around the Soviet Union, and that previous European policy had been that Polish governments must be hostile to Russia. In these circumstances either Poland had been too weak to oppose Germany or had let the Germans come through. Thus Poland had served as a corridor for the German attacks on Russia.... It is therefore in Russia's vital interest that Poland should be both strong and friendly."

Hopkins spoke of America's interests in seeing democratic freedoms in a country thousands of miles from its own borders. Stalin spoke of the need to protect his country from attack that had twice come through the nation on Russia's border. What could this mean? Were the Americans really such unbending ideologues?

Stalin offered an opening bid for a compromise. There were eighteen or twenty ministries in the Polish government. America and Britain could have four or five of them. (Molotov whispered to Stalin.) Stalin corrected himself: the Americans and British could have four posts. How about Professor Lange, an American citizen, as a member of the Polish government?

Hopkins replied dryly that he thought Lange might not want to give up his American citizenship.

At the third meeting, Poland was not mentioned; Hopkins evidently was waiting for a reaction from Washington. At the fourth meeting, Hopkins raised the subject again. There were certain fundamental rights, he said, "which, when infringed upon or denied caused concern in the United States." These were freedom of speech, freedom of assembly, freedom of movement, and freedom of religious worship. In addition, all political parties must be "permitted the free use, without distinction, of the press, radio, meetings and other facilities of political expression." Furthermore, all citizens should have "the right of public trial, defense by counsel of their own choosing, and the right of habeas corpus."

To this recital of Western political principles, Stalin calmly lied that "these principles of democracy are well known and would find no objection on the part of the Soviet government." He was sure the Polish government would "welcome them." Of course, he said, "in regard to the *specific* [italics added] freedoms mentioned by Mr. Hopkins, they could only be applied in full in peace time, and even then with certain limitations."

With that one word "specific," the fate of eastern Europe was sealed. Hopkins either did not hear it or chose to ignore it. Hopkins concluded that he thought the Big Three could settle the Polish dispute amicably. Stalin agreed — but it is not at all clear to what he agreed. He certainly did not agree to the granting of "specific freedoms" in Poland. He may have thought he agreed to pay lip service to democratic principles and give his domination of Poland the appearance, if not the reality, of democracy. He said, somewhat uncertainly, that it was necessary "for all three governments genuinely to wish to settle this matter. If one of them secretly did not wish to see it settled then the difficulties were real."

Hopkins had one more conversation with Stalin in which he returned to Poland yet again. By now, since the two men had twice agreed that they agreed, Stalin must have wondered why Hopkins kept bringing up the subject. "I told him very forcefully," Hopkins wrote to Truman, "that he must believe me when I told him that our whole relationship was threatened by the impasse of Poland.... I told Stalin further that I personally felt that our relations were threatened and that I frankly had many misgivings about it and with my intimate knowledge of the situation I was, frankly, bewildered with some of the things that were going on."

Stalin was bewildered, too. Averell Harriman cabled to the President: "I am afraid Stalin does not and never will fully understand our interest in a free Poland as a matter of principle. He is a realist in all of his actions, and it is hard for him to appreciate our faith in abstract principles. It is difficult for him to understand why we should want to interfere with Soviet policy in a country like Poland, which he considers so important to Russia's security, unless we have some ulterior motive."

One of Stalin's primary objectives for Potsdam was determined by his conversations with Hopkins: he devised sets of diplomatic ploys to test whether the Americans were naïve, or determined ideological crusaders, or had some ulterior motive.

In the midst of his conversations with Hopkins, Stalin tested the matter tentatively in a cable to Truman that urged that the Big Three establish diplomatic relations with Finland, Rumania, Bulgaria, and Hungary—in effect recognizing governments "friendly" to Russia. Truman replied by giving Finland to Stalin immediately, "because the Finnish people, through their elections and other political adjustments, have demonstrated their genuine devotion to democratic procedures and principles." The Finns had indeed salvaged something of a democratic government for themselves—principally by delivering reparations to Moscow, as Andrei Zhdanov said over dinner at the Kremlin, "on time, expertly packed, and of excellent quality. " However, Zhdanov added, "We made a mistake in not occupying Finland. Everything would have been set up if we had."

"Akh, Finland," Molotov said, "that is a peanut."

Having allowed a democratic regime in a "peanut" country, Stalin felt he had sufficiently indulged Churchill's and Truman's whims. As Truman said, "I have not found in Hungary, Rumania, and Bulgaria the same encouraging signs.... I have been disturbed to find governments which do not accord to all democratic elements of the people the rights of free expression."

"I see no reason," Stalin cabled back, "to show any preference in the matter to Finland which, unlike Rumania or Bulgaria, did not participate on the Allied side in the war against Hitler Germany." Then came the test: "As regards political regimes, the opportunities for the democratic element in Rumania and Bulgaria are not less than, say, in Italy, with which the governments of the United

States and the Soviet Union have already resumed diplomatic relations." In his reply, Truman did not mention Italy; he said, blandly, "I am giving this matter further study."

An even better test of American intentions presented itself on July 12, when word from Madrid suggested that Franco's Spanish dictatorship was in trouble. Several ministers had offered their resignations; democratic principles were openly and eagerly touted; Franco's position seemed shaky. If Truman was the ideological crusader he presented himself as being, surely he would want to join Stalin in a condemnation of the fascist Franco and encourage the Spanish people to topple the dictator. It was an acid test of American intentions, and Stalin added Spain to his list of topics for the Potsdam agenda.

Aside from this crucial testing of intentions, what Stalin wanted from Potsdam above all were concrete, tangible things. He wanted ships and factories and territories and bases. As he told Hopkins, he wanted one-third of the German Navy and Merchant Marine ships. These ships did not seem to be forthcoming, and if America and Britain rejected the Soviet "request," the results would be "very unpleasant."

Next, Stalin said, Russia would honor its commitment to enter the war against Japan three months after the end of the war in Europe. That would be on August 8. (In fact, Stalin spent many of his nighttime hours moving Russian troops into position in the Far East.) In return for this, he would expect America to honor its Yalta commitments. It has often been said that Roosevelt "sold out" American interests at Yalta. Whether he did or not — and in any case, the Americans felt great need of Russian assistance in the Far East at that time — Stalin certainly sold out the Chinese Communists. In a note Molotov gave Harriman at Yalta, Russia expressed "its willingness to conclude with the National Government of China a pact of friendship and alliance between the USSR and China." To Hopkins, Stalin said he thought Chiang Kai-shek was a good leader, and "he did not believe that the Chinese Communist leaders were as good or would be able to bring about the unification of China." In return, Stalin received a promise of Port Arthur, Dairen, the Kurile Islands, and the Manchurian railroad complex, a maintenance of the status quo in Outer Mongolia, and some other tidbits. This agreement must be honored, he told Hopkins, rubbing in the American's concern for public opinion by adding that otherwise he could not "justify entry into the Pacific War in the eyes of the Soviet people," who, of course, had never heard of the Yalta agreement. As for Japan itself, he added casually, it would be necessary to have some serious talks about "zones of occupation." Stalin would not be averse to having a zone of occupation himself.

In addition to the German fleet, there was the more

general question of reparations. At Yalta, Stalin had stunned Roosevelt and Churchill by suggesting that Germany should be stripped of 20 billion dollars' worth of reparations, including four-fifths of Germany's heavy industry. Half, 10 billion dollars' worth, would go to Russia, Stalin said calmly. In effect, Germany would pay to rebuild Russia.

Having reached all the way to Japan in the east, having begun to forge a solid phalanx of client states along his western border, Stalin then looked south. He would like to be a Mediterranean power. All that kept him from reaching the Mediterranean were the Straits of Dardanelles linking the Black Sea to the Mediterranean. Turkey controlled those straits according to the Montreux Convention, which had taken effect in 1936. Stalin wanted, at the least, an international guarantee of Russia's right to free use of the straits and, at best, his own military base there to make certain of his rights.

Once he imagined himself in the Mediterranean, Stalin picked around at various territories along the shore. He would like to discuss Syria, which controlled the major pipeline from the Iraqi oil fields, and then Lebanon; and, in line with United Nations plans to assign various powers "trust territories," he thought Russia would like to have Tripoli. Casting an eye further down the coast, Stalin's gaze encountered the International Zone of Tangier, which controlled the key entrance and exit of the Mediterranean, the Straits of Gibraltar. Stalin would like Russia to join the international organization that administered Tangier.

To obtain the items at the top of his list, Stalin was prepared to trade any number of things. He had already respected democratic sensibilities in Finland, and he would be quick to drop any claims to Tangier and Tripoli and Syria and Lebanon. They were all, for the most part, bargaining counters to be sacrificed for real gains or simply to show Stalin's reasonableness. Most often, as Stalin dropped one whimsical demand after another, he would argue with deep feeling that Russia had a right to a disproportionate share of the spoils of war because Russia had lost so many soldiers. His solicitousness for the treasure of human life could be touching at times, and it is a measure of his uncommon acting ability — his genius, really — that he could affect others with his simple sincerity. "Stalin's greatness as a dissimulator," George Ken-nan has written, "was an integral part of his greatness as a statesman. So was his gift for simple, plausible, ostensibly innocuous utterance.... The modern age has known no greater master of the tactical art. The unassuming, quiet facade, as innocently disarming as the first move of the grand master at chess, was only a part of this brilliant, terrifying tactical mastery."

Stalin was, too, a supreme realist when it came to foreign affairs. He would ditch the Communists in China, recognize democrats in Finland, and make demands only to give in on them. He believed, his biographer Adam Ulam has said, that "eventually Communism would inherit the world, but not in his time.... World domination? He was not Hitler to think in such terms, to believe the main key to power lay in military escapades. Let Russia outproduce all other countries in steel and other aspects of industrial power — again something which will not happen in his lifetime — and then there might be some sense in such speculations.

"... Could anything have made him different, made him trust and collaborate with the West? He would have found this question hilarious: he had not gotten where he was by trusting people. Of course, much of the unpleasantness could have been avoided had the West been more forthright. He understood the Americans, but their ways were exasperating. They were Indian-givers and busybodies. They gave him Poland at Teheran and then started all that fuss about elections and democratic procedures. ... He would not have disagreed with Mao's characterization of American imperialists as 'the newly upstart and neurotic.'"

Churchill had been the one to urge that a meeting of the Big Three take place. He was anxious to get together before Stalin simply took what he wanted and all chance for haggling was gone. Truman was the one to set the date for the meeting. He postponed it, perhaps to gain more time for the atomic bomb test. Stalin was the one to choose the place for the conference.

Potsdam was a convenient spot, and that was doubtless Stalin's reason for choosing it. But the place had a meaning for him, too; that escaped the notice of Churchill and Truman. Potsdam is famous not for the Cecilienhof Palace, where the conference meetings took place, but for the palace of Sans Souci, built by Frederick the Great of Prussia in 1745. It was in the small and elegantly proportioned rooms of Sans Souci, in the company of Voltaire, the latest second-rate French paintings, and a pack of sleek whippets, that Frederick doubled the size of the Prussian Army and instilled it with demanding ideals of discipline and sacrifice.

One of the officers in Frederick's army was the father of Karl von Clausewitz. Karl joined the Prussian Army in 1792 at the age of twelve, rose to the rank of general, and, in 1813, fought with the Russian Army. He is best known, however, not as a general but as the author of *On War,* an unfinished three-volume study of the art and politics of warfare. He is most frequently cited for his dictum that war is a continuation of politics by other means. The essence of Clausewitz, in fact, is the belief that political and military weapons are interchangeable and that, just as war is a continuation of the struggles of peacetime, so too can peace be understood as a continuation of war. War, he said, "is an act of social life." And social life, he might have said, is an act of war. It was an insight destined to find favor with any who admired Marx, and Lenin filled his notebooks with long excerpts from Clausewitz alongside passages from Marx and Engels. In 1933, Stalin had the Soviet government publish Lenin's notebook on Clausewitz. For Stalin, then, Potsdam was a memorial to the beginnings of Prussian militarism, the end of German military might, and the continuous struggle in peace and war for power. Potsdam was an appropriate setting for the aims of all three leaders who met to confer, though only Stalin knew it.

4
MONDAY,
JULY 16

On the morning of July 16, Babelsberg was as quiet as a small town in Missouri. The early morning was cool, the lake was still, and no breeze disturbed the leaves of the trees that shaded the gently curving streets of the town. Stalin was still making his circuitous way to the conference aboard his imperial train and he would not arrive until late in the day. Churchill was still abed. Truman was up at his customary early hour. The President had a suite of rooms on the second floor of the "Little White House" (of yellow stucco) in Babelsberg. From the sun porch adjoining his rooms, he could look out over the lawn that sloped down to the quiet lake. "Dear Mama and Mary," he wrote home, "[We are in] a beautiful house on a lake in Potsdam, which formerly belonged to the head of the movie colony. It is said that he had been sent back to Russia—for what purpose I don't know."

Jimmy Byrnes was established in a suite on the first floor of the house, and other rooms had been assigned to Leahy, Vaughan, Vardaman, Charlie Ross, Charles Bohlen, and, as Truman recalled in his memoirs, "others." Among the "others" still trying to attract the President's notice was H. Freeman Matthews, graduate of l'École Libre des Sciences Politiques.

The President dressed in a white shirt, a polka-dotted bow tie, double-breasted dark suit, and two-tone summer shoes. Everyone at the conference would be impressed by his brisk, businesslike manner. He seemed, it was said, like a chairman of the board.

The chairman took his morning walk around the American "neighborhood" of Babelsberg, had breakfast at eight o'clock, and closeted himself straightaway in conversations with Byrnes and Leahy. The sleepy suburban appearance of Babelsberg was deceptive: telephone lines kept the President in direct touch with Washington and, through the military communications center in Frankfurt, with the rest of the world. The mail pouches that went in and out of the Little White House brought mail from home, items of legislation to be reviewed and signed, and continuous intelligence reports from the State Department and the military.

Truman kept a particularly close watch on the debate in Congress over the United Nations Charter. Three troublesome senators were threatening to upset ratification of the United Nations agreements: Hiram Johnson of California and Henrik Shipstead of Minnesota, both Republicans, and James Murray, a Democrat of Montana. To ratify the Security Charter of the UN, they argued, would place the power to commit American troops to war in the hands of the UN Security Council. Thus, they said, Congress would be voting to remove from its own hands the constitutional prerogative to declare war. On July 16, the Senate Foreign Relations Committee issued its majority report: "Any attempt to give Congress power to decide every time the new world security organization could use U.S. troops against a recalcitrant would violate both the San Francisco Charter and the U.S. Constitution."

This interpretation would gradually wear away all congressional war powers until, with the passage of time and the determination of the President, those powers would come to reside exclusively in the White House. Soon enough, President Truman would commit troops to Korea—before a UN resolution called for such a measure, and before Congress had even been informed that America had gone to war. The beginning of such unchecked Presidential power dates from July 16, 1945, when the Senate voted to abridge the power of Congress to declare war — for the first time in the history of the United States.

In Babelsberg, almost everyone noticed a certain sprightliness to Truman's step. At eleven o'clock that morning Winston Churchill came to call, accompanied by Anthony Eden and Sir Alexander Cadogan. Churchill and Truman had exchanged notes and cables and spoken by telephone, and even met fleetingly when Churchill had been in Washington to see Roosevelt, but this was the first time they had met as the leaders of their two countries. Churchill was attracted by Truman's "gay, precise, sparkling manner." For his part, Truman "had an instant liking for this man. ... There was something very open and genuine about the way he greeted me." "P.M. delighted with Pres.," Cadogan noted in his diary.

Later on, Lord Moran would ask Churchill what he thought of the President. Had he real ability? Moran asked. "The P.M. stood over me. The white of his eyes showed above his pupils, his lips pouted. Looking down at me as if he were saying something he did not want to be repeated: 'I should think he has,' he said. 'At any rate, he is a man of immense determination. He takes no notice of delicate ground, he just plants his foot down firmly on it.'

"And to illustrate this the P.M. jumped a little off the wooden floor and brought his bare feet down with a smack."

The first encounter between President and Prime Minister was a smashing success — though Charles Bohlen would notice a slight change from past conferences: "Where Roosevelt was warmly friendly with Churchill and Stalin, Truman was pleasantly distant."

They settled into a drawing room in the Little White House where they were joined by Jimmy Byrnes, and their conversation turned presently to Japan. Churchill could provide forces for the Japanese war; indeed, the British were eager to help. The Americans appreciated the generous offer of assistance, but it appeared that the war in the Far East was going well enough without British help. In fact, by this time, Truman was anxious to go it alone in Japan and to have no one else in on the kill.

In a meeting of the President and the Joint Chiefs of Staff before the Americans left for Potsdam, Admiral Leahy had said that he felt the demand for unconditional surrender should be dropped. Such a demand, Leahy said, "would result only in making the Japanese desperate and thereby increase our casualty lists." The Japanese were close to defeat; if only the unconditional surrender formula were dropped, they might well stop fighting. In any case, it was clear that British aid would only be a nuisance, and, for that matter, it looked as though Russian assistance was unnecessary, too. Fleet Admiral E. J. King insisted that the Russians "were not indispensable.... While the cost of defeating Japan would be greater, there was no question in his mind but that we could handle it alone."

This impression was confirmed by the reports that came in to the President in Babelsberg. On July 15: "Guam Hq. says U.S. warships today continued shelling targets in Japan's home islands and that carrier aircraft again were active. Yesterday's shelling destroyed the Imperial Iron and Steel Works at Kamaishi, Honshu Island, and carrier planes ranging over Honshu and Hokkaido destroyed 25 and damaged 62 Japanese aircraft, *all but one of them being hit on the ground* [italics added]." The Japanese were not even getting their planes into the air: American planes could fly over Japan at will, without resistance, and bomb as much and as long as they pleased. On July 16: "Guam Hq. says Superforts from the Marianas last night attacked the Nippon Oil Co. at Kudamatsu on southern Honshu Island." The Superfortress bombers were not opposed. Japan could no longer defend itself.

The Americans knew of the urgent messages that the Japanese government was sending to its ambassador in Moscow. No, the British were not needed in the Far East; and neither were the Russians. Stalin had promised to join the war by August 8, and there was no way, really, to keep him out. But Truman would not make any special point of urging the Russians to get into the Japanese war; certainly he would not give the Russians any concessions for joining the war. And, in any event, perhaps the Japanese war would be over before August 8.

Truman was taking an awesome gamble. He needed to win the war, as one of his briefs said, "before too many of our allies are committed there and have made substantial contributions toward the defeat of Japan." He had two weapons, either of which might be equally effective: to drop the demand for unconditional surrender or, if the tests worked out, to drop the atomic bomb. To drop the demand for unconditional surrender would be, in the view of some, tantamount to "appeasement." To use the bomb, on the other hand, had the double virtue of finishing Japan and possibly, in Byrnes's phrase, of making the Russians more manageable in Europe. On the whole, it seemed worth waiting for word of the Alamogordo test.

In the meantime, Truman made it clear to Churchill that the Americans were not, as Fleet Admiral King said, going to "beg" the Russians to enter the Japanese war. Thus, if the British were not to be allowed in for the kill in Japan, at least,

Churchill could console himself, neither would the Russians. Churchill emerged from the meeting tremendously cheered up, and deeply impressed by Truman's "obvious power of decision." It was shortly after 1: 00 P.M. in Babelsberg.

It was 5: 10 A.M. at "Trinity," the code name for the test site in New Mexico. As the final countdown began, the scientists and other observers took up positions in trenches and covered their eyes with welders' goggles. Edward Teller had gone to the extra precaution of wearing a pair of dark glasses under his goggles. Hans Bethe, from the University of Munich, had smeared his face with suntan lotion. J. Robert Oppenheimer stood at the doorway of the control shack, watching the weather. "Everyone was told to lie face down on the ground," recalled General Leslie Groves, the military coordinator of the project, "with his feet toward the blast, to close his eyes, and to cover his eyes with his hands as the countdown approached zero. As soon as they became aware of the flash they could turn over and sit or stand up, covering their eyes with the smoked glass with which each had been supplied." Groves himself lay down on the ground next to James B. Conant and Vannevar Bush. The night before, Enrico Fermi had wandered among his fellow scientists offering to take bets on whether the bomb would "ignite the atmosphere, and if so, whether it would merely destroy New Mexico or destroy the world." As the countdown approached zero, he appeared eccentric, or perhaps mad, as he stood casually tearing up bits of paper. (When the bomb exploded, Fermi would drop the paper scraps and measure the distance they were carried by the shock wave to determine the force of the blast.) A short distance away stood Klaus Fuchs, a Russian spy. He had done exact calculations of the force of the bomb and knew it would not be necessary to lie on the ground for the test firing. Large, brilliant floodlights illuminated the tower on which the device had been set. William Laurence, the sole newspaper reporter allowed to witness the test, shivered in the cold dawn and took out his pencil. Oppenheimer turned to an officer in the control shack and said, "Lord, these affairs are hard on the heart."

In San Francisco Bay, the cruiser *Indianapolis* passed under the Golden Gate Bridge, and steamed toward Hawaii and the island of Tinian, known to American airmen as "the garden of paradise." Its cargo was small, consisting only of some bomb parts. Other parts were flown by Air Transport, in two C-54S, from Albuquerque to Tinian.

In Potsdam that morning, the American Joint Chiefs of Staff met to talk about the war in Japan. H. H. "Hap" Arnold said conventional bombing could end the war. General George C. Marshall thought that the Japanese should at least be forewarned so that they would have a chance to surrender before the bomb was used. Admiral E.

J. King believed a naval blockade alone would end the war by starving the Japanese into submission. General Eisenhower had told Stimson that Japan was already utterly defeated. It was, he said, "completely unnecessary" to drop the bomb, and it would only rouse world opinion against the United States to use a horrible weapon that was "no longer mandatory as a measure to save American lives." Admiral Leahy was at a loss to explain the determination to use the bomb and thought perhaps it was "because of the vast sums that had been spent on the project." As Enrico Fermi shredded pieces of paper at Alamogordo, the British Chiefs of Staff prepared for a meeting with the American Chiefs of Staff. Sir Alan Brooke urged Leahy at the meeting to reconsider "unconditional surrender." Leahy replied that the question "was clearly a political one."

No final decision had been made on the use of the bomb but, in any case, whether it was to be viewed as a military or a political weapon, the 509th Airborne Group was ready to drop it. At Tinian, the crews flew practice runs to Iwo Jima, dropping 1000-and 500-pound bombs on Rota and Guguan to sharpen their targeting skills.

At precisely 5:30 A.M. at Trinity, General Groves's "first impression was one of tremendous light, and then as I turned, I saw the now familiar fireball. As Bush, Conant and I sat on the ground looking at this phenomenon, the first reactions of the three of us were expressed in a silent exchange of handclasps. We all arose so that by the time the shock wave arrived we were standing.

"I was surprised by its comparative gentleness when it reached us almost fifty seconds later.... The shock was very impressive, but the light had been so much greater than any human had previously experienced or even than we had anticipated that we did not shake off the experience quickly."

The intensity of the light was such, as Lansing Lamont has written, "that it could have been seen from another planet. The temperature at its center was four times that at the center of the sun and more than 10, 000 times that at the sun's surface." The men at Trinity felt a sudden flush of warmth. Within eight-tenths of a second the fireball had expanded to resemble a half-risen sun — but it was larger, and it was pure white. Some tore off their goggles for a closer look and were instantly — though only temporarily-blinded by the light. Tons of sand were sucked up into "a swirling column of orange and red, darkening as it rose until it looked like flames of burning oil. Suddenly, a narrower column rose and mushroomed into a parasol of billowy, white smoke surrounded by a spectral glow of blue. Within a second or two, the blue vanished, leaving an outline of gray smoke faintly illuminated by the yellowing streaks of the dawn's early light."

"My God," said one of the men at Trinity, "the damn thing worked!"

Windows were shattered 235 miles away in Gallup, New Mexico. Tremors were felt in El Paso. Mrs. H. E. Wieselman, who lived on the Arizona-New Mexico state line saw "the sun come up and go down again."

General Groves issued a press release:

Alamogordo, N.M., July 16

The commanding officer of the Alamogordo Army Air Base made the following statement today:

"Several inquiries had been received concerning a heavy explosion which occurred on the Alamogordo Air Base reservation this morning."

"A remotely located ammunition magazine containing a considerable amount of high explosives and pyrotechnics exploded...."

"Weather conditions affecting the content of gas shells exploded by the blast may make it desirable for the Army to evacuate temporarily a few civilians from their homes."

In Wilmington, Delaware, Dr. R. M. Evans of the DuPont Company read the press item and knew the atomic bomb had been successfully tested: high explosives, pyrotechnics, and chemicals, he knew, were never stored in one magazine.

"A half-mile beyond the crater," according to Lansing Lamont's survey, "... a seventy-foot-high steel tower... lay crumpled on the ground, its mangled girders severed from one another as cleanly as a small wire snapped by pliers. The tower had been the equivalent of a six-story steel building, and when Groves later saw its wreckage he decided that the newly erected Pentagon was no longer a safe shelter from the bomb.

"The stench of death clung to the desert in the vicinity of the detonation. No rattlesnake or lizard — nothing that could crawl or fly — was left. Here and there carbonized shadows of tiny animals had been etched in the hard-packed caliche where the rampaging blaze had emulsified them. A herd of antelope that had been spotted the day before had vanished, bound, some said later, on a frightened dash that ended in Mexico. The yuccas and Joshua trees had disappeared in the heat storm; no solitary blade of grass was visible. The only green on that burned, discolored desert was the trinitite."

Some years later, looking back on what he perceived as a needless use of the bomb, Oppenheimer said, "In some crude sense, which no vulgarity, no humor, no overstatement can quite extinguish, the physicists have known sin..."

It was three-forty in the afternoon in Babelsberg. Truman, Jimmy Byrnes, and Admiral Leahy filed into the backseat of a large Chrysler convertible to drive to Berlin and see the ruins. They traveled from Potsdam along the Avus Autobahn, a broad highway that was then empty save for the bands of German nomads who trundled their salvaged belongings along in anything that had wheels. "About halfway to the city," Truman said, "we found the entire American 2nd Armored Division deployed along one side of the highway for my inspection. We stopped, honors were rendered by a band and honor guard, and I left the sedan in which I had been riding and entered an open half-track reconnaissance car. In this I passed down the long line of men and vehicles, which comprised what was at that time the largest armored division in the world. Men and tanks were arrayed down the highway in front of me as far as the eye could see. The line was so long it took twenty-two minutes to ride from the beginning to the end of it."

As they drove into the caldron of ruins that had been Berlin they were struck at once by the stench of corpses and bombed-out sewers and the acrid odor of burning. Nearly all the buildings were destroyed, and it was oddly satisfying to spot the ones that had been bombed and those that had been shelled by the final artillery barrage. The bombed buildings were smashed from the top. The shelled buildings, hit from the side, often had a wall, or part of a wall, still standing. Stunted, burned trees, twisted lampposts, snarled girders — each captured the fascinated attention of the tourists for a moment; the bombs and shells created many strange new forms.

"A more depressing sight than that of the ruined buildings," Truman said, "was the long, never-ending procession of old men, women, and children wandering aimlessly... carrying, pushing, or pulling what was left of their belongings." In the remains of the Tiergarten, an old scarecrow of a woman searched among the rubble for sticks to make a fire to heat soup for her children. In the damp basement nearby, *boîtes de nuit,* operating at highly inflated prices, beckoned to the soldiers. In the Sieges-Allee, where the statues were chipped and broken by bullets, a garden seat remained, bearing the sign: "Nicht für Juden." Not far away a notice board was propped against a wall. Pins and bits of gummed paper held offers of sale and barter, requests for information about relatives. One man pinned his offer to the board and stepped back to watch. He was going to Hamburg; in exchange for food he would take messages to relatives in Hamburg. An old woman pinned her answer to the man's notice and, after she had gone, he stepped back up to the board, took out his pen, and amended his offer to make it less generous.

Churchill was suddenly moved by the same whim that had taken Truman to Berlin. The Prime

Minister gathered Lord Moran, Cadogan, and Eden in a closed car and set off for the ruins. Truman's convertible and Churchill's closed sedan circled slowly through the city, crossing one another's paths here and there but never meeting.

Churchill wore a lightweight military uniform and kept a cigar stuck in his mouth for the whole of the tour. At the Reichstag, a crowd of Germans hung about on the steps bartering with the Russian soldiers. The Russians were treated to a vision of boots, slippers, dresses, undergarments, fountain pens, cameras, clocks, and watches. A pair of field glasses was on sale for 2, 000 marks.

Churchill got out of the car, and, to the alarm of his bodyguards, slowly threaded his way up the steps through the crowd. The Germans recognized the cigar; many of them looked away; some watched with blank faces. A shapely blonde in a brightly colored dress fell into step with the Prime Minister, eyeing him intently. One of the guards gently but firmly shouldered her aside.

As the British drove on through the streets, Lord Moran more and more "felt a sense of nausea; it was like the first time I saw a surgeon open a belly and the intestines gushed out."

As they arrived at Hitler's chancellory, Churchill recalled in his memoirs, "they all began to cheer. My hate had died with their surrender, and I was much moved by their demonstrations." In fact, the cheers came not from the Germans but from a group of British sailors and Royal Marines.

By now crowds of reporters and British and Russian soldiers had swelled Churchill's entourage to a mob. "It was frightfully hot," Cadogan said, "milling about in such a crowd, stumbling over the dusty debris with which all the rooms and passages are littered." The chancellory, Lord Ismay recalled, "was smashed to smithereens and the Russians had made no attempt to clear up the mess. Perhaps they had left it on purpose, as an awful warning." Broken window glass and remnants of chandeliers were scattered over the floor, along with an assortment of papers and ribbons and Iron Crosses, and Hitler's upturned desk — its marble top broken into hundreds of pieces.

Churchill stopped in Hitler's dining room and gazed up at the ceiling, at the spot where a bomb had crashed through the glass dome. Eden remarked idly that he hadn't been there since 1936.

Out across the courtyard and the wasteland of a former garden was the entrance to the dugout where Hitler had taken his final refuge. A guide led Churchill and his party down the dark stone steps, pointing out broken stairs with his flashlight. "Breathing the damp, acrid, foetid air," Moran remembered, "I felt my way down a lot of steps to [a] cell, strewn, as far as I could see by the light of a torch, with clothes and gas masks and every kind of litter. I picked up a burnt glove."

Water was rising in the bottommost rooms three flights down. On a table in the room that was said to have been Eva Braun's was a vase, "with a branch in it," Cadogan noted, "which had evidently been a spray of blossom." Churchill could not bear to make the full descent into Hitler's dugout. At the end of the first flight of steps, he turned and made his way slowly back up to the top where he found an old gilt chair and sat down mopping his brow. "Hitler must have come out here to get some air," he said to no one in particular, "and heard the guns getting nearer and nearer."

One of the guides pointed to a spot amidst some rusty oil cans and told Churchill that that was where the bodies of Hitler and Eva Braun were seen burning. Churchill looked for a moment and then turned away in disgust. He returned to his car in silence.

On their way through Berlin, the victors claimed some spoils. Moran picked up two Iron Crosses. Cadogan took one Iron Cross; a chunk of marble, to use as a paperweight, from Hitler's smashed desk; and a small rosette wrenched from one of the crystal chandeliers. One of the military aides got a German decoration still in its box. Another "pocketed a small piece of marble from the top of [Hitler's] desk, a fragment of his map of the world and a handful of trumpery medals from scattered heaps upon the floor."

"I was sorry that I had gone sightseeing," Lord Ismay said. "My first act on returning to Babelsberg was to plunge into a hot bath with a great deal of disinfectant in it; my second was to take a very strong drink to try to get the taste out of my mouth." The devastation of Berlin was, he said, "obscene." The whole afternoon, said Sir Alan Brooke, "seemed like a dream." On the whole, Cadogan complained, the tour was very badly organized.

Churchill reflected on the tour in his memoirs: "The moral principles of modern civilization seem to prescribe that the leaders of a nation defeated in war shall be put to death by the victors. This will certainly stir them to fight to the bitter end in any future war, and no matter how many lives are needlessly sacrificed, it costs them no more. It is the masses of the people who have so little to say about the starting or ending of wars who pay the additional cost. Julius Caesar followed the opposite principle, and his conquests were due almost as much to his clemency as to his prowess."

"That's what happens," Truman said after seeing Berlin, "when a man overreaches himself."

When Truman returned to the Little White House, he was greeted by Henry Stimson. The Secretary of War handed the President a cable from George Harrison, who had been left behind in Washington to serve as liaison between Alamogordo and Potsdam.

TOP SECRET

URGENT

WAR 32887

FOR COLONEL KYLES EYES ONLY

FROM HARRISON FOR MR. STIMSON

OPERATED ON THIS MORNING. DIAGNOSIS NOT YET COMPLETE BUT RESULTS SEEM SATISFACTORY AND ALREADY EXCEED EXPECTATIONS. LOCAL PRESS RELEASE NECESSARY AS INTEREST EXTENDS GREAT DISTANCE. DR. GROVES PLEASED. HE RETURNS TOMORROW. I WILL KEEP YOU POSTED.

"I talked to Winston while he undressed for bed," Lord Moran noted in his diary.

"'The Socialists say I shall have a majority over all other parties of thirty two.'"

"I asked him if that was a working majority."

"He replied: 'If my Government keeps being defeated I could resign. I should do so and have another election in the spring.'"

"This is a completely different tune from his

demands during the election campaign that he would not tolerate anything but a majority that gave him real power. The truth is he is much less confident and, I think, would be content to win with any majority.

"Before I put out the light I asked him what he had thought of Berlin. He answered with a smile:

"'There was a reasonable amount of destruction.'"

The special correspondent for the London *Times* sent in his dispatch for the next day's paper: There had been no "official confirmation here of the arrival of Marshal Stalin, whose movements are the subject of the strictest secrecy and security.... It may be assumed that he is now here."

The diplomatic correspondent filed a separate story: "Except when President Truman and Mr. Churchill suddenly emerged from the Potsdam compound to visit shattered Berlin, the conference of the 'Big Three' gave little outward sign of life yesterday."

5
TUESDAY,
JULY 17

Stimson now had hold of a piece of paper with which he could get the attention of anyone in the world. Early on Tuesday morning he took the top-secret cable to Jimmy Byrnes, and at lunchtime he took it to Churchill. He urged Byrnes to agree to a two-part plan: give the Japanese a strong warning about the bomb, and assure them that they could retain their emperor. Byrnes dismissed both ideas, and he apparently spoke with the authority of the President. Stimson realized he had lost both points. He dropped the subject and turned to polite conversation about Manchuria and other topics.

Down the street at Churchill's house, the Prime Minister was elated by the news. "Here then was a speedy end to the Second World War," Churchill wrote in his memoirs; and then, thinking of Russian advances into Europe, he added, "and perhaps to much else besides.

"Up to this moment," Churchill said, "we had shaped our ideas towards an assault upon the homeland of Japan by terrific air bombing and by the invasion of very large armies. We had contemplated the desperate resistance of the Japanese fighting to the death with Samurai devotion... in every cave and dug-out.... To quell the Japanese resistance man by man and conquer the country yard by yard might well require the loss of a million American lives and [if Churchill could convince Truman to let the British join in for the kill] half that number of British - or more if we could get them there: for we were resolved to share the agony. Now all this nightmare picture had vanished. In its place was the vision - fair and bright indeed it seemed — of the end of the whole war in one or two violent shocks."

Churchill's thoughts were evenly divided between Japan and Europe at the moment; "we should not need the Russians," he said. "We seemed suddenly to have become possessed of a merciful abridgment of the slaughter in the East and of a far happier prospect in Europe. I have no doubt that these thoughts were present in the minds of my American friends."

Stimson urged Churchill to agree to telling the Russians of the bomb, but Churchill would not hear of it. "I argued," Stimson said, at "some length," but the Prime Minister's mind was made up. For all of Stimson's efforts on Tuesday morning his piece of paper got him nowhere.

After Stimson left, Churchill had a sudden urge to visit Frederick the Great's palace of Sans Souci. As Moran noted, "he emerged from his room and strode into his car. " When he arrived at Sans Souci, he made it around the palace in fifteen minutes. "With quick, impatient strides, he hurried through the rooms, looking neither to the right nor the left; his eyes were fixed on the floor; his look was abstracted. His thoughts were far away on the coming conference — or was he once more counting votes?"

At twelve o'clock sharp, Stalin's car pulled up in front of the Little White House. Harry Vaughan and James Vardaman came out on the front steps to receive the Russian leader. Stalin wore a fawn uniform with red epaulets, and the Americans had to try to remember his new title; in recognition of the successes of the Red Army, Stalin had promoted himself from Marshal to Gen eralissimo. He was accompanied by Molotov and a translator. Vaughan and Vardaman escorted the Russians up the stairs to Truman's office, where the President waited with Byrnes and his translator Charles Bohlen.

Stalin was calm, cordial, soft spoken. He was straightforward and simple in his manner. Bohlen took hasty notes of the conversation:

"m. s.: LATE.

"truman:——

"s: Chinese—delayed—fly—no doctors

"T: glad to—looking forw—

"s: Personal relationship"

That is to say, Marshal Stalin (Bohlen was not yet used to thinking of him as G.S.) apologized for arriving late to the conference. Truman's response ("——") was a polite rejoinder, and Stalin lied that negotiations with the Chinese had delayed his departure and that his doctors had said "no" to flying because of a lung condition he had. Truman expressed understanding, said he was glad to make Stalin's acquaintance, he had been looking forward for a long time to meeting Stalin. The Russian said yes, personal relationships and contacts were very important, and, he added, he thought they would have no difficulty in coming to agreement on the questions they had before them at Potsdam.

"What I most especially noticed," Truman recalled, "were his eyes, his face, and his expression.... He seemed to be in a good humor. He was extremely polite...." Truman liked his directness. "I was impressed by him and talked to him straight from the shoulder. He looked me in the eye when he spoke...."

They reviewed the agenda for the conference. Stalin had several points to add to the topics for discussion, including the question of the Franco regime in Spain. Truman passed over the reference to Franco and asked what time it would be convenient for Stalin to meet for the first plenary session. Stalin said Molotov and Eden had agreed to five o'clock that afternoon, and Byrnes made a feeble joke about Stalin's habits of staying up late at night and rising late in the morning. Stalin replied courteously that his habits had changed since the war.

"s: Re Franco — I should like to explain. F. regime not result of internal conditions of Spain — imposed on Spain — by Ger — Italians — thus a danger to Uni. Nations. This regime harmful — by giving shelter to different fascist remnants — we thought it proper to break off with present regime....

"T: I hold no brief for Franco [we will give the matter further] study

"s: right."

The conversation was going well, and so Truman pushed for more warmth and friendliness. The overture seems stilted in Bohlen's notes, as it probably was when it passed through translation at the time.

"T:... I am here to—be yr friend—deal directly yes or no [I am] no diplomat

"s: good—[frankness will] help—work—USSR—always go along with US....

"T: friends—all subject differences. settle—frankly

"s: good of course difference—but.

"T: Churchill-called—

"s: *[one word illegible]*"

Stalin took advantage of this opening about Churchill to try to split the British and the Americans. He observed that the British were not really eager to do their part in the war against Japan; now it was the Russians and Americans who were the companions in arms. The British had fought hard when their interests were threatened by the Germans, but:

"s: Eng less clear Jap war—for Russians & Amer—do their duty Eng think war mainly [finished]

"T: P.M. offered [assistance]

"s: peculiar—mentality—bombed by Ger—not Japan war over for them—these feelings may work vs. P.M."

Just how these feelings were to work against Churchill is not clear, nor do Bohlen's notes of Stalin's next words make it any clearer. Was something lost in translation, or in Bohlen's ability to keep track of the conversation? Bohlen was not able to remember in later years. However, the general thrust of Stalin's remarks was certainly meant to sow doubt in Truman's mind about the reliability of the British. Stalin went on:

"US people—gave power to finish task—can Brit ask that—they believe war over—little interest in war vs. Japan—may be"

Truman was not prepared to let Stalin run down Churchill; yet, at the same time, he wanted Stalin to know that the United States was strong enough that it did not really need anyone's help. He replied casually:

"T: we are—not in dire straits as Eng was in re Germany—" Stalin replied without pause that Russia would enter the Japanese war as she had promised:

"s: we ready mid of Aug...."

We must recall again that Truman no longer felt an urgent need to have Russia join the Japanese war. It was Stalin who raised the subject of the war, and Stalin who brought up his old promise. As the Americans had thought, Russia would enter the war, needed or not, and could not be kept from doing so.

Stalin spoke at some length about his negotiations with the Chinese over the Yalta concessions.

The Chinese negotiator had not been altogether delighted with Stalin's demands:

"s: not all smooth with Chinese—that is why he went home."

The trouble with the Chinese, Stalin said, is that they "don't understand horse trading." They tried to haggle over every little point and could not see the big picture — or, as Bohlen recorded it, "try to wangle everything — big pictures—"

Truman understood. Stalin concluded:

"s: mid August—as agreed at Yalta—we keep word

"MOLOTOV }

"TRUMAN

keep words"

And so Russia was in the Japanese war, whether they were wanted or not. While Truman did not raise the subject, he could not avoid it — and now that he had been stuck with Russian help, he could at least take credit for it. In his memoirs, he wrote, "There were many reasons for my going to Potsdam, but the most urgent, to my mind, was to get from Stalin a personal reaffirmation of Russia's entry into the war against Japan, a matter which our military chiefs were most anxious to clinch. This I was able to get from Stalin in the very first days of the conference."

Truman asked Stalin to stay for lunch, and Stalin said he could not. The President, no diplomat, talked straight from the shoulder: "You could if you wanted to." Stalin stayed, and they talked of nothing in particular. Stalin complimented the President on the wine and asked to see the label. "I was glad he did," Byrnes said; "it was a California wine." Byrnes mentioned the trip the Americans had made to Berlin and asked Stalin how he thought Hitler had died. In fact, Russian soldiers had found Hitler's body and carried it away so that Russian doctors could perform an autopsy. Stalin said he thought Hitler was still alive and living in Spain or Argentina.

The conversation drifted from topic to topic and allowed Stalin and Truman to look at leisure into one another's eyes. They were both men who believed one could know a good deal from a man's eyes.

After lunch they all went out onto the balcony at the back of the Little White House and had their pictures taken overlooking the lake. Shutters snapped; several moments were frozen; heads were turned this way or that. They all looked relaxed and comfortable, like old friends on a summer vacation. And, if Byrnes or Molotov occasionally glanced to one side or another to check just where everyone stood, the eyes of both Stalin and Truman were always assured and direct.

At fifteen minutes before five that evening, Churchill's car crunched up the gravel drive to the Cecilienhof Palace. Churchill stepped out, accompanied by a plainclothes detective, and walked through the arch into the palace courtyard. There was no sign of Stalin's steel, bulletproof car or of the Russian security guards who darted ahead of it in jeeps and took up positions along the roadside to form an armed corridor through which the Russian leader was driven.

"What is the Russian cortege like?" an English aide asked of a compatriot. "When shall we see it? Where does it come from?"

"It doesn't. There is a puff of smoke, and Stalin ascends through the floor."

Truman's party came screaming up the drive with sirens and whistles and shouts. First came the outriders on their motorcycles, then the armored jeeps, then the President's car bristling with G-men on the running boards, and finally a wagonload of armed men who leaped to the ground and fanned out with guns at the ready to cover the President's entry to the palace. Truman and Byrnes emerged from the car with broad grins.

In the courtyard, the Russians had planted hundreds and hundreds of brilliant geraniums in the form of a twenty-four-foot-wide red star. The Americans circled around the edges of the red star and went directly to the main conference room where reporters and photographers and newsreel cameramen jostled and snapped and flashed and whirred from every angle. "You tell me to hold my head up when I'm being photographed!" Cadogan wrote home to his wife. "But do you realize that there are 15 sizzling hot searchlights turned on us for about 10 minutes with 40 photographers taking shots the whole time? One can't pose continuously under those conditions...."

The journalists were allowed ten minutes — that was all — and then they were hustled out of the room and banished from the conference to go back to the Berlin bars, complain of secrecy, whip up rumors, and read the dispatches that came in from other parts of the world. Admiral Chester W. Nimitz announced at Guam that "we have paralyzed the will and the ability of the Japanese Navy to come out and fight." From Washington, it was reported, "The State Department begins checking newspaper dispatches from South America reporting rumors that Adolf Hitler and Eva Braun are in Patagonia." Had Stalin been reading American newspaper dispatches before his lunch with Truman? Perhaps he thought it strange that Byrnes did not mention the State Department's investigation. On this one small point on the fate of Hitler, Stalin had the advantage of the Americans: he knew the truth, and he knew what the Americans suspected and were not saying.

When the Big Three had settled in around the baize-covered table, Stalin made the opening move. He proposed that Truman serve as chairman, thereby putting Truman in the position of moderator between Russia and Britain. Churchill, of course, seconded the motion. "So I preside," Truman wrote home to his mother. "It is hard as presiding over the Senate. Churchill talks all the time and Stalin just grunts but you know what he means. ... They all say I took 'em for a ride when I got down to presiding," the President bragged. "It was a nerve-wracking experience but it had to be done. The worst is yet to come; but I'm hoping. I have several aces in the hole I hope which will help on results...."

Sitting next to Truman were Byrnes, Leahy, Davies, and Bohlen. With Stalin were Molotov, Vishinsky, the translator Pavlov, and Gromyko—to whom Cadogan referred as "frog-face." Next to Churchill were Eden, Cadogan, the translator Major Birse, and Attlee—who reminded Bohlen of "a mechanical toy, which, when wound up and placed on the table by Churchill, would perform as predicted." In a second row of seats behind the principals were Harriman, Matthews, and other Americans, British, and Russians. Back there sat Fedor Gusev, Soviet ambassador to Great Britain. "Quite stupid and inarticulate," Cadogan said of Gusev. "Can only make up for his shortcomings by saying 'How are you?' in a voice of thunder."

As the meeting began, the room was still, and the air was warm but fresh as it came up from the lake. Gradually the smoke from Stalin's continuous chain of cigarettes and Churchill's cigars spread through the room. Papers were shuffled; whispered conversations rose a decibel or two; the voices of the translators cut through the crescendo of noise — and occasionally a slap would ring out across the room as a mosquito ran afoul of an impatient diplomat.

Truman opened with the suggestion that the Big Three agree on an agenda for the conference, and he proceeded to outline the four topics that he said urgently needed attention. The whole of American strategy was shaped around these four topics: first, the establishment of the Council of Foreign Ministers to "prepare for the peace conference" — the peace conference that Truman did not intend to have; secondly, a mandate for a Control Council for Germany that incorporated American aims in terms of Germany's strength and pliability; thirdly, an attack on Russian policy in eastern Europe; and, finally, a proposal on Italy that implied America's plan for its western European sphere of influence.

"The experience of the Versailles Conference after the First World War," Truman said, "showed that a peace conference can have many flaws unless it is prepared beforehand by the victor Powers.... That is why I propose... that we should have and now set up a special Council of Foreign Ministers, consisting of the ministers of Great Britain, the USSR, the United States, France, and China.... This Council of Foreign Ministers for preparing a peace conference should meet as soon as possible after our meeting...."

Something about the proposal seemed peculiar to Stalin. He drew on his cigarette, exhaled; his eyes drifted to the ceiling. Why should the Council of Foreign Ministers include France and China in addition to the Big Three? Would they not simply vote in any way the United States told them to vote? Of course, it was difficult to keep France out of any dealings over the peace settlements for Europe — but what was China doing in this council? What especially was China doing in the council when the Chinese were annoyed with the Russians over the Yalta "horse trading"? Churchill suggested that the heads of state refer the question to their foreign ministers to hash out. Stalin agreed with Churchill's recommendation, but said quietly that he was "not clear about the inclusion of China in the Council. After all, this is a question of European problems, isn't it?"

Truman said this could be talked over by the foreign ministers and then brought back to the meeting of the heads of state. The President pushed on with his second item, a paper on the administration of

Germany. Churchill and Stalin said they would both like a chance to read the paper.

TRUMAN: "We could discuss this matter tomorrow."

STALIN: "Indeed, we could discuss the question tomorrow."

Next, Truman read a statement attacking the Russians on their behavior in eastern Europe: "Since the Yalta Conference, the obligations undertaken... in the Declaration on Liberated Europe remain unfulfilled.... In conformity with the obligations of the Three Powers, set forth in Paragraph 3 Point 'd' of the Declaration... the Governments of the three Powers must discuss how best to help the work of the provisional Governments in holding free and fair elections. Such help will be required in Rumania, Bulgaria, and, possibly, in other countries, too."

Leahy was all but breathless with admiration for Truman: "The President, seizing [the] opportunity to take the offensive, presented at once, without permitting interruption, four of the major proposals that had been prepared.... Churchill appeared surprised at the President's forthright statement of American policy and made a long talk on the necessity for careful study."

Stalin was silent.

Truman forged ahead, saying the time had come to revise policy toward Italy. Italy, he said, should be admitted to the United Nations.

Churchill broke in and, before he quite realized what he had done, he rebuked the President. These were important matters, too important to be dealt with "somewhat too hastily," he said. He paused. Perhaps he had been too sharp. He had better explain: Britain had fought for four years against Italy. Italy had entered the war against Britain in the first instance at a very critical time. President Roosevelt himself had referred to the Italian entry into the war as a "stab in the back." Perhaps Churchill should not have referred to Roosevelt; perhaps it was wounding to Truman's *amour propre.* Churchill floundered: "I think we must have time to discuss these questions. This is the first time I have seen them. I am not saying that I cannot agree with these proposals, but there must be time to discuss them."

Truman went on doggedly reading his proposal on Italy. At the end he looked up — and it evidently occurred to him that he had plunged into his set pieces without making the proper diplomatic introductory noises. He improvised: "Because I was unexpectedly elected Chairman of this Conference, I was unable to express my feelings at once. I am very glad to meet you Generalissimo, and you, Mr. Prime Minister."

Perhaps it occurred to Truman, too, that Churchill's remark about the President's "hastiness" was an unfavorable comparison to Roosevelt, the old conference pro. Truman was self-effacing. He had, he said, stepped into "the place of a man who really was irreplaceable." He knew "Mr." Roosevelt had enjoyed the goodwill of both Stalin and Churchill. He hoped he might be able "to succeed in part to that friendship and good will."

Churchill hastened to reassure Truman. Both he and the Generalissimo "wished to renew the great regard and affection" with Truman that they'd had for Roosevelt. "This common friendship... most trying period of history... most crucial time... cordial regard and respect... hope and confidence...."

It is not recorded whether Churchill was perspiring by the end of his outpouring of regard and goodwill. Stalin broke his own silence and said very simply and quietly that he would like "on behalf of the whole Russian delegation [to express] the desire to join in the sentiments expressed by Mr. Churchill."

"The P.M.," Cadogan wrote his wife, "since he left London, has refused to do any work or read anything. That is probably quite right, but then he can't have it both ways: if he knows nothing about the subject under discussion, he should keep quiet, or ask that his Foreign Secretary be heard. Instead of that, he butts in on every occasion and talks the most irrelevant rubbish, and is giving away our case at every point. Truman is most quick and businesslike. He was only trying, at this first meeting, to establish a list of the questions we must deal with. Every mention of a topic started Winston off on a wild rampage from which the combined efforts of Truman and Anthony with difficulty restrained him."

One of the Englishmen in the second row was keeping a closer watch on Stalin. He "spoke quietly, shortly, in little staccato sentences which Pavlov, his young interpreter, translated immediately into forceful English. In the discussions Stalin was often humorous, never offensive; direct and uncompromising. His eyes looked to me humorous, and often showed as mere slits..."

Churchill suggested brightly that the Big Three review the "various points proposed for discussion and try to agree on the agenda." He seemed to have quite forgotten that he had not yet proposed any topics for the agenda himself. Truman reminded him.

TRUMAN: "We have offered what we think is most important."

CHURCHILL [recovering]: "I would like to add the Polish question."

Stalin took the meeting in hand.

STALIN: "It would be well for the three delegations

to set forth the questions they would like to discuss. Russia would like to discuss (one) the question of the division of the German merchant fleet and navy; (two) the question of reparations; (three) trusteeships for Russia under the San Francisco Charter—"

CHURCHILL: "Do you mean the territories in Europe or all over the world?"

STALIN *[without pause]:* "—We shall discuss that—(four) relations with the Axis satellite states; (five) the Franco regime imposed on Spain by the Axis. This regime should be changed. It harbors great danger to the United Nations."

CHURCHILL: "We are only discussing things to go on the agenda. I agree that the matter of Spain should be discussed."

STALIN *[relentlessly]:* "(Six) the question of Tangiers."

CHURCHILL: "Mr. Eden has advised me we can reach only provisional agreement on Tangiers in the absence of the French."

STALIN: "(Seven) the question of Syria and Lebanon; (eight) the Polish question involving the determination of Poland's western frontiers and the liquidation of the London government."

CHURCHILL *[off and running]:* "We agree the Polish question should be discussed including the winding up of the London government. We hope the Marshal and the President will recognize that England was made the home of the Polish government which fought against the Axis. England has the burden of winding up these obligations. Our objectives are similar but probably more difficult for Britain. She cannot...." And so forth, and so on.

[Silence.]

STALIN: "For the time being, the Russians have no additional points to add to the agenda."

[Pause.]

CHURCHILL: "... I suggest the foreign secretaries meet tonight to agree on the agenda for tomorrow. They can prepare a menu for us [suppertime drew near at Potsdam] better than we can at this table.... So tomorrow we will have prepared the points most agreeable."

STALIN: "All the same, we will not escape the disagreeable."

CHURCHILL *[undaunted and cheered up by his own speech]*: "We will feel our way up to them."

The diplomats sat around the table looking at one another. No one spoke.

STALIN: "What shall we do today? Shall we continue our sitting?... I think we could discuss the setting up of the Council of Foreign Ministers as a preparatory institution for the coming peace conference."

TRUMAN: "All right."

CHURCHILL: "All right."

STALIN: "... I would like an explanation of the reason for China's participation in European affairs."

TRUMAN: "China is one of the five members of the Security Council."

STALIN: "The decision taken at Crimea [i.e., Yalta] provided for quarterly conferences of the foreign secretaries. Does President Truman's suggestion supercede the Crimea proposal?"

TRUMAN: "The Crimea proposal was temporary."

STALIN: "Then the quarterly meetings of the foreign secre taries will be dropped?... I should like to know whether I am taking the correct view."

TRUMAN: "The problems to be considered by the council are quite different from the ordinary meetings of the foreign secretaries. It is intended for a specific purpose...."

STALIN: "Will it be a council preparing questions for the future international peace conference?"

TRUMAN: "Yes."

CHURCHILL: "The peace conference which will end the war. "

STALIN: "In Europe the war is over. The council will determine and suggest the date for the convocation of a peace conference."

Let us pause a moment to marvel at the direct, straight-from-the-shoulder, nondiplomatic prevarication of Truman's. There is no question that he had no intention of having a peace conference. The briefing paper outlining the idea for the Council of Foreign Ministers is explicit and repetitive on the point. And Truman did answer Stalin's questions with a forthright, unqualified "Yes"; no doubt of that. Everyone's notes — British, American, and Russian, formal transcripts and informal jottings — agree on the conversation. If Churchill made use of Britain's historic grandeur in his dealings, and Stalin used soft-spoken outlandishness, Truman unquestionably got good mileage out of his reputation as a straight shooter. Truman had thus secured the most essential element of his strategy, and he sat back poker-faced while Churchill and Stalin chewed over Chinese participation in the council. Churchill too thought China should be excluded. "Perhaps the matter can be referred to the foreign ministers," Stalin said. Truman quickly seized the opportunity to concede a point: "I have no objection to the foreign secretaries eliminating China if they think that that is best."

A glow of good fellowship embraced the Big Three. Churchill relented: "China might be present and come in when Asiatic questions are considered." And Stalin chipped in with his first joke of the conference.

STALIN: "As all the questions are to be discussed by the foreign ministers, we shall have nothing to do."

Here the conference transcript records: "[Laughter.]"

It was a good note on which to end, and Truman gave the cue.

TRUMAN: "We must specify the concrete questions for discussion at tomorrow's sitting."

CHURCHILL: "The secretaries should give us three or four points—enough to keep us busy."

TRUMAN: "I don't want just to discuss. I want to decide."

CHURCHILL: "You want something in the bag each day."

TRUMAN: "I also propose that we should start our sittings at four o'clock instead of five."

STALIN: "Four? Well, all right."

CHURCHILL: "I will obey your orders." Stalin could not resist the opening Churchill gave him.

STALIN: "If you are in such an obedient mood today, Mr. Prime Minister, I should like to know whether you will share with us the German fleet."

CHURCHILL: "... this navy should be either sunk or divided."

STALIN: "DO you want it sunk or divided?"

CHURCHILL: "All means of war are terrible things."

STALIN: "The navy should be divided. If Mr. Churchill prefers to sink the navy, he is free to sink his share of it; I have no intention of sinking mine."

On that jolly note, the first plenary session of the Potsdam conference came to an end. The delegates rose, gathered their papers, chattered, and slowly made their way into the adjoining reception room where the Russians had laid out a buffet dinner.

Eden was furious with Churchill. The whole of the German fleet was in British hands, and Eden regarded the fleet as one of Britain's better bargaining counters. Churchill, he felt, was simply flinging away the German fleet. "[I] urged him not give up our few cards without return. But he is again under Stalin's spell. He kept repeating 'I like that man.' I am full of admiration of Stalin's handling of him. I told him I was, hoping that it would move him. It did a little."

The room mellowed under the influence of champagne. Old friends from Yalta and Teheran toasted one another. Over there by the buffet! There was old Goberidge, who had supervised President Roosevelt's kitchen at Yalta, serving now as the maître d'hotel in the Cecilienhof, inspecting the Murano glasses for the champagne and sizing up the new boys from America. Cadogan might think Gusev stupid, but on the whole it was still good to be in the same room with him; these were people who grappled day by day with the great affairs of the world; this was their stage; this was where they played their parts; and the fact that this was to be the last of the wartime conferences added a sentimental warmth to the occasion.

Churchill, feeling expansive, moved toward Stalin. The Generalissimo was smoking a cigar. If anyone were to photograph Stalin with a cigar, Churchill warned with a twinkle in his eye, "everybody will say it is my influence." Vishinsky hove into view. He looked so "mild and benevolent," Churchill told him, the Prime Minister could not believe the old state prosecutor could be "fierce." He could be, Vishinsky said, "when it was necessary." No sense of humor in Vishinsky. Ah, well, that was a pity. Churchill moved on, acquiring indigestion on champagne and caviar.

As the party was breaking up, and the cars began to make their way back out of the long gravel driveway, Henry Stimson received another cable at his house in Babelsberg:

DOCTOR HAS JUST RETURNED MOST ENTHUSIASTIC AND CONFIDENT THAT THE LITTLE BOY [the bomb ready for use against Japan] IS AS HUSKY AS HIS BIG BROTHER [the exploded Alamogordo bomb], THE LIGHT IN HIS EYES DISCERNIBLE FROM HERE [Washington] TO HIGHHOLD [Stimson's farm on Long Island, 250 miles away] AND I COULD HAVE HEARD HIS SCREAMS FROM HERE TO MY FARM [forty miles away].

The officers who decoded the cable thought Stimson had just become a father and wondered whether the conference would be adjourned for a day to celebrate.

Cable in hand, Stimson walked out into the long, lingering twilight to go to Truman's villa for dinner. Had Frederick the Great still been alive, he would have been shocked. No one dressed for dinner at the Potsdam conference. The press of business and the stylistic conceits of democracy called for summer suits. Still, no more distinguished-looking man than Henry Stimson ever strolled the streets of Babelsberg. Nor was any statesman more sensitive than he was to nuance. In the course of the day, he had lost in all his efforts to substitute suasion for force. Perhaps a skillfully worded message to the Japanese would have as tremendous an effect as dropping the bomb — but that question had become strictly hypothetical. Perhaps informing the Russians of the bomb's existence would enhance their trust of the Americans — or at least not kindle their suspicions — but Churchill would block that attempt. Stimson had been thirty-three years old in 1900; he had grown up in a different world of diplomacy and historical analogy — one that knew force but preferred finesse. The finesse was gone in 1945; the bridge players had given way to poker players. It may be, after all, that secrecy, deception, and force were the only devices that Stalin respected, but Stimson was disoriented by it all.

Truman was host that evening to Stimson, General Marshall, General Arnold, and Admiral King. They all disagreed with the President's plans for the bomb. The President forestalled any conversation, however, by saying he would make no decision at all until he received a full report from General Groves. (In Washington, Groves was laboring over his report at that moment.) The conversation turned to chitchat; through the open doors from the balcony overlooking the lake came the music of Chopin. Sergeant Eugene List, flown in from Paris, played the President's favorite pieces for the piano. Truman asked for Chopin's opus 42 waltz. List did not have the music. Late that night a message was sent to Paris: Find sheet music for Chopin's opus 42 waltz and deliver it to Babelsberg soonest.

"I dined at the mess," Cadogan recorded, "(with the band of the Scots Guards playing on the lawn outside). A. [Eden] dined alone with the P.M., and says he read him a lecture and in particular urged him to try to resist giving in to Stalin (who knows *exactly* how to manage him). After dinner I had to go round for a discussion with the Americans [Matthews and another State Department officer]... with a view to clearing up some of the mess made by the Big 3. But I got to bed before 12...."

In Berlin, newspaper reporters exchanged rumors, and, since they heard so little news of the conference, they took to reporting about the other reporters. "A large gathering of international journalists are milling about all over the place," the special correspondent for the London *Times* wrote, "and it will be surprising if the conference can be carried to its conclusion without leakages of fact or fancy." The journalists read dispatches from their colleagues on the other side of the world: "The third shelling of targets in the Japanese home islands occurred late [tonight], with war planes and transport facilities along the Honshu island coastline around Hitachi, 50 to 85 miles northeast of Tokyo, being attacked, Guam Hq. says. The U.S. battleship *Iowa* and the British battleship *King George* V, most powerful in their respective navies, led the assaults, which were conducted within 10 miles of the coast. There was no Japanese retaliation."

Generalissimo Stalin stayed up into the small hours of the morning coordinating Russian troop movements toward the Far East, ordering his commanders to press on with greater speed.

6
WEDNESDAY, JULY 18, LUNCH

A T one-fifteen on Wednesday afternoon, Lord Moran was looking idly out the window of Churchill's house when he saw President Truman drive up for lunch. "His strong, friendly face," Moran said of the man who stepped energetically out of the car, "gives everyone a feeling that he is going to play a big part." The English all rushed toward the front door to shake hands with the President. Truman had brought along Vaughan, Vardaman, and Charlie Ross, and the assistants were all shepherded off to lunch with Moran while the President and Prime Minister dined alone.

Truman had with him both of the cables from Washington about the atomic bomb, and he showed them to Churchill, who was still unable to repress his delight over this "world-shaking news." The President raised the question of what to tell Stalin. He was not thinking, as Stimson was, of telling the Russians as a matter of good faith but only as a matter of avoiding the accusation of bad faith.

Still, if the Russians *were* told, they would certainly rush to get into the war against Japan and claim a share of the victory. "The President and I no longer felt that we needed [Stalin's] aid to conquer Japan," Churchill wrote. So, to keep the Russians from hurrying into the Japanese war, they must *not* be told.

The way out of this dilemma was, of course, to delay telling Stalin until the military was closer to the drop date and then to tell Stalin without really telling him. How should Stalin be told? If he were informed in writing, that would be too official; it would call too much attention to the news. Similarly, if Stalin were told at a special meeting of some sort, he would be too likely to understand the implications of the news and start rushing his troops into the Far East. Casualness was the key, some moment of bustling confusion when Stalin's mind would be on other matters, some day after a plenary session when all the diplomats were rustling papers.

"I think," Truman said over lunch, "I had best just tell him after one of our meetings that we have an entirely novel form of bomb, something quite out of the ordinary [without mentioning the word atomic], which we think will have decisive effects upon the Japanese will to continue the war." Churchill thought about it a moment, and concurred.

Truman and Churchill perceived another danger in the Japanese war: Japan might surrender through Russian diplomatic channels before the Americans had time to win. The night before, Stalin had told Churchill of the peace feeler the Japanese had sent to Moscow. "It stated," Churchill told Truman, "that Japan could not accept 'unconditional surrender,' but might be prepared to compromise on other terms."

Truman knew of this peace feeler and asked Churchill why Stalin had not told the Americans of the news. According to Churchill, Stalin did not want Truman to think that the Russians "were trying to influence him towards peace." Nor, Churchill said, did the British want the Americans to think that Britain was reluctant "to go on with the war against Japan for as long as the United States thought fit."

"However," Churchill said, "I dwelt upon the tremendous cost in American and to a lesser extent in British life if we enforced 'unconditional surrender' upon the Japanese. It was for him to consider whether this might not be expressed in some other way, so that we got all the essentials for future peace and security and yet left them with some show of saving their military honor and some assurance of their national existence..."

So it appeared that the Russians and the British would accept some modification of the unconditional surrender formula. And what if the Americans did, too? Then Japan might surrender — to *the Russians*, or at least through Russian channels. And then where would American power be in the Far East?

How was Truman to keep victory from slipping through his fingers? He needed to keep the Japanese fighting by sticking firmly to the unconditional surrender formula. Then, when he dropped the atomic bomb the Japanese would surrender to America. As the countdown proceeded, the strategy became clearer and more urgent. Stalin hastened tanks and troops to the east; Truman hoped to win before the Russians were in position.

Would this nattering about changing the surrender formula never cease? It made Truman impatient. He seized on Churchill's reference to Japanese "honor" and replied that he did not think the Japanese "had any military honor after Pearl Harbor." As far as Truman was concerned, the question was closed.

A certain plaintiveness overcame Churchill then as he contemplated the growing strength of the United States and the decisiveness and aggressiveness of this President who would run things in "the American Century." Churchill spoke of "the melancholy position of Great Britain, who had spent more than half her foreign investments for the common cause when we were all alone...."

Truman listened, the Prime Minister recalled, "with sympathy." America owed Britain a great debt, Truman said. "If you had gone down like France, we might be fighting the Germans on the American coast at the present time. This justifies us in regarding these matters as above the purely financial plane."

Just how far sympathy would move Truman above the financial plane was something else again. So Churchill added a gentle threat that he hoped would make the Americans nervous. "Until we got our wheels turning properly," the Prime Minister said, "we could be of little use to world security or any of the high purposes of [the United Nations]." The President said he would do his "very utmost" to help.

Then Truman turned the conversation to certain airfields that America had built "at enormous cost" in British territories. The Americans could not think of simply abandoning these airfields. Some "fair plan for common use" ought to be worked out. Indeed, Churchill said, he would like to work out a "reciprocal arrangement between our two countries" for airfields and other bases "all over the world. " Britain was a smaller power than the United States these days, but she "had much to give" that was left over from the great days of empire. "Why should we not share facilities for defense all over the world? We could add 50 per cent to the mobility of the American fleet."

Yes, Truman said, all this sounded very good — but Churchill was getting a bit too cozy about it. Any plan, Truman observed, would have to fit in with "the policy of the United Nations." That was all right, said Churchill, "so long as the facilities were shared between Britain and the United States. There was nothing in it if they were made common to everybody. A man might propose marriage to a young lady, but it was not much use if he were told that she would always be a sister to him."

Churchill may have thought that Britain was the young man proposing marriage in this affair. Clearly, however, Truman regarded Britain as the female in the partnership. But that scarcely mattered. Marriage was the last thing in Truman's mind. He wanted to play around in the United Nations. The President was agreeable to having a liaison — but nothing that would tie him down to Britain alone. He did not, of course, say all this to Churchill. On the contrary, he was most encouraging and left Churchill aglow with feelings for the President's "exceptional character and ability," his "simple and direct methods of speech, and a great deal of self-confidence and resolution."

Vaughan interrupted this little *tête-à-tête,* saying that the President had to go along to see Stalin. Truman was gracious in parting. It was "the most enjoyable luncheon" he had had for many years, he said. As Churchill recalled, the President had "used many expressions at intervals in our discussion which I could not easily hear unmoved."

On his way out, the President noticed a piano, and he sat down and played for a few moments, to the intense admiration of Lord Moran. Then, with some more deeply felt expressions of friendship for Churchill, the President descended the front steps and whisked off for his date with Stalin.

"Winston has fallen for the President," Moran noted in his diary. "Truman's modesty and simple ways are certainly disarming."

7
WEDNESDAY, JULY 18, 3:04 P.M

Truman arrived at Stalin's house at 3:04 on Wednesday afternoon to pay a brief courtesy call in return for the Generalissimo's visit to the Little White House. The President was accompanied by Byrnes and Bohlen, and the Americans were taken by Stalin and Molotov out to the balcony at the rear of the house to look at the lake. It was the same lake as the one to be seen from the back of Truman's and Churchill's houses and from the Cecilienhof Palace. Truman gazed at the lake and dredged up an appreciative remark about the dark trees in the background.

"I must tell you the news," Stalin said — and handed Truman a copy of the Japanese Emperor's message to his ambassador in Moscow. Truman pretended to read the message. Since Stalin had not told him of the message before, Truman may have wondered why he was being told just then. Perhaps Stalin was trying to see whether Churchill had persuaded the President to modify the surrender formula.

It did not occur to Truman that Stalin was testing American trustworthiness—but perhaps he was. Just when Stalin learned that the United States had successfully tested the atomic bomb we do not know. It may be that he knew by the time of this brief encounter. If so, perhaps he thought that the President would exchange one confidence for another.

Was it worth answering this communication? Stalin asked.

Truman replied that he had "no respect for the good faith of the Japanese."

It might be desirable, Stalin said, "to lull the Japanese to sleep, and possibly a general and unspecific answer might be returned, pointing out the exact character of the proposed... mission was not clear."

Truman appeared to be thinking.

"Alternatives," Stalin offered helpfully, "would be [to] ignore it completely and not answer, or send back a definite refusal."

Truman declared that Stalin's first suggestion was "satisfactory."

Indeed, said Molotov, it would be "factual," since it was not *"entirely* clear" what the Japanese had in mind.

So the Americans and the Russians were in a race into the Far East. Truman and Stalin and their aides looked at the dark trees on the other side of the lake.

8
WEDNESDAY, JULY 18, DINNER

In spite of everything," Churchill said of Stalin during the war, "I'd like that man to like me." On the evening of July 18, the Prime Minister got his chance to make friends with the Generalissimo. He arrived at Stalin's house for dinner at eight-thirty, and he did not leave until many drinks and expressions of good fellowship later — at one-thirty in the morning. Only their translators were with them — Major Birse for Churchill and Pavlov for Stalin.

"The Marshal was very amiable," Churchill told Moran after dinner. "I gave him a box of my cigars, the big ones, you know. He smoked one of them for three hours. I touched on some delicate matters without any clouds appearing in the sky. He takes a very sensible line about the monarchy."

"In what way?"

"Oh, he sees it binds the Empire together. He seemed surprised that the king had not come to Berlin."

There was a long pause.

"I think Stalin wants me to win the election."

At dinner, Stalin told Churchill that "all his information from Communist and other sources confirmed his belief that I should be returned by a majority of about eighty. He thought the Labour Party would obtain between 220 and 230 seats." Churchill modestly averred that he was not sure how the absentee ballots from the soldiers would come out. Oh, said Stalin, the Army preferred a strong government: they would vote Conservative. "It seemed plain," Churchill said, "that he hoped that his contacts with me and Eden would not be broken."

Churchill could not bear to receive all this flattery without giving Stalin something in return — so he gave Stalin the Mediterranean. If Eden had known, he would have been furious. "I said that it was my policy to welcome Russia as a Great Power on the sea. I wished," Churchill said, warming to the subject, "to see Russian ships sailing across the oceans of the world. Russia," the Prime Minister declared, pulling a pleasing metaphor from his rich rhetorical bank, "had been like a giant with his nostrils pinched by the narrow exits from the Baltic and the Black Sea."

The Prime Minister was well under way now, and Stalin sat back and let him rip. "I said that I personally would support an amendment to the Montreux Convention, throwing out Japan and giving Russia access to the Mediterranean. I repeated that I welcomed Russia's appearance on the oceans, and" — here the Prime Minister neatly topped himself — "this referred not only to the Dardanelles, but also to the Kiel Canal, which should have a regime like the Suez Canal, and to the warm waters of the Pacific."

What about the German fleet? Stalin prompted; Russia would like its share. Churchill played this one close; he had already been scolded by Eden for giving away the fleet. His face may have taken on the expression of the wily negotiator—clever, refusing to show his hand, flirtatious. "I did not dissent," he noted.

On October 9, 1944, Churchill had met with Stalin in Moscow and in a paroxysm of horse trading had established the principle, if not an automatically workable outline, of spheres of influence. To indicate how the world was to be divided where the spheres overlapped, "I wrote out on a half-sheet of paper," Churchill wrote in his memoirs:

Rumania	
Russia	90%
The others	10%
Greece	
Great Britain	90%
(in accord with U.S.A.)	
Russia	10%
Yugoslavia	50-50%
Hungary	50-50%
Bulgaria	
Russia	75%
The others	25%

"I pushed this across to Stalin, who had by then heard the translation. There was a slight pause. Then he took his blue pencil and made a large tick upon it, and passed it back to us. It was all settled in no more time than it takes to set it down."

"... The pencilled paper lay in the center of the table. At length I said, 'Might it not be thought rather cynical if it seemed we had disposed of these issues, so fateful to millions of people, in such an offhand manner? Let us burn the paper.' 'No, you keep it,' said Stalin."

What did Churchill think about Hungary? Stalin wanted to know now. In fact, Churchill had not thought much at all about Hungary. He would have to inquire of Eden what the "immediate situation" was.

In all the countries "liberated by the Red Army," Stalin said, "the Russian policy was to see a strong, independent, sovereign state." The Generalissimo was "against Sovietization of any of those countries. They would have free elections, and all except Fascist parties would participate."

Churchill then spoke of Yugoslavia. He and Stalin had agreed to a fifty-fifty division of "interests" in Yugoslavia. It was now "ninety-nine to one against Britain," the Prime Minister said. Not at all, Stalin replied; it was more like "90 per cent British, 10 per cent Yugoslav, and 0 per cent Russian interests. The Soviet Government often did not know what Tito was about to do."

Well, Churchill said, people were terribly anxious about Russian intentions. "I drew a line from the North Cape to Albania, and named the capitals east of that line which were in Russian hands. It looked as if Russia were rolling on westward."

Stalin was amazed. But, really! He was *withdrawing* troops from the West. "Two million men would be demobilized and sent home within the next four months. " The Generalissimo spoke of the heavy losses Russia had suffered in the war and (this was, in fact, true) of the need to bring the troops home to rebuild his devastated country.

The dinner was a huge success. Churchill had been

seduced twice in the same day, and he seemed to enjoy it. Nonetheless, whether he was being taken in, or whether he was being devilish, the net effect was the same. Chummy with Truman, chummy with Stalin, he was urging both of them on toward a confrontation with one another. He encouraged Truman to deceive Stalin, he encouraged Stalin to move into the Mediterranean and beyond—and he hoped everybody would like Churchill.

"Stalin gave his word," he said to Lord Moran that night as he got into bed, "there will be free elections in the countries set free by his armies. You are sceptical, Charles? I don't see why. We must listen to these Russians. They mobilized twelve million men, and nearly half of them were killed or are missing. I told Stalin Russia has been like a giant with his nostrils pinched. I was thinking of the narrows from the Baltic and the Black Sea. If they want to be a sea power, why not?" ("When the P.M. coins a phrase that he finds pleasing," Moran noted, "he keeps repeating it. Things must have been going pretty well when the P.M. agreed with Stalin that the Germans have no mind of their own.")

"When I said they were like sheep," continued Churchill, "Stalin told me a story of two hundred German Communists who remained rooted to a station platform for two hours because there was no one at the barrier to take their tickets." The P.M. grinned. "They never got to their meeting.

"Stalin said that people in the West wondered what would happen when he died. It had all been arranged; he had brought up good people, ready to step into his shoes. Russian policy would not be changed if he died."

The P.M. gazed at the carpet for a time.

"I think," he said, "that Stalin is trying to be as helpful as it is in him to be."

9
THE FOREIGN
MINISTERS

The professionals got their chance to try to take the world in hand at eleven o'clock in the morning on July 18, at the first of a series of meetings of the foreign ministers. Committees were appointed — drafting committees, economic committees, subcommittees on political questions — until the foreign ministers had covered all topics with an overlapping series of task forces. They had created instant bureaucracy, a remarkable feat really, which immediately began to show reassuring signs of bureaucratic life: scheduling problems arose among aides who served on more than one committee.

The ministers went straight at their work, without bothering to make complimentary speeches at one another. Molotov, his aims clearly in mind, sat forward, leaning over the table, a cigarette dangling from one corner of his mouth. Because of his stubborn stamina in negotiating sessions, Molotov was known to the Americans as "stone ass." Byrnes, the old cloakroom fixer, "plays his negotiations by ear," George Kennan once said, "going into them with no clear or fixed plan.... He relies entirely on his own agility and presence of mind and hopes to take advantage of tactical openings." Eden, the classicist, counted bargaining chips and looked for balance and symmetry.

Germany was defeated; the ministers had gathered in Potsdam to talk about Germany, and so they talked about Germany. In principle, the Big Three all agreed about Germany: it was to be administered as a unified country under a uniform policy by the United States, Britain, the Soviet Union, and France. It was divided into four zones as a matter of administrative convenience, and it was governed by a central control council on which all four powers were represented.

In fact, all three powers (and they simply assumed the right to speak for the fourth power, France) did agree on a unified policy for Germany; at least, they all agreed on the negative aspects of that policy. The foreign ministers, therefore, disposed first of those measures they all approved; Germany was to be disarmed and de-Nazified; all Nazis were to be removed from public office; all laws that discriminated on the basis of race, creed, or political belief were nullified; war criminals were to be tried; Germany was to submit unconditionally to the orders of the occupying powers.

All this was clear and simple enough, and yet, the Control Council had an inherent flaw. Whenever the four powers on the council could not agree on a unified policy, the individual zonal administrators were to do what they thought best in their own zones. And, on that bland provision, a unified Germany began to come apart at once, as all the major powers knew it would and wanted it to do. The delicacy of the operation lay in precisely the way in which Germany was taken apart.

Molotov had a nit to pick in the last sentence of paragraph 5 of the American draft of an agreement. Was there a loophole there that would permit retaining some Nazis in office? No, Eden thought, it referred only to non-Nazis. It might refer, said Byrnes, "to those who had been only nominal participants in the Nazi party or had been members of the party under duress." But he would change the offending language if Molotov wished.

It was a small matter, but it implied far larger concerns. The Russians wanted to extirpate every last vestige of Nazism — and promote members of the German Communist party to leadership positions. The Americans did not wish to be so dogmatic: after all, many German industrialists had been "nominal" Nazis, and they knew how to run the factories. The Russian zone in Germany was primarily an agricultural area. The other zones contained the lion's share of German industrial assets.

Eden suggested that they ought to add somewhere a provision that officials would retain their positions "subject to good behavior." But what did good behavior mean? Molotov turned up his nose at that, declaring that "this went without saying."

Molotov then had a quibble with paragraph 7, section *i,* which called for local democratic elections in Germany. Was it not too early to begin thinking of elections? The Control Council would decide, said Byrnes, when it was appropriate to hold elections. Perhaps so, replied Molotov, but "elections at this time would be premature." If so, Byrnes said, "they will not be held." "All would agree," Eden chimed in, "that elections at this moment are premature but that they should be held whenever possible." In that case, Molotov suggested, the paragraph could be rewritten to leave out any mention of elections. Elections could then "be left to the discretion of the occupying powers. There should be a general tendency in this direction but we should be cautious in proceeding with it."

Molotov's formula was both specific and vague. It was not clear what he meant by the "occupying powers" — whether that referred to the Control Council acting unanimously or the zonal authorities acting independently. The United States, Byrnes said, "would wish to consider this language very carefully." If the United States were to think "that a given community was ready to hold elections, to make this decision subject to the authority of the Control Council might be too restrictive.... Conditions might warrant elections in one place but not in another."

In short, the Americans wished to decide on their own, in their own zones, when to have elections. So did the Russians. Unified Germany began to show some cracks.

Molotov had tried several times during the course of the session to get Byrnes and Eden to talk about the division of the German fleet, and each time they had managed to avoid the issue. On the next day, July 19, Molotov insisted that the subject of the fleet, on which the Russians had drafted a proposal, be referred by the foreign ministers to the heads of state. Byrnes and Eden agreed — and Eden presented papers on Yugoslavia and Rumania, in which Britain had economic interests, to be passed up to the heads of state. That was done. Molotov wanted to discuss the Polish government-in-exile in London. It was to be liquidated, was it not, and all its assets transferred to the new government in Poland? The principal objective was to see that none of these assets fell into the hands of "private persons."

Eden assured Molotov that no assets would be transferred to "private persons."

The law governing these matters, Molotov said, was recent, and "many transfers might have taken place in the past."

No such thing had occurred, said Eden; the British were simply waiting for a representative of the new Polish government to arrive in London "in order that immediate discussions can begin."

Yes, Molotov persisted, but he wanted to stress the importance of "immediacy."

One could not begin discussions, Eden replied acidly, "with persons who are absent. "

Yes, well, nonetheless, Molotov wanted "a statement stressing immediacy."

The Russians wanted things, spoils, reparations, factories to ship home, Polish assets — whatever one wished to call them, whatever form they took, wherever they came from. The Americans and British kept talking about elections and "good behavior" of German officials, and it made the Russians impatient.

At ten-thirty in the morning on July 20, the economic subcommittee met. Ivan Maisky, a cherubic fellow with a goatee who had formerly been a rakish Fleet Street journalist, presented Russia's plan. The whole point of Potsdam was to settle the German question, was it? Then, "the main task of the Control Council is the elimination of the German war potential. " That seemed to follow logically enough. The general policy, therefore, "which will be carried out uniformly in all zones of occupation will be in preventing recovery of those parts of the economy which are the basis of the heavy industry...." And how did one eliminate heavy industry? Seize the factories and ship half of them to Russia as reparations!

From the point of view of America and Britain, the Russian desires posed at least four distinct dangers: a weak Germany was no barrier to Russian westward advance; a poor Germany might be a revolutionary Germany, a potentially Communist Germany; a denuded Germany was neither a good exporter, nor a good importer of American goods; and, finally, if the United States sent money and equipment into Germany to help rebuild it as a strong, prosperous trading partner and a bulwark against Russia, the United States certainly did not want its money and equipment simply to pass through Germany and go to Russia as reparations.

First, said Maisky, comes the matter of reparations. No, said the Americans, *first* comes the rebuilding of Germany, and *then,* secondarily, comes the question of reparations.

Anyway, the Americans said, the Germans would need imports to survive at all. Whatever was taken out of Germany should be applied first as payment against imports. Payments for imports must be placed ahead of reparations.

Ah, sputtered Maisky, "Everybody would say that reparations come first and imports after because we have suffered so much- capitalists want to have profits from foreign trade and don't care about reparations for those who suffered. Also when Germans know about it they will try to prove that without very considerable imports they can't live and can't export."

Will Clayton, one of the American negotiators, was a self-made man — tall, tough, blue-eyed, with his graying hair parted in the middle. His company was one of the largest cotton trading houses in the United States, with interests around the world. Several years before, the rumor in Washington was that Clayton would head a projected Department of Economic Warfare. While the department never materialized, Clayton, now an Assistant Secretary of State, remained a firm believer in aggressive capitalism. He tried to explain the American position in simple terms: "This is like the receivership of a big corporation. If a railroad company can't pay its debts, the receiver keeps that road going, issues receivers' certificates which take precedence over all creditors, for otherwise the creditors would get nothing." The bankers, Clayton explained patiently, would not finance it any other way.

Bankers, financiers, profiteers, what kind of talk was this? "We can never get the Russian people who have sacrificed so much," Clayton was told, "to understand why the Wall Street bankers have to be paid before they are!"

The economic subcommittee agreed that it could not agree — and bucked the question up the line to the foreign ministers. The economists were wrong, though, if they thought they had gotten rid of the issue. The reparations question was to rattle around Potsdam for the whole of the conference, arousing suspicion, fraying tempers, causing fights, and finally definitively splitting Germany.

By the time the foreign ministers met that morning at eleven-thirty, it was apparent that the Potsdam conference was in full swing: the professionals had got themselves into a scheduling tangle that all but completely paralyzed negotiations. Molotov started it by saying innocently that the next item on the agenda was the question of the establishment of the Council of Foreign Ministers. Byrnes asked whether the subcommittee's report was ready.

"Mr. Molotov stated that no subcommittee had been appointed.

"Mr. Byrnes pointed out that the paper had been referred back to the drafting committee established to consider it.

"Mr. Molotov asked whether there is a general drafting committee to cover all questions.

"Mr. Byrnes replied that a special committee had been appointed to draft the document on the Council of Foreign Ministers. The committee is working, and Mr. Byrnes wished to know whether they had completed their report.

"Mr. Molotov asked who was acting on behalf of the American delegation."

"Mr. Byrnes stated that Mr. Dunn and Mr. Cohen had been appointed.

"Mr. Cohen stated that because of the fact that Sobolev was busy the committee had not been able to meet until this morning and its work was not yet finished."

"Mr. Byrnes remarked that nothing could be done until the committee had reported. Mr. Byrnes then suggested that the document on the implementation of the Yalta declaration on liberated areas be placed on the agenda for the meeting of the Heads of States this afternoon."

"Mr. Molotov replied that this question would come up next and that the Russian delegation also wanted to reach agreement on the Council of Foreign Ministers.

"Mr. Byrnes stated that the American delegation is extremely anxious to reach agreement on the Council of Foreign Ministers and that he was willing to ask his appointees to leave the table to begin work immediately.

"Mr. Molotov replied that the Soviet member of the drafting committee is now in an economic meeting."

Having reached that impasse, the foreign ministers proceeded to get into a tangle over the items to be discussed at their meeting. Molotov wished to discuss trusteeship questions; Eden did not want even to mention trusteeships until he got a satisfactory answer from Molotov about British oil interests in Rumania; Byrnes would talk about anything at all, provided he could first establish the American position on the Yalta Declaration on Liberated Europe and so have a strong position that he could compromise when it came to horse trading.

The order of an agenda, like the shape of a conference table, establishes relationships among nations and issues. The foreign ministers discussed at some length just which topics they were willing to discuss until at last Molotov dropped the question of trusteeships entirely and proposed a revised agenda for the morning:

1. Italy

2. Liberated Europe

3. Rumania

The first topic would allow Molotov to cavil at the Western sphere of influence; the second would allow Byrnes to cavil back; and lastly came Eden's preferred topic.

Byrnes spoke first, and quickly: "The American position on Italy has been set forth in the President's paper of July 17," which called for full normalization of relations with Italy and an invitation to Italy to join the United Nations. There was really nothing to discuss.

Behind Byrnes's statement lay an American desire to neaten up its western European sphere of influence and have it formally recognized. The first step toward that end was to have Italy invited into the United Nations. The Russians did not really think they could frustrate this plan, but they did think the United States should be made to pay something for it.

"Mr. Molotov... asked whether Italy would be liable for the payment of reparations."

Byrnes seemed rocked by the question: "What

would they pay with?"

Molotov did not know, or did not care to say that he thought reparations would come from whatever aid America sent to Italy, but, he insisted, "somebody must consider the question of Italian reparations. "

Eden tried to evade the question by sliding smoothly into the position that "this question would be dealt with in the peace settlement."

Byrnes, however, did not want to avoid the issue. He had recovered from Molotov's thrust, and he told the Russian foreign minister that the United States had already advanced Italy 200 million dollars and would probably have to come up with another 400 to 500 million dollars more. Reparations, said the Secretary of State, "do not seem to the United States to be an immediate problem" — which was to say, no one was going to take out of Italy what America sent in.

How would it look to the world, Molotov asked, "to have small Finland paying large reparations and large Italy paying none"?

Byrnes might have told Molotov that that was Russia's problem, if the Russians wanted to strip Finland and listen to world complaints about it. He restrained himself and replied with taut courtesy that "it might be possible to work out some plan for Italy in future years to arrange some form of payment." He must say, however, "in the best spirit," that "the United States does not intend to make advances to any country in order that reparations may be paid by them."

Perish the thought! Molotov replied quickly that he had "not suggested this."

Fine. Well, Byrnes just "wanted to make the situation perfectly clear."

So that settled the business of Italian reparations—or so Byrnes thought; and then Molotov spoke again.

"Mr. Molotov suggested that the subcommittee to be appointed might consider the question of the advisability of reparations from Italy."

Had not the question of Italian reparations just been settled? Byrnes repeated what he had just said. Some questions were suited to horse trading, but not this one. The very idea that Molotov thought the United States would simply make payments to Russia via Italy infuriated Byrnes.

Very well, Molotov said, but when the subcommittee was appointed to discuss Italy, "reparations should be discussed."

The fact that Byrnes kept his temper in the face of such provocation is remarkable. He suggested, since they could not agree on the question, that the subject be referred to the heads of state. In the meantime, the foreign ministers would recommend that a subcommittee be set up to draft a statement on the admission of Italy into the United Nations.

Good, said Molotov, and when the foreign ministers reported to the heads of state on the establishment of this subcommittee, they could suggest that "the question of reparations be referred to this or another subcommittee."

Byrnes kept silent.

Next, Molotov said, they had agreed to discuss the Yalta Declaration on Liberated Europe. In Truman's statement, the President had attacked Soviet behavior in eastern Europe. Well, two could play that game. Molotov presented a Soviet draft of a statement on the Yalta Declaration that had some nasty things to say about Britain. The British were supporting the military, and very conservative groups generally, in Greece. There had been no elections in Greece, and it looked to the Soviets as though the British were keeping down the genuinely democratic forces in Greece by force of arms.

"Mr. Eden, with some warmth, stated that he would like to say at once that the description of Greece given in the Soviet proposal is a complete travesty of fact. The Soviet Government had no representatives in Greece, although they were free to go there. The press of the whole world was free to go to Greece and see for themselves and tell the world without censorship what was going on. Unfortunately this was not possible in either Rumania or Bulgaria. The Greeks proposed regular elections open to all parties. The present Greek Government had invited international observers to regulate these elections. Unfortunately the situation in Rumania and Bulgaria was not the same.

"Mr. Molotov stated that there were missions in Rumania and Bulgaria, including British representatives.

"Mr. Eden replied that these representatives had few facilities to see anything and still less to get anything done. In addition, the press was not permitted freely to operate in these countries.

"Mr. Molotov remarked that the number of British representatives in Rumania and Bulgaria was greater than the number of Soviet representatives. It was true that there were no British troops, but there were many political representatives. It was his understanding that the British Government had enough people there to keep it informed."

Byrnes then joined in to say that without freedom for the Western press to move about these eastern European countries, the United States "could not recognize them at this time."

Molotov tried to turn the criticism back again against the West, saying that there were "no excesses in Bulgaria or Rumania comparable to those taking place in Greece." What was his authority for such a statement? Why, "the American and British press." In any case, "the Soviet Government can no longer delay diplomatic recognition" of eastern European governments.

The United States could recognize them, too, said Byrnes, as soon as they had elections. No problem, said Molotov; there would be elections "as soon as candidates could be nominated. "

"Mr. Eden pointed out the difference between Greece, where all parties would participate in the elections, and Bulgaria, where the vote would be only for or against a set list. This did not meet the British idea of democracy. The press of the world could send anything out of Greece, and this included the *Tass* representative. On the other hand, British press representatives could send nothing out of Rumania or Bulgaria without extremely heavy censorship.

"Mr. Molotov stated that there was no reason to fear delay or that elections would not be free. However, the situation in Greece was different. The situation was dangerous. Mr. Molotov cited warlike speeches made in Greece against neighboring countries.

"Mr. Eden interjected that he was aware that the Yugoslav press and radio were accusing Greece of aggressive intentions. The same charges were contained in the document presented this morning by the Soviet delegation."

The argument began to heat up now.

"Mr. Molotov insisted that there is no connection between the Soviet document and the Yugoslav Government.

"Mr. Eden replied that he had only said that the language was the same. He pointed out that the Prime Minister yesterday had given figures proving that it was ludicrous to talk about an aggressive Greece. This was quite apart from the presence of British troops in Greece. He could only suppose that our Soviet Allies do not accept British assurances regarding the number of Greek troops. Greece has neither the intention nor the means to be aggressive.

"Mr. Molotov remarked that Mr. Eden's logic was correct, but the facts were that warlike speeches were being made.

"Mr. Eden replied that he was well aware of the storm of abuse coming over the Moscow and Yugoslav radios regarding Greece, but could only say that these stories were not correct.

"Mr. Molotov stated the facts had been obtained from the American and British press.

"Mr. Eden at this point stated his hope that the Soviet paper would be withdrawn. It was an unhappy paper regarding an Ally.

"Mr. Molotov replied that he was asking for consideration and for the facts.

"Mr. Eden said that it was easy for the Soviet Government to go and look at the facts.

"Mr. Molotov suggested that an end should be put to the reign of terror in Greece and that the Government should be reorganized.

"Mr. Eden reiterated that there was no terror.

"Mr. Molotov again remarked that he had read about it in the British press."

Eden's choices were very much circumscribed at this moment. He could not rise from the table and stalk out of the room; the time had not yet come to break off negotiations. Britain's foreign minister made what was, given the situation, the strongest statement he could:

"Mr. Eden stated that he wished to report on the Soviet document to the Prime Minister, since it contained grave charges against the British Government."

Molotov retreated instantly:

"Mr. Molotov denied this and stated that the charges were against the Greek Government."

But Eden did not wish to make peace. Here was an opportunity to declare a chilly war if not a hot one.

"Mr. Eden replied that Mr. Molotov knew very well that the British have troops in Greece. It was necessary to take the gravest exception to this Soviet document."

The third meeting of the foreign ministers adjourned.

Alliances among great powers are extraordinarily intricate affairs to put together. They are based, usually, on mutual military needs, on economic assistance, or cooperation, and they involve myriad compromises of economic ambitions, political autonomy, and professed ideals. Such marriages of great powers are equally difficult to take apart. As with most divorces, the issues have a way of becoming painfully entangled; differences that were clear become confused, and matters that were obscure sometimes become exaggeratedly lucid. Self-esteem plays some part; a sense of moral rectitude that has all but been forgotten is suddenly remembered, and seems, of course, to rest all on one side. The foreign ministers tried to disengage like rational, mature men of the world; but hard feelings were, perhaps, inevitable. All disentanglements do, after all, involve real rejection.

10
THE HEADS OF
STATE

According to Sir William Hayter, a member of the British delegation, "Churchill was tired and below his form. He also suffered from the belief that he knew everything and need not read briefs. Stalin was almost always late for meetings, and we spent long periods in the waiting-room allotted to the British delegation, which happened to be the Crown Prince's library. This would have been a good time to read briefs, but instead he and the Foreign Secretary read the Crown Prince's books and exchanged jokes about the comic dedications — 'to darling little Willy from his loving Great-grandmother Victoria R. I.,' that sort of thing."

As the plenary session of the heads of state opened

on July 18, Churchill tried a too obvious ploy to do a little grandstanding. He mentioned that there were 180 newspaper correspondents in Berlin trying to get information about the conference and, in their frustration, "roaming the environs in a state of fury and indignation."

STALIN: "That's a whole company. Who let them in?"

CHURCHILL [soothingly]: "They are not here, in the zone, of course, but in Berlin. Of course, we can work calmly only if there is secrecy, and we are duty bound to ensure this secrecy." Then Churchill made a magnanimous offer: "If both my colleagues agree with me, I could, as an old journalist, have a talk with them and explain to them the need for secrecy at our meeting.... I think we should stroke their wings to calm them."

Truman and Stalin were not about to let Churchill steal the headlines. "Each of our delegations has special press officers," Truman quickly rejoined. "Let them do their job."

Churchill seemed woefully hard of hearing. He interrupted; he rambled on; when he failed to understand some point Stalin had made, he would lean back in his chair and ask, in a stage whisper, for advice from his aides in the second row. If he had no ready answer to one of Stalin's points, he would ask an aide to read some part of a briefing paper to him. He could not hear; the aide would have to shout. The conference would come to a halt. The British would all look embarrassed. Then, beaming or frowning, in somber or stentorian tones, worrying over insignificant details or raising broad issues of principle, Churchill would embark upon another interminable speech. With every word he uttered he tried to widen the breach between America and Russia.

Churchill may have been exhausted and badly briefed, but he still knew how to twit and how to start arguments. If Truman and Stalin were trying to postpone a fight or blur their differences for the time being, Churchill knew how to force them into drawing battle lines. He started with definitions. Germany was mentioned.

"I want to raise only one question," Churchill said innocently. "I note that the word 'Germany' is being used here. What is now the meaning of 'Germany'? Is it to be understood in the same sense as before the war?"

Truman was cautious: "How is this question understood by the Soviet delegation?"

STALIN: "Germany is what she has become after the war. There is no other Germany. That is how I understand the question."

That was fine for Stalin; it meant that parts of Germany no longer belonged to Germany by definition. The Poles, for instance, occupied a large portion of eastern Germany. If Germany was "what she has become after the war," then part of Germany had already disappeared into Poland. By that definition, Britain and America would already have lost part of Germany before the bargaining even began.

TRUMAN: "IS it possible to speak of Germany as she had been before the war, in 1937?"

STALIN: "AS she is in 1945."

Rather than accept that definition, Truman preferred to pretend—for the sake of argument—that Germany did not exist at all.

TRUMAN: "She lost everything in 1945; actually, Germany no longer exists."

Stalin would not let Truman off the hook that easily.

STALIN: "Germany is, as we say, a geographical concept. Let's take it this way for the time being. We cannot abstract ourselves from the results of the war."

The argument was properly under way now, and Churchill sat back to enjoy it.

TRUMAN: "Yes, but there must be some definition of the concept of 'Germany.' I believe the Germany of 1886 or of 1937 is not the same thing as Germany today, in 1945."

STALIN: "She has changed as a result of the war, and that is how we take her."

TRUMAN: "I quite agree with this, but some definition of the concept of 'Germany' must be given.... Perhaps we shall speak of Germany as she had been before the war, in 1937?"

STALIN: "That could be taken formally, but actually that is not so. If a German administration should put in an appearance at Königsberg, we shall expel it, we shall most certainly expel it."

TRUMAN: "It was agreed at the Crimea Conference that territorial questions should be settled at a peace conference. How are we then to define the concept of 'Germany'?"

STALIN: "Let us define the western borders of Poland, and we shall then be clearer on the question of Germany. I find it very hard to say what Germany is just now. It is a country without a Government, without any definite borders.... Germany has no troops.... She is broken up into occupation zones. Take this and define what Germany is. It is a broken country."

TRUMAN [*insistently*]: "Perhaps we could take Germany's 1937 borders as the starting point?"

STALIN: "We can start anywhere.... Yes, we could take the Germany of 1937, but only as a point of departure."

To make certain they all understood, Churchill repeated: "Only as a starting point. " And Truman affirmed: "We agree to take the Germany of 1937 as a starting point. " They had agreed, then, to disagree by giving a definition none of them recognized as final.

Having pointed out a difference of opinion, Churchill proceeded to show how difficult it was to resolve differences. The United States and the Soviet Union were on the verge of agreement about disbanding the Polish government-in-exile.

"Mr. President," said Churchill, "I should like to explain that the burden in this matter falls on the British Government, because when Hitler attacked Poland we welcomed the Poles and gave them sanctuary." With that, the Prime Minister commenced to bore his allies with an analysis of the assets of the Central Polish Bank, an account of the living accommodations of the former Polish ambassador, the question of severance pay for former employees of the Polish government-in-exile. Stalin interrupted: "Have you read the draft of the Russian delegation on Poland?" Yes, indeed, said Churchill. "My speech is a reply to the draft" — though it was not clear just how it was a reply.

Then came another speech — this one intended, perhaps, as a warning to Truman about how much the London Poles might embarrass the American

President. "... You cannot prevent individuals, in Britain at any rate, from living and talking. These people meet with members of Parliament and have their supporters in Parliament." Not that Churchill gave them any encouragement: "... We, as Government, have no relations with them at all. Mr. Eden and I myself have never met them, and since Mr. Mikolajczyk left, I do not even know what to do with them, and never meet them.... As for us, we consider them to be nonexistent and eliminated in the diplomatic sense." But, Churchill warned, "I don't know what to do when Arciszewski walks about London and chats with journalists."

Truman was not at all worried by Polish public opinion, either in Britain or the United States. The Big Three had covered their brief agenda for the day, he declared, and could now adjourn. The Prime Minister, Cadogan noted, "wanted to go on talking at random and was most disappointed—just like a child with its toy taken away from it."

On the next day, July 19, Churchill tried to stir up Stalin by going back on his word about the German Navy. German submarines, Churchill thought, should be sunk. Submarines, after all, could only be used as weapons of war, and Britain, as an island nation, did not look favorably on having any submarines patrolling its waters. "As for surface ships," Churchill said, "they should be divided equally among us" — but there was a catch — "provided we reach a general agreement on all other questions and leave here on the best of terms." In other words, what he had just given away a few days before, the Prime Minister was now snatching back to use as bargaining chips.

Truman joined in to keep a hold on the German fleet. Ships were needed, he said, in the war against Japan. He would rather have the whole discussion postponed until the Japanese war was over. Furthermore, even after the Japanese war ended, ships would be needed to help in the supply and rehabilitation of Europe. In any case, all this could be sorted out later; after the Japanese war was over, the United States would doubtless have a "great number of merchant ships which could be *sold* [emphasis added] to interested countries."

On this point, however, Stalin was too shrewd a negotiator to be done in by Churchill and Truman. He certainly did not reckon on buying ships. He backed Truman up to the Japanese war. "Are not the Russians," the Generalissimo wanted to know, "to wage war against Japan?"

"It goes without saying," replied Truman, "when Russia is ready to fight Japan, she will be taken into the shipping pool the same as the others."

So far so good. "It is the principle we think important," said Stalin.

Churchill had already agreed on the principle and had to go along with Stalin at least that far. "I think we can reach an agreement," the Prime Minister said. "I suppose these ships could now be earmarked for each participant, and when the war against Japan is over, these ships could be handed over where they belong."

STALIN: "Which ships?"

CHURCHILL: "I mean the merchantmen...."

Stalin now closed on the ships. "The Russians should not be depicted as people who are intent on hampering the successful operation of the Allied Navy against Japan. But this should not lead to the conclusion that the Russians want to receive a present from the Allies. We want no gifts, but want to know whether the principle is recognized, whether or not the Russian claim to a part of the German Navy is considered legitimate."

CHURCHILL: "I said nothing of gifts."

STALIN: "I didn't say you did. I want a clarification of whether the Russians have a right to one-third of Germany's Navy and merchant marine. I think the Russians have this right.... If my colleagues think differently I should like to know what they actually think. . . ."

Stalin had properly trapped Churchill and Truman: they could not wriggle out from under the principle that Russia was entitled to one-third of the German fleet. Whereas Molotov could not even get Eden to discuss the subject, Stalin had moved quickly from a share in the Japanese war to a share of the German fleet. The ships were his; the bargaining was ended; Eden was again annoyed that Churchill had handled the question so badly and given away the fleet yet again — and this time definitively. Whether intentionally or not, however, Churchill had managed to drag Truman into the debate. Truman had lost, too; the first blood had been drawn.

The next item on the agenda was the Russian proposal to sever all relations with Franco Spain. Truman had already casually told Stalin he held no brief for Franco. Churchill, on the other hand, jumped in with both feet to attack the Soviet position on Spain. The Russians called for "the rupture of all relations with the Franco Government," said Churchill. "I think that, considering that the Spaniards are proud and rather sensitive, such a step by its very nature could have the effect of uniting the Spaniards around Franco, instead of making them move away from him.

"I do not think we should interfere in the internal affairs of a state with whom we differ in views," the Prime Minister further declared.

This last statement of Churchill's is such an important principle of the conduct of foreign affairs that we should pause over it for a moment. Churchill excluded from this statement of principle all countries that the Allies had defeated in the course of the war, and all countries — such as those in eastern Europe — that had been liberated by the Allies. In all other cases, however, "the world organization set up at San Francisco takes a negative attitude to interference in the affairs of other countries. It would therefore be wrong for us to take an active part in settling this matter."

Churchill's formulation is the greatest of great principles of foreign policy: everyone praises it, and almost nobody employs it. Indeed, Churchill's statement was made at what was the beginning of the very heyday of wholesale interference in the internal affairs of other countries.

Churchill was warning that Communist fifth-column forces were at work subverting governments all over Europe. And, if Franco were toppled, who would be the revolutionaries ready to take over? Communists. This was Churchill's old warning, which Truman had spurned. This was the advice from Forrestal that Truman had spurned. At Potsdam just the other day Truman had told Stalin that he held no brief for Franco. Now, however, the situation began to appear ominous. Truman went back on his word to Stalin — cautiously.

TRUMAN: "I have no sympathies for the Franco regime, but I have no desire to take part in a

Spanish civil war. I've had enough of the war in Europe. We should be very glad to recognize another government in Spain instead of the Franco government, but that I think is a question for Spain herself to decide."

STALIN: "IS that to say that there will be no change in Spain?" Stalin's motivation was obscure at best. He would have liked to see trouble stirred up in the West. He may even have wanted to see a Communist government take over in Spain — though few students of Russia believe he wanted to give himself the sort of trouble that that would have entailed. At the very least, this conversation was a test of British and American honesty about their desire to see democratic governments in Europe.

"It should be borne in mind," Stalin said, "that the Franco regime was imposed on the Spanish people from outside, and is not a regime that has taken shape in internal conditions. You are very well aware that the Franco regime was imposed by Hitler and Mussolini, and is their legacy. By destroying the Franco regime, we shall be destroying the legacy of Hitler and Mussolini. Nor must we lose sight of the fact that the democratic liberation of Europe implies certain obligations.... I am not proposing that we unleash a civil war there. I should only like the Spanish people to know that we, the leaders of democratic Europe, take a negative attitude to the Franco regime."

Perhaps Stalin had alarmed Churchill and Truman; he softened his proposal. "What are the diplomatic means that could show the Spanish people that we are not on the side of Franco but of democracy? Assuming that such a means as the rupture of diplomatic relations is too strong, can't we consider other, more flexible means of a diplomatic order?" Stalin did not want the world to think he gave his tacit blessing to Franco.

"Every government is quite free to make known its views individually," Churchill said. For Britain's part, they did not want to disturb relations with Spain; the Spanish, he said lamely, "supply us with oranges, wine, and other products, in exchange for our own goods."

Stalin proposed that the question be referred to the foreign ministers for debate. Perhaps Truman's fears were mollified, perhaps he just wanted to avoid an argument; he agreed to refer the issue to the ministers.

CHURCHILL: "I should oppose this. I think that this is a matter that should be settled in this hall."

STALIN: "Of course, we shall settle it here, but let the Ministers examine it beforehand."

TRUMAN: "I, too, have no objection to referring this matter for a preliminary examination by our Foreign Ministers."

CHURCHILL: "I consider this to be undeniable because that is a matter of principle, namely, interference in the domestic affairs of other countries."

STALIN: "This is not a domestic affair; the Franco regime is an international threat."

CHURCHILL: "Anyone can say this of the regime of any other country."

STALIN: "NO, there is no such regime in any other country as the one in Spain...."

CHURCHILL: "Portugal could be condemned for having a dictatorial regime."

STALIN: "The Franco regime was set up from outside..."

CHURCHILL: "I cannot advise Parliament to interfere in Spain's domestic affairs...."

TRUMAN: "I should be very glad if we agreed to refer the matter for preliminary examination by the Foreign Ministers...."

STALIN: "... This matter can be toned down.... Let the Foreign Ministers give some thought to the form in which it is to be clothed."

CHURCHILL: "I have not yet agreed in principle that we should make a joint declaration on this question."

Truman suggested they might return to the subject later. Stalin again proposed that they refer it to the ministers. "That's the very point," Churchill said emphatically, "on which we have failed to agree."

TRUMAN: "We pass on to the next question."

The question of Franco Spain would finally be resolved, ambiguously, by the foreign ministers. After relentless bickering, they agreed on a statement that stopped short of condemning the Franco regime, but pointedly declined to invite Spain to join the United Nations because its government had "been founded with the support of the Axis Powers. " Like Stalin's ritual bows to democratic terms in eastern Europe—perhaps, in part, as a trade for those ritual bows—the Big Three's public position on Spain was presentable and meaningless. Spheres of influence, it said in Truman's briefing book, do exist. Spain, clearly, was in the Western sphere.

With an exquisite sense of symmetry, the Big Three now turned to look at the Russian sphere of influence. The next question on the agenda concerned the Declaration on Liberated Europe as it applied to Yugoslavia. The Declaration was not being fulfilled, said Churchill, and he proceeded to have at the Russian sphere. "There is no election law, the Assembly of the Council has not been enlarged, legal procedure has not been re-established, the Tito administration is under the control of his party police, and the press is also controlled...."

Stalin neatly defended his sphere without admitting its existence. These were serious charges to bring against the Yugoslav government, he said. If Churchill wanted to make such charges, then representatives of the Yugoslav government should be invited to Potsdam to answer them.

Truman understood at once that any further conversation would be fruitless; and he recognized a Russian sphere of influence immediately by giving Yugoslavia to Stalin.

TRUMAN: "Is this matter serious enough for them to be invited over here? I find this inconvenient."

Churchill persisted, and by his persistence made lucid the difference between his strategy and Truman's. If Churchill can be said to have started shooting at the Russians, Truman was still only interested in loading the gun. The pattern of Truman's actions emerged: he intended to secure a Western sphere of influence, to recognize a Russian sphere of influence, and to object to Russian behavior — but, for the most part, to leave those objections planted in the record to use as he saw fit later on.

"We also have complaints to make," Truman said of Yugoslavia. "But," the President said, "I have not come here to judge each separate country in Europe or examine the disputes which should be settled by the world organization set up at San Francisco."

CHURCHILL: "I should like to thank Generalissimo Stalin for his patience in discussing this question. If we cannot speak of the differences which sometimes arise among us, if we cannot discuss them here, where can they be discussed?"

STALIN: "We are discussing them here. But the question cannot be settled without the accused...."

CHURCHILL: "I agree with this, but the President is opposed to inviting Tito here."

STALIN: "In that case the question will have to be withdrawn."

TRUMAN: "Today's agenda has run out. Tomorrow's sitting is at four o'clock."

In these first several days of the Potsdam conference, the Big Three engaged in a good deal of testing and probing. As they probed, they met, recognized, and — except for Churchill — respected resistance. Gradually, vague outlines of opposing spheres of influence took shape. On the next day, Friday, July 20, another kind of probing surfaced — within the Western sphere, between Churchill and Truman.

The President asked once more to have his Allies accept the American proposals to bring Italy into the United Nations. Stalin, all goodwill and cooperation, agreed, and said that he only wished to have discussed, "along with the question of Italy, the question of Rumania, Bulgaria, and Finland." Truman replied that he was "in full agreement with Generalissimo Stalin on this point."

"Our stand on the question of Italy," Churchill declared, "is not quite identical with that taken by my two colleagues." Although the Prime Minister did not say so, Britain's dispute with America dated back some time. In the summer of 1944, the Italian left-wing Committee of National Liberation, led by a conservative named Ivanoe Bonomi, refused to cooperate with the government led by Pietro Badoglio. Churchill backed Badoglio; Roosevelt backed Bonomi. A new Italian Cabinet was formed, excluding Badoglio. In the autumn of 1944, Roosevelt extended 100 million dollars in credit to Italy, and Bonomi told the Americans that "Italy looked for guidance more to the United States than to any others." Then Bonomi's Cabinet ran amok of Italy's traditional political chaos. For a time, the British seemed to have the upper hand, and Churchill's dreams of leading a western European bloc were revived. Great Britain's resources, however, could not support Churchill's diplomatic aims, no matter how cleverly they were pursued. Four-fifths of all relief supplies for Italian civilians came from the United States; more was promised by way of the United Nations Relief and Rehabilitation Administration. As Byrnes had just been telling Molotov, the United States had poured several hundred million dollars into Italy by the time of Potsdam, and more was on the way.

Churchill had a message for Truman: America had better not push Britain around too much, or the Prime Minister would start flinging monkey wrenches. He started in on a marathon speech. "Italy attacked us in June 1940, " Churchill said, "at a time when we ourselves were threatened with invasion. We lost many warships and merchantmen in the Mediterranean. We had heavy losses on land, on the coast of North Africa.... Without support from anyone we had to undertake the campaign in Abyssinia. ... Special squadrons of Italian air force were dispatched to bomb London. It should also be mentioned that Italy undertook an absolutely unwarranted attack against Greece.... All that took place when we were absolutely alone."

If sympathy for Britain standing alone and suffering great losses would not move the President, then Churchill would threaten to undermine Truman's position on democratic governments: "I also note that the present Italian government has no democratic basis arising from free and independent elections. It merely consists of [American-backed] political figures who call themselves leaders of various political parties." If that barb failed to find its mark, Churchill also raised some questions that remained to be settled, such as "the future of the Italian fleet, Italian colonies" — and *reparations*.

And, if Truman thought he could easily bring Churchill to heel, Churchill could suddenly drop his pose of speaking for the whole of the British Empire and point out how independent the dominions were. "I must say that the terms of surrender were signed not only by Great Britain, but also by other states within the British Empire; they were signed by the dominions — Australia, New Zealand, and others, who suffered losses during the war."

At the end of Churchill's speech, Truman sat silently — and left it to Stalin to reply to the Prime Minister.

"It seems to me," Stalin said quietly, "that the question of Italy is one of high politics."

Stalin then proceeded to explain "high politics" to Churchill. "The task of the Big Three is to dissociate the satellites from Germany, as the main force of aggression. There are two ways of doing this. First, the use of force. This method has been successfully applied by us, and the Allied forces are in Italy, and also on the territory of other countries. But this method alone is inadequate for dissociating Germany's accomplices from her.... It is therefore advisable to supplement the force method with that of easing the position of these countries. This, I believe, is the only means, if we view the question in perspective, of rallying these countries round us and dissociating them from Germany for good.

"Such are the considerations of high politics. All other considerations, such as those of revenge and injury, no longer arise."

Then, looking around the table at his allies, Stalin told them what considerations *did* arise in high politics, whether between Russia and eastern Europe, or Russia and the West, or Britain and America:

"Feelings of revenge or hatred or a sense of compensation received for injury are very poor guides in politics. In politics, I believe, one should be guided by an estimation of forces."

That evening, after the meeting had adjourned, Moran fussed about Churchill's room while the Prime Minister changed for dinner. Churchill was muttering about the "election business" back home. "It hovers over me like a vulture of uncertainty in the sky," he said.

"For three days, " Moran noted, "the P.M. has been certain that Truman's firmness has changed everything. Stalin has been very fair and reasonable. Now Winston is less certain about things."

Churchill invited Moran to join him for dinner with Eden. "He warned me," said Moran, "that Anthony had just had a telegram to say that his boy [Simon Eden of the Royal Air Force], who was missing, had been found dead by the wreckage of his plane. During dinner nothing was said of this.

They talked until nearly midnight as if nothing had happened."

11
AN ESTIMATION
OF FORCES

Charles L. Mee Jr.

Henry Stimson waited for a full report on the bomb from General Groves, and, while he waited, he fretted. He did not know what to think. As time went on, he gradually came to rationalize whatever it was that Truman had already decided.

On the question of whether to inform the Russians about the bomb, Stimson was still several steps behind the President. Whereas Truman had decided both to inform and simultaneously not to inform Stalin about the new weapon, Stimson was still stuck back in the old simplistic either/ or dilemma. He had finally concluded that the Russians should not be informed, because a police state and a free society could not possibly maintain permanently good relations, and thus it would be dangerous to give weapons secrets to Russia. But, if it were deemed necessary for some reason to share atomic secrets with Russia, it ought to be done cautiously; and the secrets should be used, somehow, as a lever to pry open the Soviet state and make it a more democratic, free society. This new, magical notion of using the atomic bomb to change the nature of Russian government appealed to Stimson's imagination, and he wrote up a memo about it for the President.

Next, the Secretary of War applied himself to a close analysis of the Proclamation that was to be put out calling for Japan's surrender. Stimson had originally advocated telling the Japanese that they could retain their emperor by including a specific reference in the Proclamation to "a constitutional monarchy under the present dynasty." Now, more than a week after Truman and Byrnes had cut that phrase from the Proclamation, Stimson recommended cutting the phrase.

The Secretary of War had by this time taken both sides of nearly every question that had come to his attention; and still his mind would not stop churning the same points over and over. Stimson's torturous arguments with himself were at last mercifully put to rest on the morning of July 21, at eleven-thirty, when General Groves's report reached him at Potsdam. Stimson did not manage to get to the Little White House before lunch. After lunch, the President was busy with some shopping. The officer in charge of the VIP post exchange had brought over a selection of items from which the President was able to buy gifts to take back home to his family.

At three o'clock, in the sun room of the Little White House, Stimson finally got his chance to sit down with Truman and Byrnes and read General Groves's report to them. Truman and Byrnes kept utter silence, and Stimson's excitement so overcame him that he often stumbled over the words:

MEMORANDUM FOR THE SECRETARY OF WAR

Subject: The Test.

1. This is not a concise, formal military report but an attempt to recite what I would have told you if you had been here on my return from New Mexico.

2. At 0530, 16 July 1945, in a remote section of the Alamogordo Air Base, New Mexico, the first full scale test was made of the implosion type atomic fission bomb. For the first time in history there was a nuclear explosion. And what an explosion!...

3. The test was successful beyond the most optimistic expectations of anyone. Based on the

data which it has been possible to work up to date, I estimate the energy generated to be in excess of the equivalent of 15,000 to 20,000 tons of TNT; and this is a conservative estimate. Data based on measurements which we have not yet been able to reconcile would make the energy release several times the conservative figure. There were tremendous blast effects. For a brief period there was a lighting effect within a radius of 20 miles equal to several suns in midday; a huge ball of fire was formed which lasted for several seconds. This ball mushroomed and rose to a height of over ten thousand feet before it dimmed. The light from the explosion was seen clearly at Albuquerque, Santa Fe, Silver City, El Paso and other points generally to about 100 miles. Only a few windows were broken although one was some 125 miles away. A massive cloud was formed which surged and billowed upward with tremendous power, reaching the substratosphere at an elevation of 41,000 feet, 36,000 feet above the ground, in about five minutes, breaking without interruption through a temperature inversion at 17,000 feet which most of the scientists thought would stop it.

Groves was no poet, and so, after he had given a rundown on the effects of the blast, he quoted a description of the test written by Brigadier General Thomas F. Farrell:

"The effects could well be called unprecedented, magnificent, beautiful, stupendous and terrifying. No man-made phenomenon of such tremendous power had ever occurred before. The lighting effects beggared description. The whole country was lighted by a searing light with the intensity many times that of the midday sun. It was golden, purple, violet, gray and blue. It lighted every peak, crevasse and ridge of the nearby mountain range with a clarity and beauty that cannot be described but must be seen to be imagined. It was that beauty the great poets dream about but describe most poorly and inadequately. Thirty seconds after the explosion came, first the air blast pressing hard against the people and things, to be followed almost immediately by the strong, sustained, awesome roar which warned of doomsday and made us feel that we puny things were blasphemous to dare tamper with the forces heretofore reserved to The Almighty."

Both Truman and Byrnes, Stimson noted in his dairy, "were immensely pleased. The President was tremendously pepped up by it.... He said it gave him an entirely new feeling of confidence and he thanked me for having come to the conference and being present to help him in this way." Stimson did not quite realize it, but Truman had just dismissed him. Two days later, finding another opportunity to speak to the President, Stimson complained that he was being excluded from the critical meetings about policy on the bomb. Truman said Stimson could go back home any time he liked. The President had the information he wanted; he no longer wanted to listen to Stimson's advice.

Now, for the first time, Truman really knew what he had. Talk about using the bomb to intimidate the Russians in Europe could now be tested in the knowledge that Truman really had the atomic power to back up his words. The atomic bomb worked potently on the imagination. Churchill had been transported by his vision of its impact. Truman was cooler; but the fact of the weapon nonetheless became a force to be balanced along with all the other factors and dreams and images and fantasies that formed, dissolved, and reformed in the minds of the Big Three.

That evening at the plenary session, Truman again took the offensive — or perhaps we should say that he attempted a counter-offensive against Stalin's initiatives in Europe. If Stalin did not intend to have his Red Army march all the way to the shores of the Atlantic Ocean, his Army had, in any case, already penetrated to the heart of Europe. His technique for securing and legitimizing his position in Europe was straightforward enough. The Red Army moved in to fight the war. Behind the Army, "friendly" governments were established. Stalin then made a persuasive case to have these governments recognized by Britain and America. Then, when the Army was pulled back, the client governments would remain as the legitimate, recognized governments of Europe.

This technique worked well enough in Rumania, Bulgaria, Poland, and elsewhere. Stalin wished, however, to stretch the technique just a bit farther and secure a slice of eastern Germany; for that plan, Stalin was employing the Poles. As the Russian Army advanced across Germany toward Berlin, the Poles moved along behind them and settled into eastern Germany.

The Poles had no "right" to be in eastern Germany. That Stalin had put them there was uncommonly aggressive. Nonetheless, he could justify it—if only very tenuously. A large part of eastern Poland had already been ceded to Russia by previous agreement; at Yalta, the Big Three had agreed to compensate Poland for this loss of its territory. The Poles were to take from Germany a chunk of territory that would make up for what they had lost to Russia. It was a simple bit of legerdemain to perform: the Big Three had only to agree to move the western boundary of Poland further west, into Germany. The only point of contention among the three powers was just how far west to move this new Polish border. Since Poland was on its way to becoming a client state of Russia, Stalin wanted Poland to take a large piece of Germany. To be certain Poland got what he wanted, Stalin moved the Poles in to occupy the real estate he had decided to have.

Truman, "pepped up" by the report on his new weapon, set out to nail the Generalissimo. "Allow me to make a statement," the President said, "concerning Poland's western border. The Yalta agreement established that German territory is to be occupied by the troops of the four Powers — Great Britain, the U. S. S. R., the U. S. A., and France — each of whom is to have its zone of occupation. The question of Poland's borders was touched upon at the conference, but the decision said the final solution of the question was to be made at a peace conference. At one of our first sittings we decided that as the starting point of a discussion of Germany's future borders we take Germany's borders as of December 1937.

"We have delineated our zones of occupation and the borders of these zones. We have withdrawn our troops to our zones as had been established. But it now appears that another government has been given a zone of occupation and that has been done without consulting us.... I take a friendly attitude to Poland and will possibly fully agree to the Soviet Government's proposals concerning her western borders, but I do not want to do this now, because there will be another place for doing this, namely, the peace conference."

The conversation is going to become very complicated in a moment unless we sort out what "peace conference" meant to Truman and what it meant to Stalin. When Truman spoke of a peace conference he referred to something that would never occur. He meant, therefore, that he was putting a problem off to become a permanent bone of contention. In the meantime, however, he was eager to use the idea of a peace conference to show that Stalin had already violated an agreement to wait for a peace conference. If he could show that Stalin had violated an agreement, then he would be able to renege on an agreement, too. In this case, as we shall soon see, Truman wished to deprive Stalin of any reparations from western Germany. Truman might, as he said, "possibly fully agree" to surrender part of eastern Germany to Poland; the price for that would be reparations: western Germany would keep its wealth to rebuild after the war.

Stalin's understanding of a peace conference was different, but just as cynical. In his view, the Big Three would decide whatever it wanted, and then a peace conference would dignify those decisions with a rubber stamp.

STALIN: "The decisions of the Crimea Conference said that ... Poland was to receive substantial accretions to her territory in the north and west. It was further stated that... the new Polish Government of National Unity will be asked for its opinion on the question of the size of those accretions.... The Polish Government... has expressed its opinion on the western border. Its opinion is now known to all of us."

The new Polish borders, Stalin implied, could now be recognized, and that would be the end of it. Were there technical violations of some sort? Stalin would walk boldly over them and maintain they should be ignored, forgotten, made meaningless by the simple expedient of legalizing what had been done.

TRUMAN: "NO official statement has ever been made on this western border."

STALIN: "I am now speaking of the Polish Government's opinion. Now we all know what it is. We can now agree on Poland's western border, and the peace conference is to take the final formal decision on it."

TRUMAN: "Mr. Byrnes received the Polish Government's statement only today. We have not yet had any time to study it."

If Truman did not want to press to dislodge the Poles, it was all the same to Stalin. So the Americans would not agree to Stalin's border for Poland. Never mind. The Poles were there; they could stay; a *fait accompli* would become an established government; eventually Britain and America would have to recognize what they could not change. "It makes no difference," the Generalissimo said, "whether we express our opinion today or tomorrow."

In the meantime, Truman ought not to imply that the Russians had done anything underhanded. "As for the question that we have granted the Poles an occupation zone without having the consent of the Allied Powers, it has not been stated correctly." Stalin had had nothing to do with letting the Poles into Germany; it had simply happened; it was the result of an inevitable, implacable, abstract tendency.

STALIN: "... The American Government and the British Government have repeatedly suggested that we should not allow the Polish Administration to enter the western regions until the question of Poland's western border is finally settled. We could not do this because the German population had gone to the west in the wake of the retreating German troops. The Polish population, for its part, advanced to the west, and our army needed a local administration in its rear, on the territory which it occupied. Our army cannot simultaneously set up an administration in the rear, fight, and clear the territory of the enemy. It is not used to doing this. That is why we let the Poles in.

"... We were also inclined to do this in the knowledge that Poland was getting an accretion of land to the west of her former border. I don't see what harm there is for our common cause in letting the Poles set up their administration on a territory which is to be Polish anyway. I have finished."

Truman slid smoothly into his counterpunch: "I have no objections to the opinion expressed concerning Poland's future border. But we did agree that all parts of Germany must be under the control of the four Powers. And it will be very hard to agree to a just decision of the question of reparations if important parts of Germany are under an occupying power other than one of these four Powers."

Did Truman refer to reparations only from eastern Germany? That gave Stalin no problem. If eastern Germany was to be under Polish control, Stalin would just take whatever he wanted. "Is it for reparations that you are apprehensive? In that case, we can waive reparations from these territories."

Stalin had not yet caught the drift of Truman's argument. The President did not want to interfere with reparations from just "these territories" but from all territories.

Stalin went on. He had established — he hoped — that the Poles did not have an occupation zone. Now he argued that he had not violated any understanding on a final determination of borders: he had not unilaterally moved Poland's borders to the west. "There has been no decision on the western border," he said; "the question has remained open. There was only the promise of extending Poland's borders to the west and north."

TRUMAN: "It is up to the peace conference to determine the future borders."

Stalin agreed, of course. Nonetheless: "It is very hard to restore the German administration in the western strip; everyone has run away."

How pathetically helpless Stalin seemed to be. Truman could not resist a sly dig. "If the Soviet Government wants to have help in reestablishing the German administration in these territories, this question could be discussed."

Stalin ignored the barb and offered a fuller explanation of the irresistibility of broad historical trends: "Our concept... is as follows. The army fights, it goes forward and has no worries except winning the fighting. But if the army is to move on it must have a tranquil rear. The army fights well if the rear is tranquil and if the rear sympathizes with it and helps it. Consider for a moment the situation in which the German population is either on the run behind the retreating troops, or is engaged in shooting our troops in the back. Meanwhile, the Polish population follows in the wake of our troops. In such a situation the army naturally desires to have an administration in its rear which sympathizes with it and helps it. That is the whole point."

Stalin was all but whining. Truman was gently condescending: "I understand this and sympathize."

STALIN: "There was no other way out. This does not mean, of course, that I lay down the borders myself. If you do not agree to the line which the Polish government has proposed, the question will remain open. That is all."

Truman would not let go of the question so easily, not until he had caught Stalin in the wrong. "I want to know," the President said, "whether the areas now being dealt with are a part of the Soviet zone of occupation. I think that at the appropriate time we shall be able to reach agreement concerning Poland's future borders, but now I am interested in the question of these areas during the occupation period."

Stalin squirmed. If he admitted the area was still part of Germany and was strictly under Russian occupation, Truman might insist the Poles be dislodged, to lose their foothold in Germany and, perhaps, never regain it. If he admitted the Poles had taken possession of the territory, he would be admitting a violation of an agreement. He took the best way out: he had it both ways.

STALIN: "On paper they are still German territory; actually, *de facto*, they are Polish territory."

If Stalin would not be pinned down on the question of whose government governed where, then Truman had another way to define what had been done—by speaking of the people. He asked his question with apparent offhandedness: "What has happened to the local population? There must have been three million of it."

STALIN: "The population has gone."

The population had to have gone somewhere. They must have gone west, into the British and American zones. Then the British and Americans would have to feed these people. That would strain the resources in the western zones. Thus, reparations from the western zones would have to be reduced. Churchill chimed in to spell out the implications: "... We agreed to compensate Poland at Germany's expense for the territory which has been taken from her [and given to Russia] east of the Curzon line. But the one must balance the other. Poland is now demanding much more than she is giving away in the east.... At any rate, the Poles have no right to create a disastrous situation in the food supply for the German population.... We don't want to be saddled with a large German population without any food resources."

Stalin was not moved by the prospect of hungry Germans. "Anyhow," he said, "Germany cannot do, and has never done, without grain imports."

CHURCHILL: "Of course, but she will be even less able to feed herself if the eastern lands are taken away from her."

STALIN: "Let them buy grain from Poland."

CHURCHILL: "We do not consider this territory to be Polish territory."

STALIN: "The Poles live there, and they have cultivated the fields. We can't demand of the Poles that they should work the fields and let the Germans have the grain. "

In the meetings of the foreign ministers and the economic subcommittee, the Americans had begun to split off western Germany and bring it firmly into an American sphere of influence. Now, in the meeting of the heads of state, Stalin made it clear that he had already sliced off a piece of eastern Germany for the Russian sphere and that he intended to keep it. Churchill continued to argue that the resources of eastern Germany should be available to all Germans, but the argument had obviously become a mere formality now.

CHURCHILL: "... I have been told... that the Poles are selling Silesian coal to Sweden. They are doing this when we in Britain have a shortage of coal and are faced with the coldest and harshest winter without fuel. We start from the general principle that the supply of Germany within her 1937 borders with foodstuffs and fuel must be shared proportionally to the size of her population, regardless of the zone in which this food and fuel is located."

STALIN: "And who is to mine the coal? The Germans are not doing it; it is the Poles who are...."

CHURCHILL: "But they are working in Silesia."

STALIN: "The masters have all run away from there."

CHURCHILL: "They have gone because they were afraid of military operations, but now that the war is over they could return."

STALIN: "They don't want to, and the Poles have not much sympathy with the idea. I am afraid the Poles would hang them if they returned."

Stalin could not have made his position any clearer: Germans sent back to eastern Germany would be hanged. Truman was quick to recognize the finality of the Generalissimo's statement, and equally quick to define the potential bargain. "It seems," said the President, "to be a *fait accompli* that a considerable part of Germany has been handed over to Poland for occupation. What in that case remains for the exaction of reparations?" The three heads of state batted the question around a while longer and, at the conclusion of the session, Truman repeated the terms of the deal that would have to be made: eastern Germany could not be given to Poland without payment; the question "must be considered in connection with reparations and the supply problems of the whole German people."

STALIN: "Are we through today?"

The plenary session of July 21 was adjourned.

The atomic bomb, it must be admitted, had done very little for the United States. It had bucked up Truman's spirits, and Truman had been unyielding with Stalin. Anthony Eden remarked, "This has been the President's best day so far." But it did not cause Stalin to retreat at all.

The next day, when Stimson gave General Groves's report to the Prime Minister, Churchill was again transported by enthusiasm. "Stimson," the Prime Minister boomed with a wave of his cigar, "what was gunpowder? Trivial. What was electricity? Meaningless. This atomic bomb is the Second Coming in Wrath." Now he knew, Churchill said, "what happened to Truman.... I couldn't understand it. When he got to the meeting after having read this report, he was a changed man. He told the Russians just where they got on and off and generally bossed the whole meeting."

Yet, Truman had not in fact "bossed the whole meeting." He had managed a confrontation and the outlines of a deal, but he had not forced Stalin to yield on anything at all. The problem was that the vaunted power of the bomb existed only in the imaginations of Churchill and Truman. It had the power of a vision or a nightmare, but, unless one actually dropped the thing on the Russians, it had no power over Stalin in fact. The nightmare of the bomb—if Truman and Churchill could eventually plant it firmly in Stalin's mind — might one day still achieve some magical power. But it was, and as far as Russia was concerned it was destined to remain, a chimera.

In truth, the plenary session of July 21 showed exactly what the American bomb and Russian possession of territory could do: they could hold each other at a standoff. Truman could stomp a foot and threaten; Stalin could stomp a foot and threaten; but neither felt he could charge the other. As the Cold War developed, it would be characterized by endless permutations of this foot-stomping routine, none of it really very threatening, all of it done from behind the lines painstakingly delineated at Potsdam. By the end of the session of July 21, it seems safe to assume — though it is only an assumption — that both Stalin and Truman understood the ritualized nature of their histrionics, and that neither would spoil the game.

Churchill, of course, still wanted to spoil the game, and he was alternately exhilarated by news of the bomb, depressed when Truman refused to go for the jugular, hopeful when Truman and Stalin fought, fretful when they seemed on the verge of a deal. That night, Stalin gave a dinner for the heads of state at his villa. Truman had a fine time; Churchill was unhappy.

"Stalin gave his state dinner," the President wrote home to his mother and sister, "... and it was a wow. Started with caviar and vodka and wound up with watermelon and champagne, with smoked fish, fresh fish, venison, chicken, duck and all sorts of vegetables in between. There was a toast every five minutes until at least twenty-five had been drunk. I ate very little and drank less, but it was a colorful and enjoyable occasion."

Truman had given his own dinner party for Stalin and Churchill on a previous evening. To entertain his guests, Truman had brought in a pianist and a violinist. Stalin, for his dinner party, escalated the entertainment, doubling Truman's forces. "... Stalin sent to Moscow and brought on his two best pianists and two feminine violinists. They were excellent. Played Chopin, Liszt, Tchaikovsky. I congratulated him and them on their ability. They had dirty faces though and the gals were rather fat...."

The President did not tell his mother that he sat back with Admiral Leahy and made nasty cracks about the gals. Leahy confided to his diary that "the Pres. and I estimated they weighed about 200 pounds each."

Churchill could not bear all the jollity. Nor did the Prime Minister, whose one great love was talking, like to sit still and listen to music. "When are you going home?" he mumbled to Truman. The President was having a wonderful time: "I'm going to slay until our host indicates the entertainment is over."

The Prime Minister drank his brandy, smoked his cigar, sulked, and plotted. As the party broke up, he whispered to Leahy that he would "get even" with Truman and Stalin for all this music. Not long after Churchill returned to his villa that night, a directive went out for entertainers for a dinner party the P.M. planned to give: for music, he ordered up the whole of the Royal Air Force Band.

12
THE DREADFUL PEOPLE

In principle, it was agreed: Russia was to swallow Poland; Poland was to swallow a chunk of Germany; and the remainder of Germany was to be carved up according to a plan yet to be determined. Such was the broad outline; yet many of the niceties remained to be worked out.

Both the outline and the niceties were based, to some extent, on realities, on assessments of political possibility, military strength, economic needs, and other irreducible facts. The positions of the various armies, the number of ships in various fleets, the productivity of various factories — all these were immutable realities for the Big Three. Nonetheless, a great deal was neither fixed nor certain. Neither the Polish border nor the amount of reparations to be given to Russia was an invariable factor in the world. Either could, on the contrary, be adjusted, rebalanced, and shifted at will. The final settlement of all these shifting factors would depend not only on their inherent reality but also on how they were combined in the minds of the Big Three to make some ideal or acceptable image.

On July 22, Truman, Churchill, and Stalin joined in a world of pure imagination and vied with one another to impose their conceits upon the hard facts.

They had, in principle, agreed to move a line about on a map and define a new border for Poland. It is not difficult to draw and redraw lines on maps, but one would expect the draftsmen to be forced to confront the unpleasant fact that real people with real faces and histories and wishes are affected by those shifting abstractions. After all, Germans who suddenly found themselves standing on Polish soil would have to pick up and move to the west to get back within the new German borders.

For a moment, this reality seemed to intrude itself into the Potsdam conference. There were, Churchill said, some eight or nine million Germans in the east who would have to be uprooted and moved into the west. Such a vast number of people is no inconsiderable fact — if it is a fact. Stalin snorted at Churchill's willful exaggeration, and exaggerated in return. No Germans whatsoever remained in the east, he said; they had all gone, or been killed in the war. Someone else said there were two and a half million Germans in the east who would have to be moved west, and someone else mentioned one and a half million.

These elusive numbers drifted back and forth across the conference table. No one suggested that a census be taken. No one suggested that experts be consulted or that a rough head count be made by the occupying armies. Real numbers of real individuals did not matter. Numbers were simply a manner of speaking. They were bargaining counters, of greater or lesser magnitude — and all of the Big Three could agree to increase or decrease the German population depending upon other imaginary constructs. Vast populations could not only be moved from one place to another; they could be invented, or, if need be, made to vanish entirely. If Stalin agreed that there were nine million Germans to be moved from east to west — where they would presumably have to be fed and kept warm — then reparations for Russia from the western zones would have to be proportionately reduced. Were there nine million Germans? Then there was not 10 billion dollars' worth of reparations in the west: it simply did not exist. But, if there were two and a half million Germans, then perhaps there was several billion dollars' worth of reparations. According to Churchill, there were nine million Germans and no reparations; according to Stalin, there were no Germans and 10 billion dollars' worth of reparations. The facts would ultimately have to submit to a compromise that was a sheer expression of imagination and desire.

And what of the Poles, meantime? They, too, were an imaginary people, with imaginary needs, imaginary rights and powers. Stalin insisted that the Poles needed to be heard from, to determine how far west the Poles wanted their border to go. They should be invited to Potsdam to present their case. Such a hearing would clearly be supererogatory, since the Poles would say whatever the Russians told them to say. No one, however, was impolite enough to point that out. Churchill maintained that for the Poles to have much added territory "will not benefit Poland," and, in any case, the Poles should not be asked what they want, because the Poles "will demand much more than we can agree to." Truman did not want the Poles to be brought to Potsdam, because whatever they said would be irrelevant — since borders could not be determined until "a peace conference." Anyhow, Truman wondered, "Is it necessary to settle the question so urgently?... What I do not know is how urgent the question is." The whole thing might be postponed until the first meeting of the newly formed Council of Foreign Ministers, which had just been established by the Big Three at Potsdam and whose first meeting had been scheduled for September. Stalin agreed to that: "Let us refer the questions to the Foreign Ministers' Council. That would not be superfluous."

"Mr. President," said Churchill, "with all due respect to you, I should like to note that there is a certain urgency about the question. If the settlement of the question is deferred, the *status quo* will be fixed. The Poles will start exploiting this territory, they will settle down there, and if the process continues, it will be very difficult to adopt any other decision later.... If the Foreign Ministers' Council, after hearing the Poles, also fails to reach agreement, the question will be postponed indefinitely. Meanwhile, winter will set in...."

Winters in Germany are harsh affairs. There was a problem with coal. Berlin itself might suffer; some of its coal, said Churchill, came from Silesia. No, said Stalin, Berlin's coal came from Saxony. For that matter, Berlin could take coal from Zwickau.

CHURCHILL: "IS that so-called brown coal?"

STALIN: "No, it is good hard coal. Brown coal is good for use in briquettes, and the Germans have good briquette factories."

Somehow, this talk of brown coal and hard coal and briquettes assumed the dimensions of mysterious and elemental facts of life that had to be confronted. Churchill ruminated about coal for a few moments, and then concluded that after all, on the whole, it would be a good thing to invite the

Poles to Potsdam to present their own case on their new border. Truman agreed; he had no objection to inviting the Poles.

Thus an invitation was sent to the Poles to come to Potsdam. Despite the invitation, the Poles were not welcome; they had no power to affect the course of their fate; their advice and pleadings would be listened to by no one. In fact, while it was all very pleasant to speak about the Poles as a figment of one's imagination, they were a damned nuisance in the flesh. When Churchill's turn came actually to meet with the Poles, he was appalled. "I'm sick of the bloody Poles," the Prime Minister said. "I don't want to see them. Why can't Anthony talk to them?" But the Poles came to Potsdam, proud and demanding as usual, to play their part in an elaborate, ironic ritual in which they were both victims and conquerors. They were the helpless victims of the visions and designs of others; they were the conquerors of new territory — won not by virtue of their strength, but because of their weakness. They were constrained to make certain predictable demands for territory; and, constrained as they were, this would be virtually the last occasion on which they had freedom of speech. Just to add the final touch of cruelty, the Poles had no idea that the fate of Poland had already been settled in broad outline, and so they argued their case as though their very lives and souls depended on it. With the invitation to the Poles, Potsdam diplomacy was transmuted into theater.

"It got hotter and more and more oppressive this afternoon," Cadogan wrote home, "till a thunderstorm burst at about 5. All the streets of our village are littered with trees — there was a most frightful squall....

"As I was driving back from the meeting this evening," Cadogan went on, "when I was halfway out of the park of the Cecilienhof, I was held up by Russian sentries at a crossroad. From the road on the left emerged a platoon of Russian tommy-gunners in skirmishing order, then a number of guards and units of the N. K. V. D. army. Finally appeared Uncle Joe on foot, with his usual thugs surrounding him, followed by another screen of skirmishers. The enormous officer who always sits behind Uncle at meetings was apparently in charge of operations, and was running about, directing tommy-gunners to cover all the alleys in the ark giving access to the main road. All this because Uncle wanted 5 minutes' exercise and fresh air, and walked out to pick up his car 500 yards from the Palace!"

While the Big Three waited for the Polish delegation to arrive, they spruced up their proposals on other issues; the subcommittees labored on; the heads of state ran through peripheral concerns; and, on the evening of July 23, Churchill played host at another dinner party. By this time even the supernumeraries were well practiced in their parts. Half an hour before Stalin arrived, Russian soldiers poured into the grounds surrounding Churchill's house, machine guns at the ready. The British were no longer alarmed by the maneuvers of the Red Army. But just to avoid any untoward incident, British sentries around the house were withdrawn and regrouped on the terrace. There, standing under bright lights, they were less likely to be inadvertently shot.

Everything was in good order at Churchill's house except, apparently, the plumbing. The rainstorm that hit Potsdam had knocked over a lime tree just outside the Prime Minister's house. According to Cadogan, "It appears to have been planted... just over the water main, on which its roots had got a complete grip. So when it bent it cracked the pipe.... P. M. very annoyed at not being able to have a bath. He says it is 'a most unwarranted act of Providence.'"

Earlier in the day, Churchill had reviewed the menu for dinner and found it wanting, and he had some cold ham flown in from England. Once the ham had arrived, no one knew quite what to do with it. Nonetheless, the Prime Minister had ordered ham, and so, after the main course was finished, the ham came in, momentarily bewildering some of the guests, as a sort of special added attraction.

Churchill loved soldiers and uniforms, and he had carefully deleted from the guest list everyone who did not have a uniform — or almost everyone. The three foreign ministers wore business suits, as did the Russian and American translators. (Churchill's translator was a major.) And Truman, of course, wore his double-breasted suit. Otherwise the dinner table was surrounded by splendid uniforms full of ribbons and medals.

The dinner guests had no sooner sat down to the table than, one by one, they began popping up again to deliver complimentary toasts and speeches. The speakers all had to raise their voices, for, in the background, blared Churchill's Revenge: the full Royal Air Force Band, playing continuously and at full volume — "Ay-ay-ay [Mexican Serenade]" by Friere, "Carry Me Back to Green Pastures" by Pepper, "Sons of the Soviet" by Curzon, "Serenade Espagnole," "Irish Reels," "Skye Boat Song." Every once in a while Stalin would lean over and ask Churchill if the band knew anything "lighter," and finally the Generalissimo tried to take the band under control by strolling over to the conductor, raising a toast to the band, and requesting a few favorite (quiet) tunes.

It was a good, happy, boisterous party, and it got louder and more boisterous as it went on. Churchill was having a fine time, and, after he had gotten quite a few toasts under his belt, he rose, glowing, and heaped praise on Stalin, working himself into such a state of eloquence that the only way he could come to a suitably socko finish was to proclaim the Russian leader "Stalin the Great."

The military men were not ignored; on the contrary, they were celebrated extravagantly. If the British Navy was toasted, so were the Russian and American Navies; then the Army, all three Armies in turn; then the Air Forces. Truman proposed a joint toast to Field Marshal Sir Alan Brooke and General Antonov. Brooke replied, reminding Stalin of his Yalta toast to "those men who are always wanted in war and forgotten in peace." Brooke studied Antonov's face (he went on awkwardly, trying to find a way out of the complicated toast he had begun) and thought Antonov had not been forgotten. He hoped soldiers would never be forgotten.

Stalin rose and replied briefly to the point that soldiers would never be forgotten. Then Stalin proposed a toast of his own. The Russians knew, he said, that it would not be right to let the British and Americans shed their blood in Japan without help from the Soviets. He drank to all of the Big Three joining forces against Japan. Churchill and Truman choked down their thoughts and lifted their glasses with the Generalissimo.

The President offered a toast to the Prime Minister. Truman was, he said, "naturally a timid man"; when Churchill and Stalin had made him the chairman of the conference he had been "literally overwhelmed." It was, Truman said, "a great privilege and pleasure" for him, "a country boy from Missouri, to be associated with two such great figures" as the Prime Minister and Generalissimo Stalin.

Stalin replied that "modesty such as the President's was a great source of strength and a real indication of character" — particularly since it was coupled with "real strength and character and honesty of purpose."

The evening went smoothly, with only one difficult moment. A colloquial phrase cropped up in a toast — no one could later recall just what it had been; some thought it was "second to none." Stalin felt he had been insulted. He asked his translator Pavlov for a rephrasing. The guests fell silent while Pavlov and Major Birse argued heatedly over the meaning of the phrase. But the moment passed, smiles returned, and toward the end of the evening Stalin got up from the table with his menu card in hand and asked everyone for their autographs. Dutifully, Churchill and Truman circulated their cards, too. The soldiers and statesmen wandered around the table clutching their menu cards, borrowing fountain pens, bumping into one another, laughing and looking shy. To some it seemed an intensely poignant moment, rather like the day that schoolchildren take their last yearbooks around to collect the signatures of their classmates.

Much sentiment was displayed; British officers who had not exchanged an intimate word for years presented their cards to one another as though this were to be the only moment in all their careers that they would confess to personal affection. Major Birse boldly complimented Truman on his piano playing, and Truman replied expansively, "Ah, my boy" — this to a man several years his senior — "I have always been interested in music. I wish I had taken it up as a career, instead of politics."

Not long after midnight, the band played three national anthems; and the party broke up; and the Russian Army vanished from the grounds of Churchill's villa.

President Bierut of Poland led his delegation into the meeting of the Big Three's foreign ministers at noon on July 24. Bierut was described by Arthur Bliss Lane, then ambassador to Poland, as being "about five feet seven inches in height, with a small, closely cropped brown mustache and a weak mouth... not... a dominating personality.... He spoke easily and gracefully, enunciating his phrases in a low but clear, well-modulated voice." When he spoke, Bierut had difficulty in looking directly into another person's eyes and usually averted his gaze.

Bierut's Communist credentials were in good order. He grew up in Lublin, then part of Russia, and he went underground as early as the First World War to escape the Czarist police. He was jailed several times during the twenties for illegal political activities. During World War II he was head of the Polish section of OGPU in Moscow and was later dropped into Poland by parachute to organize resistance to the Germans. Most of those who met him were immediately struck by his resemblance — physically, but in no other way — to Hitler.

Of the colleagues who accompanied Bierut, two stood out at Potsdam, Foreign Minister Rzymowski and that old friend of America and Britain, Mikolajczyk. Rzymowski, said Lane, was a tall, spare man, slightly stoop-shouldered, with a "scholarly looking face," occasionally lit by "a shy smile." Mikolajczyk was a light-complexioned man, stocky, with a "slow, delicate manner of speech," calm and tenacious.

All the talking was left to these three members of the Polish delegation. Each one of their small, set speeches tidily supplemented the others, and in sum they presented such a cogent and mildly eloquent little plea for Poland, it is a shame the exercise was a charade. Their meeting with the foreign ministers would otherwise have made a neat turning point in the negotiations.

Bierut played the hardheaded numbers man. Poland had ceded 180,000 square kilometers to Russia, he pointed out. In return, the Poles were actually asking for less. Poland had been a country of 388,000 square kilometers; according to the Polish plan to have a new border far to the west, along the Oder and Western Neisse rivers, Poland would become a country of 309,000 square kilometers. Before the war, the population density of Poland was 83 persons to 1 square kilometer. Now Poland would lose some population — a good many Ukrainians and White Russians and Lithuanians had been given to Russia along with eastern Polish real estate. In addition, some Germans would be leaving the east and resettling in the west. Bierut estimated the number of Germans to be sent packing at one or one and a half million — which was less than Churchill's nine million, but more than Stalin's none. Anyhow, when all this was sorted out, Poland would need 314,000 square kilometers to achieve the same population density it had had before the war; yet, Bierut concluded with a statistical flourish, the Poles asked for only 309,000 square kilometers. Bierut may well have been the most boring head of state in the world, but the point came through the talk of square kilometers that the Poles were not being greedy.

Foreign Minister Rzymowski opened his plea with a modestly eloquent recollection of recent history. World War II began, Rzymowski said, with Hitler's attack upon Poland. Poland had been under Nazi occupation longer than any other country, and the Nazis had tried utterly to destroy Polish civilization. "It was the only country in which there were so many death camps. The Germans had tried to kill off the population to obtain *Lebensraum* for Germans and had attempted to destroy Polish culture." If the Big Three still had left even a bit of a lust for vengeance, Rzymowski was saying, here was the occasion for "an expression of historical justice."

Furthermore, Rzymowski argued, the industries of Silesia had been a source of German armaments; under the peace-loving Poles, these industries would be turned to peaceful purposes.

Toward the end of his presentation, Rzymowski petered out with some miscellaneous secondary points: the proposed new boundary line would be the shortest possible line between Germany and Poland and thus the easiest to defend; a potential unemployment problem would be averted if Poland acquired Silesia and sent Poles to work in Silesian industries.

It was left to Mikolajczyk, friend of the capitalist countries, to conclude with an economic argument. "The Germans had two bases for their imperialism," he said. "One was the armament industry and the second the profit which they made as an intermediary between other nations." Giving Silesia to Poland helped eliminate German military strength. Extending the Polish border to the Oder and Western Neisse rivers gave Poland control of the river traffic that had produced profits for Germany as an intermediary trader among nations.

That was all the Poles had to say, and the foreign ministers of the Big Three hardly had anything to respond; yet, some sort of cordial remarks seemed necessary to the occasion. Molotov said that he thought the views of the Polish government were "just" and that the Soviet Union favored the Polish request.

"Mr. Eden said that as the matter was before the Big Three he had no comments to make.

"Mr. Byrnes said that they would present to the Heads of Government the views expressed by the Polish delegation."

Somehow, none of this came out sounding quite as cordial as it should have; the foreign ministers each took one more turn at trying to say something nice.

"Mr. Molotov repeated that the Soviet position was a special one and that they had certain obligations to Poland.

"Mr. Byrnes pointed out that although the United States was not a neighbor of Poland they had always been a friend of Poland.

"Mr. Eden said that it was because of Poland that Great Britain had entered the war. "

At last there really was no way to swell the scene or add a speech or two. The meeting was adjourned, and the Poles trooped out at about two-thirty in the afternoon.

The trouble with the Poles was that, once they had been invited to Potsdam, they would not go back home again. They stayed on, and stayed on, lobbying every British or American diplomat they could corner, cadging drinks or dinner here and there, pressing again and again to win their suit after they had long since been handed the victory behind their backs. They batted around the British and American houses in Babelsberg like weekend guests who didn't know when to leave.

After they had met with the foreign ministers, the Poles descended on Churchill. The Prime Minister had been out of sorts that morning, but after two stiff whiskeys and a snort of brandy he was back in fine fettle. Indeed, he was feeling positively conversational. Stalin and Truman kept cutting Churchill off at the plenary sessions, but on this afternoon the Prime Minister found himself facing an earnest and attentive audience, a genuinely captive audience. He delivered a soliloquy.

"I began by reminding them," Churchill recalled, "that Great Britain had entered the war because Poland had been invaded, and we had always taken the greatest interest in her..." But, despite all these feelings of good fellowship, said the Prime

Minister, Britain was not favorably impressed with Poland's request to take over "one quarter of the arable land" of Germany. "Eight or nine million persons would have to be moved, and such great shiftings of population not only shocked the Western democracies, but also imperilled the British zone in Germany itself, where we had to support the people who had sought refuge there."

Churchill plunged into his store of balanced rhetorical flourishes and tossed one before Bierut and his entourage: "The result would be that the Poles and the Russians had the food and the fuel, while we had the mouths and the hearths."

The Prime Minister rumbled on impressively. There were questions of free elections, of the freedom of many democratic parties to participate in these elections. "What was the definition of democratic parties?" the Prime Minister asked himself. "I did not believe that only Communists were democrats. It was easy to call everyone who was not a Communist a Fascist beast; but between these two extremes there lay great and powerful forces...." Churchill ran on and on.

At last, immensely pleased with himself, the Prime Minister subsided, and Bierut spoke up. The Poles, said Bierut, did not ask for much. Before the war Poland's population had been 83 persons per square kilometer. Now Poland was asking only for an amount of territory in the west that would compensate for what had been lost in the east. In truth, when one measured the actual square kilometers....

Something is peculiar about Bierut's speech: a striking sense of *déjà vu* overwhelms it. Perhaps he was simply repeating, verbatim, like a well-programmed automaton, what had just been said at the meeting of the foreign ministers. Or could it be that Churchill, when he came to write his memoirs, refreshed his recollection of the Polish requests by reading over the transcript of the foreign ministers' meeting? It is some measure of the strictly ritualistic character of the Polish mission that it really does not matter.

At four-thirty in the afternoon, Bierut and company arrived at the Little White House to meet Truman. Again Bierut recited his case for extending the Polish border west to the Oder-Neisse line. Truman replied brusquely that, although he had "great interest in Poland and its future," border questions "must be determined at the peace settlement." The Russians and Poles were handling the whole question in an "arbitrary manner," the President said, and "a disagreement would be a source of trouble in the future." Truman mentioned no conditions on which the Poles would enjoy American goodwill; he spoke neither of free elections nor a free press nor other democratic reforms, but left the Poles with the stark prospect of future trouble. Averell Harriman noted that "as the Poles were fifteen minutes late, having been with Prime Minister Churchill, and as the President had a meeting of the Big Three, the conversation lasted only fifteen to twenty minutes."

Historical determinism will not explain the fate of Poland in 1945 and later. The naïveté of Poles who desired a Socialist system and thought they could have Soviet assistance without Soviet control played a part. Vainglory, wishful thinking, pusillanimity, and dangerous flirtation all figured into what Mikolajczyk called "the rape of Poland." Nonetheless, the very geographical location of Poland determined its destiny to a great extent. For several centuries, Poland had seemed always to be caught in the crossfire between two powerful nations. The Poles always seemed to believe, or to hope, that the contending powers would want to have a large and strong Poland to balance and check the expansion of its neighbors. In the sixteenth century, the Poles had hoped England would help them hold the Muscovites in check. A memo that caught Napoleon's attention referred to the Poles as a possible ally against Russia. Karl Marx thought a strong Poland might be useful as a barrier to Czarist Russia. But of all the notions of what to do with Poland, the Due de Broglie wrote of the one that seemed most consistent with Truman's ideas in 1945; in the eighteenth century, he said, "It suited the French cabinet to sacrifice Poland, but to sacrifice that unhappy country, since it could no longer be defended, noiselessly; and, so to speak, without making or letting it cry."

To this formulation, Truman contributed one addendum: he would reserve the right to complain about the sacrifice, and to blame the Russians and the Polish Communists for the fate of Poland. In short, the President made a deal to sacrifice Poland, but he neither acknowledged that he made a deal nor intended to live with it noiselessly. It was thus that hapless Poland, the nation over which World War II had begun, was to become one of the essential *casus belli* of the Cold War.

Powerless people, and especially powerless people of whom one has taken an advantage, have a way of becoming contemptible. By late evening of July 24, the Poles had become not only farcical but contemptible. "I had to be back at A's [Anthony Eden's] house at 10:30," Cadogan wrote home to his wife. "Found no one there, so sat down to read a newspaper, but in about five minutes the Poles streamed in — dreadful people all of them, except Mikolajczyk. So I had to entertain them as best I could, and went on entertaining them — no signs of A. He didn't turn up till 11:30.... So then we got down to it, and talked shop till 1:30. Then filled the Poles (and ourselves) with sandwiches and whiskies and sodas and I went to bed at 2 A. M."

13
DIVIDING GERMANY

When Truman arrived at Gatow airfield in Berlin on July 15, he got into a car for the drive to Babelsberg with Byrnes, Vardaman, and Vaughan, and one other man who went unnoticed. The other man was Edwin Pauley, and he was invited to ride in the President's car for a reason.

Born in 1903 in Indiana, Edwin Pauley grew up in Alabama. He worked his way through to a master's degree in business from the University of California and started his career as a mucker in the California oil fields in 1923. After an airplane crash left him with more than thirty broken bones and 9 thousand dollars' worth of medical bills, he went back into the oil business with an enhanced sense of drive. Within fifteen years he was president of Petrol Corporation of Los Angeles, Fortune Petroleum Corporation, Golconda Petroleum Corporation, a member of the board of People's Bank of California, and a director of Griffith and Legg Construction Company. "Some of his business methods," *Current Biography* delicately noted, "have been called into question by political opponents." He was a big, six-foot-three-inch, broad- shouldered man, an easy talker.

He worked for Roosevelt in 1932 and 1936, directed fund raising in the western states in 1940, was appointed treasurer of the Democratic National Party in 1942, and was one of Senator Harry Truman's most aggressive backers for the Vice-Presidential nomination at the 1944 convention. In April 1945, President Truman named Pauley the head of the American delegation to the three-power Allied Reparations Commission in Moscow.

The whole vexing business of reparations was so complex that we would do well to recall once more its broad outlines. If America was to have an internationalist foreign policy after World War II, it required a set of means, or a "machinery" as it was often called, to achieve this end. This machinery, in turn, had its own requirements — and, like so many metaphors, it acquired its own set of characteristics and imperatives. It had an economic engine to make it go — and, as Alfred P.

Sloan, the chairman of General Motors, said — the "spark plug" of this engine was Germany.

No other country served this role of spark plug in Sloan's view. In these terms, France might have been a radiator, Italy a fan belt — Sloan did not attempt to drive his Rube Goldberg contraption too far — but only Germany could be considered the spark plug. In addition to being the spark plug of the western European economy, Germany was important, by virtue of its geographic position, as a bulwark against possible Russian military expansion. As a political matter, it seemed essential to the British and the Americans to keep Germany from "going Communist" and threatening to infect other parts of western Europe with Communism.

For political, geographic, and economic reasons, then, Germany was of immense importance. Playing with stakes as high as these, Roosevelt had said at Yalta — almost casually it would seem — that the Big Three could, in speaking of reparations to be taken from Germany, use 20 billion dollars as a starting point. In the time between Yalta and Potsdam, the Americans gradually came to realize, and with an increasing sense of alarm, that the removal of 20 billion dollars' worth of reparations would denude Germany and blow the spark plug.

To the most imaginative of the worriers, a set of cascading implications followed. The German economy would collapse; thus the European economy would collapse; thus American exports would collapse; and thus America would be buffeted by vast unemployment, unrest, perhaps political upheaval, possibly even a revival of American Communism or Populism. Charles P. Taft, the brother of the isolationist senator, joined economics, American political stability, and internationalism in a quintessential remark of the time. "Free enterprise," the internationalist Taft declared, "cannot be confined within even our wide borders and continue to exist. The destruction of free enterprise abroad, like the destruction of democracy abroad, is a threat to free enterprise and democracy at home."

Political leaders customarily speak of foreign affairs in terms of votes back home. How one deals with the future of Poland presumably affects the "Polish vote" in America; what one does about Italy theoretically influences the "Italian vote" back home. Politicians speak less often of those larger issues — such as economic turmoil in Europe and its effect on employment in the United States. These larger issues, however, are the more dangerous ones. They threaten not merely to trim this or that bloc vote, but to put the whole game up for grabs. Nothing, in this view, is more unsettling than widespread unemployment and an upsurge of, say, Populists — who belong to no party or union or ethnic bloc that can be maneuvered around or balanced against another bloc. German reparations, then, and the entire internationalist structure of which the German economy was a keystone, had a direct connection, at least in the minds of some, to the future of the two parties back home and Harry Truman's career in Washington. This is a philosophical view of the world that is informed by modern notions of progress and its corollary of growth: it insists that political power must expand or collapse. Many, and maybe most, negotiators at Potsdam accepted this view of the nature of things as a truism.

Having committed themselves to a figure of 20 billion dollars as a starting point, the Americans now had to find a way to start backing away from that sum. The first tactic for backing away was to deny the validity of any fixed dollar figures at all; the second tactic was to place a "first charge" against the German economy before any reparations were taken from the country.

Edwin Pauley had just spent a couple of weeks in Moscow haggling over these matters. On June 19, he had cabled Washington: "In numerous informal conversations with Mr. Maisky, he keeps coming back to the 20 billion dollar sum that was discussed at Yalta of which the Soviet Union would receive 10 billion or 50%, the British and the US 8 billion or 40%, and all others 2 billion or 10%. Inasmuch as Roosevelt, Stalin, and Churchill agreed at Yalta to use this as a basis of discussion, I have not officially resisted this basis. At this moment, however, I am strongly of the opinion that... a formula [should] be adopted which will emphasize percentages, rather than dollars...." He suggested at the same time that the Big Three keep all reparations in their own hands and agree among themselves just how leftovers were to be divided up among "all others." So, in Pauley's revised percentage formula, the 10 percent for all claimants other than the Big Three was redistributed: Russia was to have 55 percent of reparations, Britain *22½* percent, and America *22½* percent.

The United States was not interested in reparations in quite the same way as was Russia, whose industries had been damaged by the war. In fact, there was some question what the United States would do with reparations if it got the share Pauley was demanding. Pauley admitted as much in his cable, and said, "We must claim all we can accept. The US might well demand more reparations except that we are limited as to the kind and type of thing we can take. We cannot use plants, machinery and labor. But we can take and should assert to the fullest extent our demand for gold currencies, foreign assets, patents, processes, technical knowhow of every type."

In Washington, Joseph C. Grew, Acting Secretary of State, ruminated on all this and replied that none of this was exactly acceptable. The Acting

Secretary of State went on juggling numbers of dollars instead of Pauley's suggested percentages, and said, too, that France would have to be added into a reparations formula. Grew picked away at Pauley's plan in some detail, and added as an afterthought that the United States did not really need any gold.

Whoever may have been guiding Grew in all these questions, it is clear that Pauley enjoyed Truman's blessing. America's man in Moscow pressed on with his scheme. He did not bother to reply to Grew. Instead he cabled Jimmy Byrnes, then aboard the S.S. *Augusta* on his way to Potsdam. France could not be included in reparations discussions, Pauley cabled; as for the continuing talk of putting dollar values on reparations, he planned to go ahead with a deal based on percentages. As for Grew turning up his nose at gold, Pauley would continue to stake a claim to gold.

If talking percentages instead of dollars was one way to back away from a reparations commitment, another way was to insist on a first charge for imports. The first-charge principle was the wrinkle that cotton dealer Will Clayton tried to explain to Maisky by talking about railroad receiverships. Pauley explained the idea even more clearly in a letter he wrote to Maisky: "Surely we both understand there can be no current annual reparations from Germany except as more goods are shipped out of Germany than are shipped in, that is, there must be a large export balance. An export balance cannot be produced in Germany without some imports, such as food, alloys, cotton, etc. If these indispensable imports (without which there would be no exports of certain highly important types) are not a charge against the exports, then you, or we or some other economy will have to pay for the imports. ... Mathematically it may be stated as follows: current Reparations equal German current Production less the sum of Occupation costs, minimum essential German Consumption and Imports required to achieve the production permitted by the Allies. In symbols this reads:

$$R = P - (O + C + I)$$

... When we say that essential imports are a prior charge on exports, this is not because we think that imports are more important than reparations. Quite the contrary. All we are saying is that you must feed the cow to get the milk. The food is a 'prior' charge, it comes first in time, but it is not more important.

"Without carrying this simile too far we could say that you want a plan which will give lots of milk. We both expect that the cow will lose both horns and will get mighty thin. We want to be sure that the small amount of fodder required will be paid for with some of the milk...."

Joseph Grew, and others back in Washington, might have lost the drift of the argument somewhere between the spark plug and the railroad receivership and the fodder, but metaphors, no matter how thoroughly mixed, did not distract Maisky. The Russian negotiator perceived two dangers in the American's argument: first, percentages of no fixed sum could end up being percentages of nothing; second, a big first charge for imports could easily eliminate all reparations, as Pauley's mathematical formula clearly demonstrated. To accept either one of these two principles in a reparations plan would be to give up any definite claim to reparations. The essential question really was whether America and Russia did agree about the cow losing its horns and growing thin. Would the cow grow thin while Russia was fattened? Or would the cow be fattened up to America's advantage while Russia stayed thin? Talk of percentages and first charges for imports indicated that the Americans had no intention of letting the cow lose weight.

While Maisky understood all this, it is not clear whether the people back in the State Department grasped just how shrewd their man in Moscow was being. On board the *Augusta*, Truman and Byrnes worked over the briefing paper on reparations, scratching out some paragraphs, adding new provisions. H. Freeman Matthews worked over his copy of the briefing paper, too, deleting different paragraphs, adding different ideas. Reparations was a tricky affair, and it appears that everyone was confused — everyone except Maisky and Pauley.

If Byrnes and Truman did not understand the subtle technicalities of reparations, they certainly understood what they wished to achieve. One paragraph in the briefing paper stated: "No action shall be taken in execution of the reparations program or otherwise which would tend to support basic living standards in Germany on a higher level than that existing in any one of the neighboring United Nations." In Byrnes's copy, a notation was made in the margin next to this paragraph: "out." The word was evidently passed to Matthews; in his copy the paragraph was stricken out. The reparations program would, if the United States had its way, support higher living standards in Germany than among its neighbors. Maisky was right to be worried; the Americans wanted to fatten the cow.

Pauley seems to have been several steps ahead of most others in his thinking about the means to be used to achieve the American goal. His cables went unanswered for several days, and then a message was relayed from the *Augusta:* "Instead of replying now to the questions raised in your [cable number] 2418... [Byrnes] suggests that these issues be discussed and decided when you join President at Berlin."

Thus Pauley was the one man to join the inner circle of Byrnes, Vardaman, and Vaughan for the drive to Babelsberg in the President's limousine. "The extent to which the handling of reparations," Samuel Lubell wrote in 1946, "... produced the effects of an economic iron curtain splitting Europe in two is not generally appreciated." Truman and Byrnes and Pauley appreciated it.

By July 23, the testing and probing and bluffing had located some hardened positions—and then the trading began. If the Russians and Americans could not agree on a reparations plan to be applied uniformly to all of Germany, perhaps Germany should be divided so that America would adopt its plan in the west and Russia its plan in the east. Byrnes met with Molotov.

BYRNES-MOLOTOV MEETING, MONDAY, JULY 23, 1945, 10:30 A. M.

PRESENT

United States Soviet Union

Secretary Byrnes   Foreign Commissar Molotov

Mr. Bohlen   Mr. Pavlov

Bohlen Minutes

TOP SECRET

The Secretary said he had asked to see Mr. Molotov because he was deeply concerned at the development of the question of reparations from Germany. He said that as Mr. Molotov knew the

United States government had always favored and still favored the adoption of a friendly overall policy for the Three Powers which would treat Germany as an economic whole. He said, however, after listening to the discussions here and hearing the report of the Reparations Committee he did not see how certain of the positions taken by the Soviet Government could be reconciled with the adoption of an overall reparations plan. For example, the question of the transfer now to Polish administration of a large part of 1937 Germany would expose the British and Americans in their zones to serious dangers in connection with an overall reparations plan.

The Secretary continued that he was also very much afraid that the attempt to resolve these conditions in practice would lead to endless quarrels and disagreements between the three countries at a time when unity between them was essential.

The Secretary said that under the circumstances he wondered whether it would not be better to give consideration to the possibility of each country taking reparations from its own zone. For example, according to their estimates, about 50% of the existing wealth of Germany was in the Soviet zone and that, therefore, the Soviet Union could receive its share of reparations from its own zone. He added that if they wished to obtain certain equipment or materials from the British or American zones they could do so in exchange for food or coal needed to feed and warm the German population in the west. He added that Marshal Stalin had indicated some such proposal when he had said yesterday that if the British wished to obtain coal from Silesia they could do so by exchanging other goods with the Poles.

Faced with this extraordinarily forthright statement, Molotov broke and started to deal. He understood that the Americans did not want to send goods into Germany only to have goods removed to Russia. Yet, Stalin "strongly favored" a unified, overall reparations plan for Germany. Perhaps, Molotov said, Russia could consider reducing its reparations claims.

Having broken through their fixed positions, Byrnes and Molotov immediately parted and agreed to get together again in the afternoon. At four o'clock, they met once more. This time they had invited the British to join the conversation, and Byrnes brought Pauley, and Molotov brought Maisky.

Byrnes moved very quickly and confidently to take advantage of Molotov's concession of the morning. Let the Soviets cut their reparations demands from 10 billion to 9 billion dollars, said Byrnes. Then the other powers would cut their demands by the same percentage, and total reparations would amount to 18 billion dollars. It was still a mystery to him, Byrnes said, "where any such amount of reparations was to come from."

He returned to his proposal of the morning: "If each country should take reparations from its own zone, it would be possible to exchange goods between the zones. In this manner the Soviet Union would get its share from its own zone and the United States and Great Britain from theirs and would be able to take care of the needs of France, Belgium, Holland, etc." According to American figures, Byrnes said, about 50 percent of German resources lay in the Soviet zone in any case. (Byrnes's advisers had told him that the Soviet zone contained "31 percent of Germany's movable manufacturing facilities and 35 to 39 percent of the total prewar manufacturing and mining, and 48 percent of the agricultural resources of Germany" — but Byrnes persisted in rounding those figures off to 50% of Germany's total wealth.)

Molotov retreated precipitately. The Russians would reduce their figure to 8½ billion or 8 billion dollars, but they wanted to be certain of 2 billion dollars from the industrialized Ruhr. Molotov was on the run, and Byrnes had no wish to close a deal until he had done even better. He declined to notice Molotov's sacrifice of yet another billion dollars. The Secretary of State was worried, he said, "that quarrels would develop between the Soviet, British, and American governments over these matters...." Moving to clinch the first-charge principle on imports, he said "there would obviously be a disposition on the part of the Soviet authorities to question the need for imports which would reduce the amount available for reparations from the western zones."

Byrnes had gone too far, and Molotov began to squirm. The Russians were willing to reduce their figure (perhaps even more?), but they must insist on a fixed quantity of reparations from the Ruhr. The foreign ministers had arrived again at an impasse; they needed to retire and consult among their advisers before making any more moves. The meeting was adjourned.

Here the argument over reparations rested for several days. The loose ends of that argument lay scattered about, unanswered, untidied, with the loose ends of many other arguments. It is something of a marvel to see how diplomats are able to leave so much business so unfinished for so many days: this is the sort of work that calls for vast resources of patience, of imperturbability amidst chaos, and for minds agile enough to keep a myriad of details suspended in a fluid relationship in their imaginations.

The many differences of opinion were beginning, however, to assume a new form. Positions that had been frozen began to break up, and the various elements began to reassemble in new relationships. We can already begin to see that a bargain over Poland and a bargain over reparations was shaping up into one interrelated bargain. We can see, too, that the emerging Poland reparations bargain had within it a deal to divide Germany. And we can see that over that divided Germany loomed the implacable images of an atomic bomb and a Russian Army. We can begin to see very dimly the contours of the Cold War that the Big Three were designing.

14
FANCIES AND NIGHTMARES

The hardest questions, the toughest negotiations, revolved around Germany. The next hardest involved spheres of influence in Europe. The differences that were easiest to resolve were those over the peripheral interests of the Big Three. With the beginnings of a break in the negotiations over Germany, the flotsam and jetsam were quickly sorted out.

At the Teheran conference, Roosevelt and Churchill had agreed to give the East Prussian port of Königsberg to Russia, and at Potsdam Stalin asked to have this agreement confirmed. According to an American record of the conversation, "The Russians had complained that all ports of the Baltic froze. They froze for a shorter or longer period but they froze. The Russians had stated that it was necessary to have at least one ice-free port at the expense of Germany." Both Truman and Churchill readily agreed, and, in the easy-going, deal-making atmosphere on Monday, July 23, they confirmed the Teheran arrangement.

George Kennan, who was not present at Potsdam, was bewildered when he heard of this agreement. In fact, Kennan observed, Russia already had three "substantially ice-free" ports: Ventspils, Lepaya, and Balitsky. "Königsberg, on the other hand, lies forty-nine kilometers from the open sea, at the end of an artificial canal which is frozen several months of the year and has to be kept open, if it is to be kept open at all, by icebreakers. Königsberg is, furthermore, accessible only to moderate-sized vessels, with a draft not exceeding about twenty-five feet. In both of these respects its qualities are not materially different from those of the major port of Riga, which had already fallen to the Soviet Union...."

None of these facts got in Stalin's way, however, and no one thought to contradict him. On the contrary, when Truman returned to the United States, he patiently explained to the American people that he thought it was right to "satisfy the age-old Russian yearning for an ice-free port." Such was the power of the Big Three, that they could not only move borders, create spheres of influence, cause millions of Germans to exist or disappear — they could also melt ice at Königsberg. This mutual fantasy was eventually made into a fact in the *Soviet Encyclopedia* of 1953, which, unlike the earlier edition of the encyclopedia, described Königsberg as "ice-free." Kennan drew the obvious conclusion: "If anyone thought, after 1945, that he saw ice in the canal at Königsberg, he didn't. It was an illusion fed by anti-Soviet prejudice."

Truman matched Stalin's fantasy with one of his own. The President agreed, he said, to revising the Montreux Convention so that the Soviet Union would be able to use the Black Sea straits freely. He wished to link that question, however, to his proposal to open up "free and unrestricted navigation along all the international inland waterways." He had been studying history, Truman said, and he had asked himself, "What has been the cause of all these wars? In the last 200 years, they have all started in the area between the Mediterranean and the Baltic Sea, between France's eastern frontiers and Russia's western frontiers." What was the explanation for this? Truman thought it had something to do with water, with straits and canals and rivers. He advocated that "free and unrestricted navigation... be established for internal waterways running through the territory of two or more states, and... regulated by international agencies on which all the interested states are represented...."

The President suggested that the first waterways to be internationalized should be the Black Sea straits, the Kiel Canal in northern Germany, the Rhine, and the Danube, which flowed from western Europe across Bulgaria and Rumania to the border of Russia. If this was Truman's idea of a beginning, there was no telling where it would end. The Bug River, for instance, ran from Russia into Poland; the Dniester, too, flowed through both Poland and Russia. In the east, rivers flowed from China through India, from China through Burma, and down through Cambodia and Vietnam. Along the Russian-Chinese border, rivers flowed through both countries. If the Truman plan were applied all over the world, then countries all over the world would be opened up to some international agency. The notion was either fantastically aggressive or else Truman had very little understanding of the implications of it. Either way, it struck the others as something to be got around as swiftly and delicately as possible.

Stalin reacted to the idea very gently and cautiously, as though he were not sure just how mad Truman was. "The President's proposals should be given a closer reading," Stalin said; "it is hard to catch everything by mere listening."

There was no doubt that Truman had hold of a harebrained scheme, and most of the diplomats tried to make it go away by ignoring it. Churchill was more gallant — or more eager to ingratiate himself with the President — and he quickly agreed that the four specific waterways the President mentioned should be internationalized. There the subject lay, with everyone trying to avoid further talk about it. Truman kept bringing it up from time to time, but he could not get anyone even to agree to discuss it. On one occasion after Stalin had rebuffed Truman on the idea, the President turned to the American advisers in the row behind him and said, "I don't understand that man." As the days wore on, the President came to feel frustrated when his pet idea was repeatedly and callously dismissed. Though he never became angry about it, he did get irritated, and it was clear that his feelings had been hurt. Years later, when Charles Bohlen sat in his parlor in Washington reminiscing about Potsdam, the subject was still faintly embarrassing. Bohlen shrugged and said, "Well, that was the President's own idea..." There seemed to be nothing else to be said about it. Everyone has these little flights of fancy; sometimes they simply go so far beyond the realm of the possible that it is best just to let them pass.

On the topics of Syria and Lebanon, Churchill had a speech to make. He talked fast. In the course of the war, the major powers had all recognized Syria and Lebanon as nations in their own right, independent of any colonial powers. One of the colonial powers most affected by this decision was France. As Churchill said, France had long had both commercial and cultural interests in these countries. "The French have their schools, archaeological institutes, etc., there. Many Frenchmen have lived there for a long time, and they even have a song, 'Let's Go to Syria.' They say that their claims date back to the time of the Crusades."

At the end of the war, Syria and Lebanon were occupied by British troops. Churchill intended to withdraw, but, in withdrawing, he wanted to recognize that France had some "special privileges" in Syria and Lebanon. Who was Churchill to grant favors to France in independent countries? In truth, he was not exactly in any position to do this. Nonetheless he wanted to exercise the power so that he would have a bargaining counter in his own side-dealings with the French. He did not have the temerity to claim he had any rights over Syria and Lebanon. He observed simply that British troops were there. Since British troops were there, Britain would deal with French claims.

Why did Churchill not simply withdraw his troops from Syria and Lebanon and let the French enter their own negotiations for privileges from these independent countries? "If we were to withdraw our troops now," he explained, "there would be a massacre of French citizens" who were there. This would "cause great unrest among the Arabs" which would in turn "upset law and order in Saudi Arabia and Iraq." This would then "lead to disorders in

Egypt as well." And, as if that alone were not bad enough, disorder in Egypt would lead inevitably to having the Suez Canal "placed in jeopardy," and it was through the Suez Canal that "arms and reinforcements for the war in the Far East are moving." Obviously, then, by a direct line of logic, if Britain removed its troops from Syria and Lebanon, the conduct of the Japanese war would be imperiled! Thus, the British must stay where they were and do their own dealing with France. "Of course," the Prime Minister said in concluding this inventive scenario, "if the United States wished to take our place we should only welcome it."

TRUMAN: "No thanks."

The conference transcript records: *"[Laughter.]"*

Churchill's little fantasy was breathtaking, and, to Truman and Stalin, captivating. Stalin had suggested that Russia and America might enter into an adjudication of French claims. After hearing Churchill's marvelous justification for keeping the whole matter in his own hands, Stalin withdrew his suggestion.

The Americans were not quite as sporting about it all. When Churchill said he would give France "special privileges" in Syria and Lebanon, the second row of American delegates quietly stirred, and George V. Allen leaned over to whisper something to James C. Dunn.

George Allen was a not-very-remarkable-looking career State Department man. He was forty-two years old, and he had joined the government as an editorial clerk in the Census Bureau in 1929. In 1930, he entered the State Department Foreign Service and was successively stationed in Kingston, Jamaica; Shanghai; Patras and Athens in Greece; and in Cairo. In 1944, he was named chief of the Middle East Division of the State Department. He was the expert on this question of Syria and Lebanon, and, while we cannot pinpoint any other occasion on which his advice got to the new President, we can watch this whispered message of Allen's travel straight to the top.

The man who listened to the whispered message, James C. Dunn, was born in 1890 of wealthy parents and had had a smooth, sure rise as a diplomat. In 1928 he was appointed chief of the Division of International Conference and Protocol; he was acknowledged to be an accomplished dealer and shuffler of place cards and was known as the "Capitol's social fixer." His brown hair was parted in the middle and firmly slicked down; his trousers were pressed to razor sharpness; his conversation sparkled with "innocent gossip"; his manner was gentle; and he had a talent, it was said, for doing everything "in good taste." It was James Dunn who handed down the famous decision in the 1930s that Vice-President Curtis's half sister Dolly Gann was "entitled to precede Speaker Longworth's wife to the dinner table."

Dunn had married Mary Augusta Armour, and he and his wife were known for having the most lavish dinner parties of anyone in the State Department and for decorating their dinner parties lavishly with members of the European nobility. With these credentials—and with membership in the Metropolitan, the Alibi, the Burning Tree, the Chevy Chase, and the Brook—Dunn rose to a measure of prominence in the State Department, and he received some attention for siding with Franco in Spain. As Max Lerner wrote, he was "the chief target of the attacks on State Department 'fascists'...."

Nothing indicates that Truman ever listened to Dunn; the President seemed to share Capitol Hill's general disdain for the "spat-wearing career boys of the State Department." Nonetheless, Dunn wrote Allen's whispered message down on a piece of paper and passed it up to the front row at the Big Table, to Jimmy Byrnes. Byrnes read the message and handed the slip of paper to the President. Truman read the message, and, when Churchill finished speaking, the President replied to Churchill's proposal to give France "special privileges" in Syria and Lebanon.

TRUMAN: "We believe that no state should be given any privileges in these areas. These areas should be equally accessible to all states...."

CHURCHILL: "And you, Mr. President, will you prevent Syria from granting any special rights to the French?"

TRUMAN: "Of course I won't prevent it if the Syrians want to do so. But I doubt that they have such a desire." *"[Laughter.]"*

In the laughter, Allen's point was lost, the heads of state moved on to the next item on the agenda, and Churchill slid by the faint American objection and got his way.

If the first half of this plenary session was fantastical, the latter half was illusionistic. The subject of Iran was addressed. Iran possessed a good share of Middle Eastern oil.

At the end of a war, when farms and factories have been destroyed, one economic treasure remains as before: natural resources. The United States controlled 57 percent of the world's oil in 1945; Britain controlled 27 percent; and Russia had 11 percent. During the war, Russian oil production dropped by one third; it was for that reason, among others, that Russia seized and held eastern Europe, where refineries in Rumania, Austria, and Hungary continued to operate. One-third of the world's oil resources lay in the Near East. Of that, England controlled 74 percent, America 24 percent.

All three of the major powers had troops in Iran. All three had agreed to withdraw their troops.

Churchill and Stalin were reluctant to withdraw; Truman was eager to withdraw, urged that the others do likewise, became the champion of Iranian independence, and ended up Iran's closest friend. As it turned out, Truman's strategy was the most effective.

When the heads of state discussed Iran on July 23, they vied with one another to show the greatest indifference. Truman said American troops would leave Iran. Stalin suggested that Teheran at least could be evacuated immediately. Churchill agreed and suggested that further withdrawals be considered by the Council of Foreign Ministers when it met in September. The issue was given to the drafting subcommittee who wrote one of the blandest paragraphs they could on oil-rich Iran.

"The Near East," it said in Truman's briefing book, "is rapidly developing into one of the vital danger spots in world relationships." At Potsdam, the Big Three agreed to leave Iran as it had been — a potential trouble spot, the cause of later conflict.

At the end of the plenary session that day, Churchill spoke of the worry that had been nagging him for so long. In just three days, the vote tally in Britain would be completed. Truman and Stalin, said the Prime Minister, "must be aware... that Mr. Attlee and I are interested in visiting London on Thursday of this week. [Laughter.] That is why we shall have to leave here on Wednesday, July 25.... But we shall be back by the afternoon sitting on July 27, or at least some of us will. *[Laughter.]*"

The Prime Minister put up a brave show of it, and everyone at the conference said he was certain to be reelected. And yet, in the days at Potsdam, he had been turning slowly into a figure of pathos if not of tragedy. It was Churchill who did most of the talking at Potsdam, and, for all his lapses and meanderings, he spoke well. Eugene List, the pianist who played for the Big Three at Truman's dinner party, remembers being struck by the way Churchill spoke in fully formed, perfectly balanced paragraphs. This profusion of Churchillian paragraphs could not disguise, however, his weakness in the face of the soft-spoken Stalin or the brisk Truman, both men of few words. Churchill had not won many points at the Big Table. On July 23, Truman and Stalin had allowed him to have his way in Syria and Lebanon, to act as power broker with France. It was a crumb they had given him — one of the few he took away from Potsdam.

Perhaps it was because Churchill felt his weakness so keenly that he was so excited by American possession of the atomic bomb, and so sure that this weapon conferred limitless power on the United States. The Americans proceeded deliberately and confidently that day with their plans for the bomb, and Churchill peeked in on them with something of the mixed admiration and envy small boys feel for football stars.

In Washington on July 23, General Groves tried his hand at drafting the order to drop the bomb. "To General Carl Spaatz, CG, USASTAF: 1. The 509 Composite Group, 20th Air Force, will deliver its first special bomb as soon as weather will permit visual bombing after about 3 August 1945, on one of the targets: Hiroshima, Kokura, Niigata and Nagasaki...."

In China, Chiang Kai-shek waited for a message from Truman. The Chinese and Russians had been negotiating over the terms on which Russia would enter the war against Japan. In Chiang's view, the Russians were demanding too many concessions from China in exchange for their projected participation in the war. Chiang had asked Truman to intercede with Stalin on China's behalf. Truman was thus put in an intriguing situation. Did he want to help China and Russia come to a speedy agreement so that Russia could enter the war soon, or did he want to let the negotiations drag on so that Russia's entry into the war would be delayed?

At lunch that day in Babelsberg, Truman directed Stimson to ask General Marshall whether the Russians were still needed in the Japanese war. After lunch, Stimson sat down with the general and listened to his ambiguous reply. The atomic bomb made Russia unnecessary, Marshall said.

Nonetheless, the Russians would march into Manchuria whether they were needed or not, and take whatever they wanted. Furthermore, although the Russians were not needed, they would be useful in containing the Japanese in Manchuria. As far as the last point was concerned, however, the Russians had probably already achieved the most important goal simply by their presence on the Manchurian border. Their massed forces there had already drawn a good part of the Japanese army away from other fronts—which was the most crucial factor as far as Marshall was concerned.

This carefully hedged advice was brought back to Truman, and the President reached a decision quickly. He instructed Byrnes to cable Chiang: "If you and Generalissimo Stalin differ as to the correct interpretation of the Yalta agreement, I hope you will arrange for Soong [Chiang's negotiator] to return to Moscow and continue your efforts to reach complete understanding." In brief, Truman decided to embroil Stalin and his military plans in lengthy negotiations. "I had some fear that if they did not," Byrnes recalled, "Stalin might immediately enter the war, knowing full well [and here it all becomes rather complex] that he could take not only what Roosevelt and Churchill, and subsequently Chiang, had agreed to at Yalta, but — with China divided and Chiang seeking Soviet support against Chinese Communists — whatever else he wanted. On the other hand, if Stalin and Chiang were still negotiating, it might delay Soviet entrance and the Japanese might surrender. The President was in accord with that view."

None of this was to be revealed to the Russians, of course. Far from it. Truman and Churchill reviewed, approved, and informed the Russians of the recommendation of the British-American Combined Chiefs of Staff: the Soviet Union was to be "encouraged to enter the war; and such aid to its war-making capacity as might be needed and practicable was to be provided."

The end of the war in the Far East began to look like a mirror image of the end of the war in Europe. Where the Russian Army had rushed in to hold the position of power in Europe, the American bomb would hold it in the Far East. The conflicting spheres of influence were about to be extended around the entire globe; and although these spheres were still nothing but imaginative constructs, the Japanese were about to feel a tangible effect of mental inventiveness.

Churchill was again euphoric. Others might have shared his dream — Byrnes, for one, seemed to share it — but once again it was Churchill, the man who spoke in paragraphs, who gave it voice. He was especially pleased to be able to reveal the news to his generals, and Sir Alan Brooke recalled, "He had absorbed all the minor American exaggerations and, as a result, was completely carried away. It was now no longer necessary for the Russians to come into the Japanese war; the new explosive alone was sufficient to settle the matter. Furthermore, we now had something in our hands which would redress the balance with the Russians.... Now we had a new value which redressed our position (pushing out his chin and scowling); now we could say, 'If you insist on doing this or that, well.... And then where are the Russians!'

"I tried to crush his over-optimism," Brooke said, "based on the result of one experiment, and was asked with contempt what reason I had for minimizing the results of these discoveries. I was trying to dispel his dreams and as usual he did not like it.... He had at once painted a wonderful picture of himself as the sole possessor of these bombs and capable of dumping them where he wished. Thus all-powerful and capable of dictating to Stalin!"

To Lord Moran, all of these vaunting fancies had turned into a nightmare. When Churchill told him about the bomb, Moran was dismayed, and he sat down to make a long entry in his diary:

"I own I was deeply shocked by this ruthless decision to use the bomb on Japan. I knew I was hopelessly illogical. From bows and arrows to bullets, and shells, and gas-shells, and gas, to a torpedo which might send a thousand men to the bottom of the sea; and finally, to an atomic bomb; there could be no one point when the process of destruction becomes immoral. It was all to no purpose. There had been no moment in the whole war when things looked to me so black and desperate, and the future so hopeless. I knew enough of science to grasp that this was only the beginning, like the little bomb which fell outside my hut in the woods near Poperinghe in 1915, and made a hole in the ground the size of a wash-basin. It was not so much the morality of the thing, it was simply that the lynchpin that had been underpinning the world has been half wrenched out. I thought of my boys.

"Rowan came into the room and I found myself listening to his conversation with the P.M. as one hears the voices around when going under an anaesthetic, voices very far off and not like real people. I went out and wandered through empty rooms. I once slept in a house where there had been a murder. I feel like that here."

15
THE BIG TWO

A t ten-twenty in the morning on July 24, Henry Stimson paid a visit to the President in the Little White House. The Secretary of War had received some more reports from Washington, and he was now able to tell the President that the first atomic bomb would be ready to drop some time after August 3. Truman was delighted; that would fit in perfectly with his plans. He had asked Chiang Kai-shek to look over the draft of the Proclamation demanding Japan's surrender and join in signing the Proclamation, and Truman expected to hear from Chiang soon. The moment he heard, the President said, he would send out the warning.

When Truman mentioned the Proclamation, Stimson took the opportunity to raise again the question of letting the Japanese understand that they could retain their emperor. Stimson had agreed before that the phrase of reassurance to the Japanese should be deleted; but he had reconsidered the whole issue and now he thought that an offer should be made to the Japanese after all. Of course, he knew it was too late actually to revise the Proclamation, but he thought the President should keep a close watch on the situation; if the Japanese seemed to balk at that one point, then a verbal message might be put through diplomatic channels. Truman said he would certainly keep a watch on the situation and do just as Stimson advised should the appropriate occasion present itself. The President must have been relieved when Stimson finally headed for the door.

If Stimson felt excluded from the President's councils, he was not alone. Truman seemed to be systematically excluding all advisers save a few. Some of the American delegates wondered why they were being kept so much on the periphery of the dealings. One rumor around the American compound was that Harry Vaughan had told Truman that every time the Americans added one adviser to the group around the Big Table at the plenary sessions, the Russians added *two!* According to this rumor, Truman deliberately cut back the American delegation to see what Stalin would do. Another rumor had it that Vaughan alarmed the President by suggesting that the notes

made of conversations at the plenary sessions might
be leaked. Whether or not Vaughan unsettled
Truman with that prospect, Truman restricted
distribution of plenary session notes to himself and
one or two others, and so the American diplomats
took to filching copies of the minutes distributed
by the British.

For much of the conference, then, a good many
American delegates were confused, or simply
ignorant. Few could see how their little pieces of
the negotiations fit into the larger plan in Truman's
mind. The President was playing the conference
close, and few of his colleagues knew enough to
correct his misapprehensions or share his vision.
American policy had come to be locked inside the
heads of only a very few people. But, then, if many
of the American diplomats were kept in the dark
about negotiations, so, too, were the British.

At midday on July 24, the foreign ministers,
Byrnes, Molotov, and Eden, had lunch together.
Over lunch, the conversation was general and
polite. After lunch, Eden had to leave. Byrnes and
Molotov stayed on, with only their translators
present. Byrnes, it turned out, had something to
say. No one had asked him, but he wanted Molotov
to know that he and Truman thought they should
all "avoid a peace conference made up of delegates
from fifty-odd nations. Such a conference would
result in endless discussions and in no satisfactory

results. Small nations not having direct interests in important European questions should not be given opportunity to air their views thereon." The British did not appear to agree with this idea, Byrnes said blandly, but they would doubtless go along "when they had given more thought to the matter." As far as the Americans were concerned, said Byrnes, the new Council of Foreign Ministers could settle problems on an *ad hoc* basis. The Big Three would form the core of the council. (The fact that they formed the core would be partially disguised by inviting China and France to join; but China and France, since they were not "signatory to the terms of surrender" imposed on Germany, would be written into the council in a way that limited their participation.)

Molotov may have wondered why Byrnes was telling him at this late date — after days of conversational references to a general peace conference — that there would be no peace conference. And we might wonder, too, since the American deception seemed to be working so well, why Byrnes upset the whole, apparently useful ruse.

Perhaps the President's conscience had begun to bother him, and he had decided to be candid and open about his plans. Or perhaps he saw some usefulness in moving beyond the ploy of a peace conference that was not to be and clearing the way to a new, more positive level of confrontation. In either case, Molotov and Stalin could draw only one conclusion from this startling announcement: the Americans believed that they and the Russians would settle all problems between the two of them. In case the Russians had any illusions about British-American relations, they should understand that the Americans would do what they wanted, and the British would just have to go along. In case the Russians had any illusions that the Americans *really* cared for the rights of small nations — and here was the heart of the message — the small nations were to be excluded from any peace conference. They could speak only when asked by the Council of Foreign Ministers. And thus Truman shoved aside Britain and all the little nations of the world — and there he stood, he and Stalin alone, face to face.

Molotov carried the message back to Stalin, and while the Generalissimo thought about it and prepared for the plenary session that evening, the Combined Chiefs of Staff of the United States, Great Britain, and the Soviet Union had their big meeting at the Cecilienhof Palace.

It was a hot afternoon, and the British chiefs were kept waiting in a stuffy room lined with calf-bound books. Field Marshal Sir Alan Brooke, Marshal of the Royal Air Force Portal, and Admiral of the Fleet Cunningham reconnoitered the shelves and plucked out a few choice volumes as spoils.

Admiral Leahy presided at the meeting, and, as the British secretary, Lieutenant-Colonel Mallaby recalled, he "opened the proceedings, extending an elaborate and polysyllabic welcome of the Chiefs of Staff of what he called, by a drowsy slip of the tongue, 'Our gallant ally Japan.' It was growing very hot. It did not matter. The interpreters were not such fools and the Russians easily sustained their blank and uncomprehending stares."

Army General Antonov replied by saying that Soviet troops were at that moment massing in the Far East and would be "ready to commence operations in the last half of August. The actual date, however, would depend upon the result of conferences with Chinese representatives which had not yet been completed." What Antonov said was exactly what the Americans had counted on, but it was good to have it confirmed. The Japanese, Antonov continued, had about thirty divisions in Manchuria in addition to about twenty Manchurian divisions — and this confirmed General Marshall's opinion that the Russians had already accomplished the major objective of drawing Japanese forces away from other fronts.

Leahy then called on General Marshall to give American estimates of ground troop strength in China. The United States chief of staff, said Marshall, estimated that there were about one million Japanese in China; "heavy movements of Chinese troops have been made from Burma to China. The movement of troops and supplies to China has been undertaken in order to have ready by August 15, Chinese divisions of 10,000 men each equipped with American arms, trained by American officers and enlisted men, and directed under American guidance." The Chinese, then, were preparing for large-scale attack on the Japanese.

Lieutenant-Colonel Mallaby nodded and started awake. The room was hotter and stuffier.

Marshall droned on. A few interesting points were buried in his report: American aircraft had reduced the normal Japanese sea traffic "from ports as far south as Indo-China to Japan from forty convoys a day to none whatsoever..." And "the Japanese have been compelled to stop all operations at sea except minor operations in the Sea of Japan...." And "the attacks upon Japan from the air and the sea are now proceeding in tremendous volume, but the intensity of these attacks would increase each week." In short, Japan was dying.

British General Ismay had fallen sound asleep. General Hollis nudged Mallaby and smiled at Ismay. A moment later, Hollis's smile faded and he, too, dozed off.

Field Marshal Brooke reported that the British were clearing Burma and Siam; Admiral Cunningham said that "only remnants of the Japanese Fleet in the

Southeast Asia area remained...." Marshal Portal said that "the British and United States air forces in Southeast Asia maintained complete supremacy over the Japanese air forces in that area...."

Mallaby woke with a start and jabbed Hollis, Hollis woke and jabbed General Pug awake. The meeting was adjourned.

"Thus finished our Combined Chiefs of Staff meeting in Berlin," Brooke noted in his diary, "where we had never hoped to meet in our wildest dreams of the early stages of the war. And now that we are here I feel too weary and cooked even to get a kick out of it. It all feels flat and empty. I am feeling very, very tired and worn out." Brooke was doubtless feeling irrelevant, too, for all the decisions were political ones by this time.

The way was now cleared for the Big Three to return to the heart of their differences. They had disposed of the military business. They had settled, for the most part, the peripheral issues. At the plenary session that evening they moved back toward the center of Europe. Once again they took up the Yalta Declaration on Liberated Europe as it applied to Rumania, Bulgaria, Hungary, and Finland.

At an earlier meeting of the foreign ministers, Byrnes had said that the ministers should discuss a document having to do with the admission of Italy to the United Nations. Molotov had replied that he would not discuss the document because it contained no mention of admitting Rumania, Bulgaria, Hungary, and Finland to the United Nations. Byrnes suggested that the United States would "meet the desires of the Soviet delegation" by adding these sentences: "The Three Governments also hope that the Council of Foreign Ministers may, without undue delay, prepare peace treaties with Rumania, Bulgaria, Hungary, and Finland. It is also their desire, on the conclusion of peace treaties with responsible democratic governments of these countries, to support their application for membership in the United Nations Organization."

Molotov was not, of course, content with such words as "hope," "may," "desire," or with the qualifying "responsible" in front of "democratic governments." All these words seemed to the Russians to be loopholes that the Americans would use to avoid recognizing the eastern European governments or giving them a vote in the United Nations.

"One gets the impression," Stalin said, "of an artificial division: on the one hand, Italy, whose position is eased, and on the other, Rumania, Bulgaria, Hungary and Finland, whose position is not to be eased.... In what way is Italy more deserving than the other countries? Her only 'merit' is that she was the first to surrender. In all other respects Italy behaved worse and inflicted greater harm than any other [German] satellite state.

"... As regards the Government in Italy, can it be said that it is more democratic than the Governments in Rumania, Bulgaria or Hungary? Of course not. Has Italy a more responsible Government than Rumania or Bulgaria? No democratic elections have been held either in Italy or any of the other states. In this respect they are equal."

Stalin had a suggestion: Italy was to have its "position eased" in two ways; it had been given diplomatic recognition, and now it was to be taken into the United Nations. Stalin proposed that just the first of these two favors be granted to the eastern European countries. Let diplomatic relations be restored immediately.

"I should like to say," Truman replied, "that the difference in our views of the Government of Italy, on the one hand, and the Governments of Rumania, Bulgaria and Hungary, on the other, is due to the fact that our representatives have not had an opportunity to obtain the necessary information in respect of the latter countries.... In addition, the nature of the present Government of these countries does not allow us to establish diplomatic relations with them at once. But in the documents submitted we have tried to meet the Soviet delegation's desire and not to place the other satellites in a worse position than that of Italy."

STALIN: "But you have diplomatic relations with Italy and not with the other countries."

TRUMAN: "But the other satellites too can obtain our recognition if their Governments satisfy our requirements."

STALIN: "Which requirements?"

TRUMAN: "Concerning freedom of movement and freedom of information."

STALIN: "None of these Governments hinders or can hinder movement and free information for members of the Allied press. There must be some misunderstanding. With the ending of the war the situation there has improved...."

TRUMAN: "We want these Governments reorganized...."

STALIN: "I assure you that the Government of Bulgaria is more democratic than the Government of Italy."

TRUMAN: "... We proposed the same formulation in respect of Rumania, Bulgaria, and Hungary as in respect of Italy."

STALIN: "But this... does not include... diplomatic relations."

TRUMAN: "I have said many times already that we cannot resume diplomatic relations with these Governments until they are reorganized as we consider necessary."

Stalin was nonplussed by Truman's directness, and

for a moment the Generalissimo turned snippity. He suggested that the word "responsible," wherever it was applied to Italy, should be deleted. "This word tends to belittle the Italian Government's position." Nonetheless, Truman replied, the United States could not support any application for UN membership from a government that was not responsible and democratic. But, said Stalin, "In Argentina the Government is less democratic than in Italy, but Argentina is nevertheless a member of the United Nations Organization. If it is a government, it is a democratic government, but if you add 'responsible,' it turns out that this is some other kind of government."

Frustrated in this line of argument, Stalin subsided and tried a more insinuating approach. He proposed that the Big Three declare themselves ready merely to "examine" the question of resuming diplomatic relations with the eastern European countries. This did not mean that all three of them would actually resume relations at the same time, only that they would all examine the question of doing so "sooner or later." This was, for instance, what had actually been done in Italy, said Stalin. Russia and America had ambassadors in Italy, but Britain did not. It was not essential for all of the Big Three to send ambassadors to other countries simultaneously.

Churchill did not quite agree with Stalin's characterization of the case. "We consider that our representative in Italy is fully accredited.... The status of that representative cannot be fully equated with that of an ambassador.... But we do call him ambassador."

Stalin was extraordinarily quick to seize on the opening Churchill had unwittingly given to him.

STALIN: "But not of the kind as those of the Soviet Union and the United States."

CHURCHILL: "Not quite. About 90 percent."

STALIN (savoring the moment before he pounced): "Not quite, that's true."

CHURCHILL: "But the reason is a formal and technical one."

STALIN: "That's the kind of ambassador that should be sent to Rumania—such a not-quite ambassador." *"[General laughter.]"*

The laughter faded quickly. Truman brought the conversation back to a somber tone. He wanted to do everything he could to get to the point of resuming diplomatic relations with the eastern European countries, but "I have already explained the difficulties in solving this problem." Stalin's response was cold and hard: "The difficulties were there before, but they are no longer there. We find it very hard to adhere to this resolution in its present form. We do not want to adhere to it."

Truman and Stalin had reached an impasse, and now Churchill piped up — and made it worse. He wanted to say a few words on Italy's behalf, the Prime Minister said. Italy had dropped out of the war two years before, he said, and had since been fighting with the Allies. Relations with the Italian government had developed satisfactorily and there was "no political censorship there. The Italian press frequently attacked me only a few months after Italy's unconditional surrender." Thus, said Churchill, Italy obviously had a responsible democratic government. But the trouble with eastern Europe was that it was so tightly closed to Western representatives that Britain could not even find out what sort of governments were there. "I must say," the Prime Minister concluded with an offhandedly harsh attack, "that we know nothing concerning Rumania, not to mention Bulgaria. Our mission in Bucharest was placed in conditions of isolation reminiscent of internment."

Stalin bridled: "How can you say such things without verifying them?"

And Churchill announced the theme of the Cold War: "We know this from our own representative there. I am sure the Generalissimo would be surprised to learn of some of the difficulties of our mission in Bucharest. An iron fence has come down around them."

STALIN: "All fairy tales!"

Admiral Leahy sat in silence next to the President. Stalin would not budge from his position: he wanted recognition of the eastern European governments. Truman would not budge from his position: the governments would not be recognized unless they were "reorganized." Leahy understood the portentousness of the moment. "The result was a complete impasse," he later recalled, "and might be said to have been the beginning of the cold war between the United States and Russia."

Still, the time had not yet come to declare open war; the hint of an open break had to be papered over. Byrnes proposed a formula.

BYRNES: "In the hope of reaching agreement, I propose that the words 'responsible government' should be replaced by the words 'recognized government.'"

STALIN: "That is more acceptable. But I think we should also adopt a decision that the three governments are willing to examine the question of establishing diplomatic relations with these four countries...."

Churchill, however, was not at all interested in papering over any differences. To suggest, the Prime Minister said, that the Big Three would agree even to examine the question would "clash with what we have just said here." No, said Stalin, each country would simply be saying that it would take up the question of recognition entirely independently.

TRUMAN: "I have no objections."

STALIN: "In that case, we have none either."

CHURCHILL [*stubbornly*]: "I think there is a contradiction. I understood the President to say here that he does not now want to recognize the governments of Rumania, Bulgaria and the other satellite countries."

TRUMAN: "It says here that we undertake only to examine the question."

CHURCHILL: "This tends to mislead public opinion." STALIN: "Why?"

CHURCHILL: "Because it follows from the meaning of the statement that we shall soon recognize these governments; as it is, I am aware that this does not reflect the stand either of the government of the United States or the government of the United Kingdom."

Stalin had another syllogism to propose that went at the problem from a different set of assumptions. The Big Three had agreed, said the Generalissimo, that the Council of Foreign Ministers, at their meeting in September, would prepare peace treaties with the eastern European countries. "We all believe," Stalin said, "that a peace treaty can be concluded only with a recognized government.

Consequently, we must mention this recognition in some way, and then there will be no contradiction. If we fail to say that the three governments intend to raise the question of recognition in the nearest future, we shall have to delete the clause about preparing peace treaties...."

Well, said Churchill, he wanted to know if the President thought the Council of Foreign Ministers would discuss peace treaties with representatives of "the present Governments" of the eastern European countries.

Truman hedged: "The only government that can send its representatives to the Council of Foreign Ministers will be the government which is recognized by us."

CHURCHILL: "The present governments will not be recognized and that is why it will be impossible to prepare the peace treaties with them."

STALIN: "What makes you think so?"

CHURCHILL: "It follows logically."

STALIN: "NO, it does not."

CHURCHILL: "... It seems to me that it does."

The governments might or might not be recognized, said Stalin. "No one knows whether they will or will not be recognized." The question would be examined, that was all, and then peace treaties could be signed after the governments actually were recognized.

"Anyone reading this clause," said the Prime Minister, "will not understand that the U.S. Government does not wish to recognize the present governments of Rumania and Bulgaria.... You must excuse me for insisting on the point in this way, but I ask you to bear in mind that if the document is published, it will have to be explained, especially by me, in Parliament. We say that we shall conclude peace treaties with governments to which we accord recognition, but we have no intention of recognizing these governments. I find this almost absurd."

At last, Stalin found the way to hide all their intentions: "Nothing is said here at all about the conclusion of peace treaties; it says here about preparation. Why cannot a treaty be prepared, even if the government is not recognized?"

Churchill, with his fund of ready words, came up with the proper construction: "Of course, we can prepare the peace treaty ourselves. In that case, I propose that we replace the preposition 'with' by the preposition 'for,' so that it should read not 'peace treaties with Rumania, Bulgaria,' etc., but 'peace treaties for Rumania, Bulgaria,' etc."

STALIN: "I have no objection to 'for.'"

CHURCHILL: "Thank you."

STALIN: "Don't mention it."

And so, the Big Three agreed to issue a statement that sounded vaguely as though the eastern European countries were to be recognized and were to have peace treaties with the Big Three but that in fact guaranteed no such thing. The Big Three agreed to write peace treaties that they might not sign for countries that they might not recognize because of differences that they might not resolve. They had just approved one of the essential causes in their mutual declaration of war, and no one who read the public statement issued in their names would ever guess.

Here, according to the conference transcript, occurred "[*General laughter*]."

At the end of that day's plenary session, Truman got up from the big table and sauntered casually around to Stalin. He had nothing important to say—the fact that he had left his interpreter Bohlen behind proved that.

"I was perhaps five yards away," Churchill remembered, "and I watched with the closest attention the momentous talk. I knew what the President was going to do. What was vital to measure was its effect on Stalin. I can see it all as if it were yesterday."

Byrnes, too, was watching: "At the close of the meeting... the President walked around the circular table to talk to Stalin. . . ."

Leahy tried not to appear to be watching the conversation.

"I casually mentioned to Stalin," Truman said in his memoirs, "that we had a new weapon of unusual destructive force. The Russian Premier showed no special interest. All he said was that he was glad to hear it and hoped we would make 'good use of it against the Japanese.'"

"I was sure," Churchill said, "that [Stalin] had no idea of the significance of what he was being told.... If he had had the slightest idea of the revolution in world affairs which was in progress his reactions would have been obvious. Nothing would have been easier than for him to say, 'Thank you so much for telling me about your new bomb. I of course have no technical knowledge. May I send my expert in these nuclear sciences to see your expert tomorrow morning?' But his face remained gay and genial and the talk between these two potentates soon came to an end. As we were waiting for our cars I found myself near Truman. 'How did it go?' I asked. 'He never asked a question,' he replied."

Truman could now claim that he had been an honest and trustworthy ally; he had informed Stalin about the atomic bomb. At the same time, he and Churchill believed that Truman had successfully deceived Stalin. According to the Russian General Shtemenko, the deception did indeed work: after the plenary session of July 24, the Russian Army "general staff received no special instructions." Stalin did not guess what Truman meant until after the first bomb had been dropped on Japan.

Marshal Zhukov remembered it differently: "On returning to his quarters after this meeting, Stalin, in my presence, told Molotov about his conversation with Truman. The latter reacted immediately: 'Let them. We'll have to talk it over with Kurchatov and get him to speed things up.' I realized they were talking about research on the atomic bomb."

Very few turning points of history can be specified precisely. When Rome began to decline, when it can be said to have fallen, when the Renaissance began or even exactly what the Renaissance was — all these questions become murky as they shade off into questions of preconditions and antecedents and are examined from different points of view. But, whether Stalin knew exactly what Truman was talking about that evening or whether he only came to realize it later on, here is one turning point in history that can be dated with extraordinary precision: the twentieth century's nuclear arms race began at the Cecilienhof Palace at 7:30 P. M., on July 24, 1945.

16
CHURCHILL DEPARTS

On July 25, Churchill awoke depressed. "I dreamed that life was over. I saw — it was very vivid — my dead body under a white sheet on a table in an empty room. I recognized my bare feet projecting from under the sheet. It was very life-like.... Perhaps this is the end." This was the day Churchill was to leave Potsdam and return to England, to be present when the votes from the general election were counted.

The meeting of the Big Three had been set for eleven o'clock that morning, and just before the session began Truman, Churchill, and Stalin posed for the photographers in front of the Cecilienhof Palace. Truman stood between the other two and, crossing his arms, he was the center of a triple handshake. His right hand crossed over to his left side and grasped Stalin's hand; his left hand crossed to the other side to take Churchill's left hand.

The President stood smartly at ease. He was dressed in a crisply tailored and well-pressed dark, double-breasted suit, with a four-in-hand tie. The hint of a handkerchief graced his breast pocket. He inclined ever so slightly toward Stalin, and he and the Generalissimo had a firm grip on one another's hands. His head was turned away from Churchill; his eyes were fixed on Stalin; his smile was broad, confident, forthright.

Stalin stood as though he had been lowered into position by a crane. He leaned neither toward nor away from Truman. He looked out past the photographers into the crowd around them. He wore his cream-colored military jacket, with its five shiny brass buttons up the front and stiff epaulets on his shoulders. His lips were slightly parted, as though he might smile if only his moustache were not so stiff. His eyes smiled. Perhaps it was his firm grip on Truman's hand that was pulling the President toward him.

Churchill held Truman's left hand tenuously, even limply. The Prime Minister's weight was shifted totteringly away from the President. He, too, looked out into the crowd. His light-colored military uniform needed pressing and, around the Prime Minister's ample stomach, the jacket strained and bunched and wrinkled. His smile looked soft and pudgy and toothless. He seemed — and this in a black-and-white photograph — very pink. He looked a bit as though the air had gone out of him. This was no longer the bulldog Churchill of the famous Karsh portrait. This was the Churchill of second childishness.

The conversation at the plenary session that day was desultory. The heads of state gave the impression that they had met only to be photographed together and to lend a touch of formality to Churchill's departure. There were few topics that they could profitably discuss in any case. So many negotiating positions had broken in the past few days that the Big Three needed to give their foreign ministers and the assorted subcommittees time to catch up and draft new papers to be used in the next round of bargaining.

Churchill again raised some questions about Germans displaced from Poland, and Stalin replied that he thought "the supply of the whole of Germany with coal and metal is of much greater importance..."

CHURCHILL: "If coal is supplied from the Ruhr to the Russian zone, it will have to be paid for with food deliveries..."

STALIN: "If the Ruhr remains a part of Germany it must supply the whole of Germany."

CHURCHILL: "Why then can't we take food from your zone?"

STALIN: "Because that territory goes to Poland."

These were the same old inflammatory issues, but they failed to take fire that morning—perhaps because the heads of state were beginning to get bored going over all the same old arguments, or perhaps just because Churchill and Stalin were not very fiery in the morning. Both of them were better at night than they were in the early daylight hours.

Talk about the Ruhr and coal led Churchill to complain about coal shortages in Britain. Stalin seemed surprised. "Britain has always exported coal," he said. Yes, said Churchill, but the miners had not been demobilized; there was a labor shortage.

STALIN: "There are enough POWs. We have POWs working on coal. It would be very hard without them…. You have 400,000 German soldiers in Norway, they are not even disarmed, and I don't know what they're waiting for. There you have manpower."

These 400, 000 German soldiers were a surprise. What indeed were they waiting for? Was this part of Churchill's German Army that he had been keeping in reserve to go into war against Russia? That pugnacious thought had faded long ago; it seemed by this time to have been the most impossible sort of fantasy.

"I didn't know they had not been disarmed," said Churchill — and it is quite possible that he did not. "At any rate, our intention is to disarm them."

That odd army from what now seemed the ancient past did not deflect Churchill from his path for more than a moment. "I want to repeat," the Prime Minister said, recollecting his train of thought, "that we are short of coal because we are exporting it to France, Belgium and Holland...."

"I am not in the habit of complaining," Stalin complained, "but I must say that our position is even worse. We have lost several million killed, we are short of men. If I began to complain, I am afraid you'd shed tears, because the situation in Russia is so grave. But I do not want to worry you."

The talk meandered, as it does among people who are thinking more of the clock than of their conversation while they wait for a plane. Afterthoughts popped out, and, as is often the case when the mind is distracted, the afterthoughts betray profound worries. The disconnected chatter skittered over the same knotty problems — over the Polish question; coal and food and reparations; the specter of starving Germans, denuded Germany, cold and impoverished Britons — but the minds of the heads of state all seemed to be elsewhere. Truman proposed one more time that the foreign ministers discuss his idea for internationalizing inland waterways—and this time Stalin and

Churchill agreed, absent-mindedly it would seem, to have it considered.

Only one moment stood out as peculiar in the morning's discussion. Truman read into the record a prepared statement outlining the constitutional authority of an American President. "I am sure it is understood that... treaties under our Constitution must be made with the advice and consent of the Senate of the United States. Of course, when I indicate my support of a proposal, I shall use my best endeavors to secure its acceptance. That naturally does not guarantee its acceptance. Nor should it preclude my coming back and informing you when I find that political sentiment at home on a proposition is such that I cannot continue to press its acceptance without endangering our common interests in the peace."

Even this statement slipped by casually. Stalin asked if the statement applied "only to peace treaties or to all questions discussed here." Truman answered that "we can settle any question here unless it must have the ratification of the Senate." Truman's answer was ambiguous, for there were few questions which could not be construed as requiring Senate ratification. If matters of reparations, diplomatic recognition, trade agreements, redrawn borders, and so forth, were ever to find their way into treaties, they would all require Senate approval. And it would be up to the President to persuade, or quietly dissuade, the Senators on all these issues. What Truman had actually just told Stalin and Churchill was that he reserved the right to renege on any agreement they had made at Potsdam. On the morning of July 25, that amazing statement, too, passed all but unnoticed.

Truman has always had a reputation for being a straight-forward, honest man, and, from his behavior at Potsdam, we can see why he deserved his reputation: he very often told people when he was going to cheat.

Churchill had made his last speech. He picked over the business of coal once more, and then he subsided. "I am finished," the Prime Minister declared. "What a pity," Stalin said.

CHURCHILL: "I hope to be back."

STALIN: "Judging from the expression on Mr. Attlee's face, I do not think he looks forward avidly to taking over your authority."

Churchill returned to his house in Babelsberg and meandered around there for only a short time before he announced he was heading for the airport. He asked Eden to join him, but his foreign minister "was going later and separately."

The Prime Minister had both time and solitude on the flight home to think about the conference he had left behind. In his memoirs, he wrote, "A formidable body of questions on which there was disagreement was... piled upon the shelves. I intended, if I were returned by the electorate, as was generally expected, to come to grips with the Soviet Government on this catalogue of decisions. For instance, neither I nor Mr. Eden would ever have agreed to the Western Neisse being the frontier line. The line of the Oder and the Eastern Neisse had already been recognised as the Polish compensation for retiring to the Curzon Line, but the overrunning by the Russian armies of the territory up to and even beyond the Western Neisse was never and would never have been agreed to by any Government of which I was the head. Here was no point of principle only, but rather an enormous matter of fact affecting about three additional millions of displaced people.

"There were many other matters on which it was right to confront the Soviet Government, and also the Poles, who, gulping down immense chunks of German territory, had obviously become their ardent puppets. All this negotiation was cut in twain and brought to an untimely conclusion by the result of the General Election. To say this is not to blame the Ministers of the new Government, who were forced to go over without any serious preparation, and who naturally were unacquainted with the ideas and plans I had in view, namely, to have a 'showdown' at the end of the Conference, and, if necessary, to have a public break rather than allow anything beyond the Oder and the Eastern Neisse to be ceded to Poland."

But this was all hot air, written a long time after the Potsdam conference, after Churchill was powerless to affect any of the decisions concerning Poland, and he knew it. For Churchill, and for Churchill's British Empire, the Potsdam conference had been a complete, unmitigated defeat. In a few days, Attlee would return to the conference with fresh ideas and energies—but Attlee's program was precisely to abandon the empire Churchill fought to preserve, or re-create. The Labour Party had just run on a platform of giving independence to India. That Attlee had been elected at this moment would have been a crucial turning point in British history were it not for the fact that everything he wanted to give away had already been lost in any case.

The Potsdam conference provides as convenient a point as any other to mark the end of the British Empire. The sterling bloc was finished; India was about to lead the former colonies to independence; British forces were only just allowed to take a small part in the end of the war in the Far East; the United States was busily taking the Middle East away from Britain; Churchill's plans to draw western Europe around British leadership had been reduced to blather; the British economy was shattered; the British people were exhausted by the war; Truman had been either cagey or evasive about helping

Britain to rebuild; and Churchill had just proved that not even the most inventive bluff and bluster could hold the old imperial power together. No wonder Churchill dreamed of seeing his dead body under a white sheet.

Freud has said that no single cause can account for any given effect. Rather, said Freud, many causes converge to "overdetermine" an effect. The end of the British Empire was certainly overdetermined; no individual, Churchill included, could have stood against all the forces converging to produce that end. If we are to believe that men affect history, we must nonetheless recognize that they are often overpowered. Churchill met with two other men who had not only personal visions and energy on their sides but also the force to make their visions impress themselves on the world. And yet Churchill did affect the appearance of the postwar world. If he did not succeed in bringing America to the rescue of the British Empire, he did succeed in stirring up and exacerbating suspicion and antagonism between America and Russia. This man who loved war and struggle, who perceived history as a battle between great forces of good and evil, helped by the power of his rhetoric to persuade those who had other powers that the world was divided into two huge and hostile camps, separated by an "iron fence." Even as he dreamed that he and the empire were dead, the force of his imagination was one of the determining causes of the Cold War, and we live still, to some extent, with the legacy of his dreams and nightmares.

Back at Number 10 Downing Street, a communications center had been established in the map room. Churchill checked in to see that all was in order to receive the early returns and then he had a quiet dinner with his wife Clemmie and his daughter Mary. "The latest view of the Conservative Central Office," he said, "was that we should retain a substantial majority.... On the whole I accepted the view of the party managers, and went to bed in the belief that the British people would wish me to continue my work...."

"However, just before dawn I woke suddenly with a sharp stab of almost physical pain. A hitherto subconscious conviction that we were beaten broke forth and dominated my mind. All the pressure of great events... would cease and I should fall.... I was discontented at the prospect, and turned over at once to sleep again. I did not wake till nine o'clock, and when I went into the Map Room the first results had begun to come in."

The earliest returns were unfavorable, and as the morning went on it became clear that the trend was against the Conservatives. By midday, it was evident that the Socialists had won the election. "It may well be a blessing in disguise," Clemmie said to her husband. "At the moment," said Churchill, "it seems quite effectively disguised."

Lord Moran heard the news as he was walking along Pall Mall to the College of Physicians. There had been a landslide, a friend told him on the street, "like 1906." After lunch, when the fellows of the college were having tea, Moran read out the three o'clock results to his colleagues. "They were so taken aback they stood there in complete silence," Moran noted. "One fellow so far forgot where he was as to emit a low whistle."

Eden was out driving around his own constituency as the news reached him bit by bit. At one o'clock, he stopped in Snitterfield to get the latest reports. "Worse than ever," he said. "It is evident that we are out. Rang up Winston and said what I could." Eden wondered who would take over as foreign minister. He wrote later that he hoped it would be Ernest Bevin. He had once asked Bevin what office the latter would take if his party won, and Bevin had said he wanted the Treasury. Eden: "Whatever for? There will be nothing to do there except to account for the money we have not got."

Sir Alan Brooke was disconsolate. "I feel too old and weary to start off any new experiments." When he finally got a chance with the other chiefs of staff to see Churchill, Brooke kept a tight rein on his emotions. "It was a very sad and very moving little meeting at which I found myself unable to say much for fear of breaking down. He was standing the blow wonderfully well."

Moran hurried over to see Churchill. "He was sitting in the small room next to the secretaries', where I had never seen him before, doing nothing. He was lost in a brown study. He looked up. 'Well, you know what has happened?' I spoke of the ingratitude of the people. 'Oh, no,' he answered at once, 'I wouldn't call it that. They have had a very hard time.'"

Back in Potsdam, Cadogan was rocked by the news. "The election will have come as a terrible blow to poor old Winston, and I am awfully sorry for the old boy. It certainly is a display of base ingratitude, and rather humiliating for our country. " Or so Cadogan wrote his wife. Later on, he confessed to Eden what was really troubling him: "I've hardly got the resilience of youth to make a fresh start with a lot of new bodies, and I feel rather miserable."

The most resilient man in England turned out to be Winston Churchill. He had lost before; he had been down and out and in disgrace many times. The Conservatives had lost the government, but Churchill had retained his own seat in Parliament. Now he would be leader of the Opposition. That night after dinner, Clemmie had gone to bed with a migraine headache, and Churchill sat up with his daughter Mary and with Robin Maugham, Somerset Maugham's nephew. "The new government will have terrible tasks," the old war-horse rumbled, refusing still to lay aside the burdens of office. "Terrible tasks. We must do all we can to help them." But then the public man collapsed, and Churchill spoke self-pityingly like an abandoned figure, shrunk to the dimensions of private life. "It will be strange tomorrow," said the former Prime Minister pathetically, "not to be consulted upon the great affairs of State."

Sick and exhausted, punished by too much brandy and war, the old man still spoke late into the night of "great affairs of State," still saw the world as a great stage for a brilliant historical pageant, still cast himself in a role to rouse pity and terror—and then, too, he did still have that amazingly irrepressible will. Was the great man to be retired to private life? Then what would be the proper role for a statesman cast aside by the world? "I shall return to my artistic pursuits," Churchill said at last to no one in particular; and then, to his daughter, "Mary, get the picture I did the other day in France."

17

"MOKUSATSU"

On July 25, at seven in the evening, Tokyo time, the Japanese foreign minister cabled Ambassador Sato in Moscow. Since the Big Three conference was in recess until the British returned to Potsdam, Sato was instructed to take advantage of the moment to go anywhere, to meet any time with Molotov, and to impress the Russians "with the sincerity of our desire to end the war."

This message, which was intercepted by American intelligence and sent up the line to Byrnes and Truman, specified that it was not possible for the Japanese to accept unconditional surrender — retention of the emperor was still the sticking point — "but we should like to communicate to the other party through appropriate channels that we have no objection to a peace based on the Atlantic Charter." The tone of the cable became plaintive: "Also it is necessary to have them understand that we are trying to end hostilities by asking for very reasonable terms in order to secure and maintain our nation's existence and honor." From the Japanese point of view, the question of keeping their emperor was a question of national "existence and honor." The Japanese understood that retention of the emperor had only formal meaning and no practical, political significance. Nonetheless: "Should United States and Great Britain remain insistent on formality," the cable to Sato said, "there is no solution to this situation other than for us to hold out until complete collapse because of this one point alone."

Eisenhower told Stimson that Japan was only searching for a way "to surrender with a minimum loss of face." It must seem extraordinary that the Japanese were prepared to go on fighting, to continue to sacrifice so much in the hope of saving so little. Yet, to the Japanese, it seemed auspicious that the Russians had not yet declared war against Japan. The Russians were still, in fact, a neutral power and might still intercede on Japan's behalf to modify the unconditional surrender formula. As long as Russian mediation remained even a remote possibility, the Japanese government predictably wished to try to rescue some vestige of its "existence and honor."

That night in Moscow, Sato called on Molotov's deputy, Lozovsky. Did Sato want the Russians to mediate? Lozovsky asked. Sato did. In that case, Lozovsky wanted to know whether the proposed mission of Prince Konoye to Moscow would cover only those matters relating to the end of the war or whether it would also deal with Russo-Japanese relations. Sato's instructions covered this question: the cable from Japan had said that Sato should "make it clear that we are fully prepared to recognize the wishes of the Soviet Union in the Far East."

But the Russians were in no hurry to help the Japanese. If Stalin knew anything, he knew that he would rather have his troops well positioned than to rely upon promises or paper agreements. The Russian troops were not yet all in position in the Far East. Lozovsky encouraged Sato to think the Russians might be of some assistance; if the Japanese ambassador would put his thoughts down on paper, Lozovsky said that he would see that Sato received an answer.

While the Japanese government tried to get its message through to Potsdam, President Truman looked over the draft of the order to General Spaatz for the bombing of Japan. Attached to the draft order were one-page descriptions of each of the four potential targets (Hiroshima, Nagasaki, Kokura, and Niigata) along with a map of Asia, cut out from a large *National Geographic* map, on which the targets were located. The British had already given their approval of American plans to use the atomic bomb, and, as Churchill later wrote, "the decision whether or not to use the atomic bomb... was never even an issue." Some of the scientists who had worked on the project had begun to worry about the political and moral implications of the weapon—but their concerns had not been communicated to the President, and Truman never dreamed of having any reservations on his own.

In some sense, the atomic bomb existed as two bombs — one was merely a weapon, more powerful than others, that would be used as a matter of course when it was ready. There was never any "decision" to drop this bomb; its use had been inevitable from the moment work began on its development. It was in another, second sense that the atomic bomb was different and required any special consideration. In this second sense, the bomb so surpassed any previous weapon in power as to become different in kind, to become the "ultimate" weapon, and so to have psychological effects even in excess of its physical destructiveness. It was this second aspect of the bomb that so excited Churchill when he called it the "Second Coming in Wrath," that moved the Alamogordo witness to speak of doomsday, that caused Stimson's voice to quaver when he read the report of its test to Truman and Byrnes, and that caused some of the scientists on the project to urge that the bomb not be used after all.

Truman later spoke of the bomb as though he only thought of it in its first sense, as a mere weapon, not as a doomsday machine. "I regarded the bomb as a military weapon," he said, "and never had any doubt that it should be used."

In truth, though, the President did understand the bomb as a doomsday machine, too. The so-called Interim Committee that had studied and recommended American policy on the bomb had said as early as June 1 that the bomb should not only be used on Japan but that it should be used on a dual military-civilian target — a military installation surrounded by workers' houses — in order to have maximum psychological effect.

By July 25, the bomb-as-weapon was generally believed to be unnecessary — as Truman had by then been told by Leahy and Eisenhower and King and Arnold and Le May and others. General Douglas MacArthur, then Supreme Commander of Allied Forces in the Pacific, was not asked for his opinion whether the bomb was of any military use against Japan. After the war, he volunteered that he thought it was not. Only General Marshall continued to hedge on the question, and he was profoundly disturbed at the thought that the attack was to be a surprise. He would later say that the bomb shortened the war "by months"; Le May said it shortened the war by two weeks. Churchill was to say, "It would be a mistake to suppose that the fate of Japan was settled by the atomic bomb. Her defeat was certain before the first bomb fell...." The United States Strategic Bombing Survey said after the war, "Japan would have surrendered even if the atomic bombs had not been dropped, even if Russia had not entered the war, and even if no invasion had been planned or contemplated."

It was no longer necessary to drop either the bomb-as-weapon or the bomb-as-doomsday-machine on Japan. However, if the weapon were not dropped on Japan, the doomsday machine could have no psychological effect on Russia. The bomb was therefore dropped on Japan for the effect it had on Russia—just as Jimmy Byrnes had said. The psychological effect on Stalin was twofold: the Americans had not only used a doomsday machine; they had used it when, as Stalin knew, it was not militarily necessary. It was this last chilling fact that doubtless made the greatest impression on the Russians.

The President approved the bombing order on July 25, before the final warning had been sent to the Japanese, because he needed "to set the military wheels in motion." He also instructed Stimson, the President said, "that the order would stand unless I notified him that the Japanese reply to our ultimatum was acceptable" — a possibility the Americans all believed to be very remote. "The atomic bomb was 'no great decision,'" Truman later said, "... not any decision that you had to worry about."

Henry Stimson's work was finished, and on July 25 he, too, left Potsdam for home. He left as he had arrived, still worrying, He thought back over the advice he had given the President, and he thought of the way Truman had handled the Russians — of how the Russians had not been told about the bomb, of what Stalin would conclude from its use by the Americans, of the way in which the "pepped up" President was trying to use the doomsday machine psychology against the Russians, and the way in which Truman was shouldering aside all others in his race to control the Far East. Stimson concluded that all this was terrifying. The Secretary of War was seventy-seven years old, and he was exhausted. He felt it was time to retire, and within weeks of the end of the Potsdam conference he submitted his resignation. Yet he had also decided by then that "I was wrong," and so, before he left his post, he wrote one last memorandum to the President:

"The advent of the atomic bomb has stimulated great military and probably even greater political interest throughout the civilized world. In a world atmosphere already extremely sensitive to power, the introduction of this weapon has profoundly affected political considerations in all sections of the globe....

"To put the matter concisely, I consider the problem of our satisfactory relations with Russia as not merely connected with but as virtually dominated by the problem of the atomic bomb....

"Those relations [Stimson's italics] *may he perhaps irretrievably embittered by the way in which we approach the solution of the bomb with Russia. For if we fail to approach them now and merely continue to negotiate with them, having this weapon rather ostentatiously on our hip, their suspicions and their distrust of our purposes and motives will increase....*

"The chief lesson I have learned in a long life is that the only way you can make a man trustworthy is to trust him; and the surest way to make him untrustworthy is to distrust him and show your distrust.

"If the atomic bomb were merely another though more devastating military weapon to be assimilated into our pattern of international relations, it would be one thing.... But I think the bomb instead constitutes merely a first step in a new control by man over the forces of nature too revolutionary and dangerous to fit into the old concepts. I think it really caps the climax of the race between man's growing technical power for destructiveness and his psychological power of self-control and group control — his moral power. If so, our method of approach to the Russians is a question of the most vital importance in the evolution of human progress....

"My idea of an approach to the Soviets would be a direct proposal... that we would be prepared in effect to enter an arrangement... to control and limit the use of the atomic bomb ... and so far as possible to direct and encourage the development of atomic power for peaceful and humanitarian purposes."

Truman whiled away the time on July 26 by flying to Frankfurt to inspect troops there. At 7:45 a. m. he boarded his plane, *The Sacred Cow*, with Charlie Ross, Fred Canfil, Harry Vaughan, and a few others. Presumably by this time Vaughan had finished his business in Berlin and was ready for a holiday. While the heads of state met at the Cecilienhof, Vaughan had been hustling on the black market. Aside from the lively trade in cigarettes and watches, Vaughan had discovered there was a demand for clothing, and he had sold all of his spare clothes for "a couple thousand bucks," as he was to brag to the folks back home when he returned from the conference.

Eisenhower joined the President's party for lunch at Weinheim (soup, fried chicken, French fried potatoes, peas, green salad, wine, and coffee), and, after lunch, Truman inspected the 84th Infantry Division. He made a short speech and ended by saying he would not keep the men out in the hot sun any longer, "since I'm not running for office, and since you can't vote anyway." At Frankfurt, the President stopped in at Eisenhower's headquarters, a large, yellow building that was, as one of the President's aides observed, "noticeably unbombed amid Frankfurt's general desolation. This building had once housed the central offices of the vast I. G. Farben industries."

When the President returned to Potsdam, he was greeted with the news that Chiang Kai-shek had approved the Proclamation calling for Japan's surrender. At seven o'clock that evening, copies of the Proclamation were given to the press for release at 9:20 P.M.

"... The time has come for Japan to decide whether she will continue to be controlled by those self-willed militaristic advisers whose unintelligent calculations have brought the Empire of Japan to the threshold of annihilation or whether she will follow the path of reason.

"Following are our terms. We will not deviate from them. There are no alternatives. We shall brook no delay.

"There must be eliminated for all time the authority and influence of those who have deceived and misled the people of Japan...."

The Proclamation specified that Japan would be occupied until its "war-making power is destroyed"; its sovereignty would be limited to its home islands "and such minor islands as we shall determine"; the Japanese military would be permitted to return home to lead "peaceful and productive lives." Japan was not to be "enslaved as a race or destroyed as a nation," but reconstructed along democratic lines. In conclusion, the Proclamation said, "We call upon the Government of Japan to proclaim now the unconditional surrender of all the Japanese armed forces, and to provide proper and adequate assurances of their good faith in such action. The alternative for Japan is prompt and utter destruction." The document was signed by Truman, Churchill, and Chiang Kai-shek.

Stimson had advised the President that Stalin should also be asked to sign the Proclamation. If the Japanese pinned some final hope on Russia's neutrality, Stimson reasoned, then this hope should be closed off. When the Japanese realized that all the major powers were at last arrayed against them, they would doubtless give up. Both General Marshall and former Secretary of State Cordell Hull agreed with this advice and urged Truman to obtain the additional Soviet "sanction" for the Proclamation. Before the Potsdam conference began, alternative phrases, including Russia as a signatory to the warning, were drafted for the Proclamation. Before the Proclamation was released, Truman had the optional phrases deleted.

Various advisers had suggested three different elements for the Proclamation, any one of which, their advocates felt, might be sufficient to occasion Japanese surrender: Stalin's signature, a guarantee to retain the emperor, specific mention of the atomic bomb as the source of the threatened destruction. Not any one of those elements appeared in the Proclamation.

The Russians were not informed about the Proclamation until, immediately after it was released, Byrnes sent a copy over to Molotov. Molotov's translator telephoned to inquire whether the Proclamation might be held up for two or three days.

On the next day, July 27, Molotov called on Byrnes.

"The secretary said first of all he wished to tell Mr. Molotov that his request for a two or three day postponement in the issuance of the statement on Japan had only reached him this morning when it was too late.

"MR. MOLOTOV replied that he had sent the word last night as soon as he had received the Secretary's letter.

"The secretary explained that even then it would have been too late since at 7: 00 o'clock the statement had gone to the press for early morning release. He explained that the President for political reasons had considered it important to issue an immediate appeal to the Japanese to surrender. Two days ago he had discussed it with the Prime Minister and he had received his consent to the issuance of the statement and had cabled Chiang Kai-Shek. On his return yesterday from Frankfurt the President had found a telegram from Chiang Kai-Shek agreeing to the issuance of the statement.

"MR. MOLOTOV said that thus they had not been informed until after the release.

"The secretary said that we did not consult the Soviet Government since the latter was not at war with Japan and we did not wish to embarrass them.

"MR. MOLOTOV replied that he was not authorized to discuss the matter further."

Byrnes chose this moment to raise once more the question of reparations, and to confirm the implication that the American plan on reparations would lead to the division of Germany.

"The secretary then said that he had also wanted to discuss privately with Mr. Molotov the difficult question of reparations. He said he had closed off the discussion at the Foreign Ministers meeting this afternoon since nothing could be accomplished until the new British delegation had returned to the Conference.

"MR. MOLOTOV agreed.

"The secretary asked Mr. Molotov whether he had had an opportunity to think over the suggestion which the Secretary had made, namely, that each country would obtain its reparations from its own zone and would exchange goods between the zones.

"MR. MOLOTOV said would not the Secretary's suggestion mean that each country would have a free hand in their own zones and would act entirely independently of the others?

"The secretary said that was true in substance but he had in mind working out arrangements for the exchange of needed products between the zones, for example, from the Ruhr if the British agreed, machinery and equipment could be removed and exchanged with the Soviet authorities for goods — food and coal-in the Soviet zone. The Secretary said that he felt that without some such arrangement the difficulties would be insurmountable and would be a continued source of disagreement and trouble between our countries.

"MR. MOLOTOV... said that he had had in mind the impression that they had received at Yalta, namely, that the United States was in accord with the Soviet view that we should exact as much reparations as possible from Germany.... He said now at this Conference the Soviet delegation had received the impression that the United States no longer held that view....

"The secretary replied that there had been no change in view on the part of the United States Government and that we were still willing to discuss the Soviet proposal but that he must agree that many conditions had changed since Yalta. There had been first of all the extent of the destruction in Germany and secondly questions as to definitions of war booty and then the *de facto* alienation to Poland of a large and productive part of former Germany. He said that our aim remained the same and that all he was trying to do was to find a way which would on the one hand be acceptable to all and would on the other take cognizance of existing realities.

"MR. MOLOTOV in conclusion then said that, as he understood it, what Mr. Byrnes suggested was in fact an exchange of reparations between the zones.

"The secretary said this was correct."

Molotov would soon learn that that was almost correct. The specifics, however, were less important than the general message Byrnes conveyed to the Russians—that the United States, too, could settle matters unilaterally, and not just in eastern Europe but in both the eastern and western hemispheres.

Before dinner that evening, President Truman stood out in the cooling breeze on the back porch of the Little White House and listened quietly as the buglers played "Colors. " At the end of the bugling, the President, full of emotion, walked down the back steps and across the lawn to the base of the flagpole to congratulate the buglers

T/S H. J. Wagner of Buffalo, New York, and Pfc. Victor Edmunds of Arcade, New York. As he came back up the steps and into the dining room, the President explained to pianist Eugene List who was standing by, "That isn't easy to play, you know."

At six in the morning, Tokyo time, on July 27, Japanese radios picked up the transmission of the Potsdam Proclamation. The Japanese government assembled hastily and spent the whole day discussing the meaning of the Proclamation.

Foreign Minister Togo felt the Proclamation was "evidently not a dictate of unconditional surrender," and he advised the Emperor to treat the ultimatum "with the utmost circumspection." Admiral Toyoda argued that the government should issue a statement at once saying they "regarded the declaration as absurd and would not consider it." The Admiral had, of course, been called a self-willed, unintelligent militarist in the Proclamation.

For those who wished to regard the Proclamation favorably, however, two arguments were especially persuasive. First, the Soviet government had not signed the document and was therefore still neutral and might negotiate on behalf of the Japanese; secondly, the phrase "unconditional surrender" only occurred one time in the Proclamation and occurred then only in speaking of the "Japanese armed forces."

Prime Minister Suzuki agreed with Togo that the Proclamation called for a response of the "utmost circumspection." The problem for the Japanese government, then, was how to respond, to whom to respond. The Proclamation had not been sent through any diplomatic channels, through a neutral country, for example. It had been released to the newspapers and the radio.

The hawks and the doves in the Japanese Cabinet reached a temporary compromise. For the moment they would simply release a cut and edited version of the Proclamation to the newspapers, without any comment from the government — without, that is, any criticism or rejection of the ultimatum.

One Japanese newspaper, *Mainichi,* put a headline on its story: "laughable matter." The *Asahi Shimbun* editorialized, "Since the joint declaration... is a thing of no great moment, it will merely serve to re-enhance the government's resolve to carry the war forward unfalteringly to a successful conclusion!"

Foreign Minister Togo was enraged. He suspected that the military had gotten to the newspaper editors to distort the Japanese government's reaction to the Proclamation. While thousands of leaflets were dropped from American airplanes threatening the Japanese with horrible destruction, Togo faced the military leaders with his accusation. The military men replied by insisting that the Prime Minister must clearly and definitely reject the Proclamation.

Yet another compromise was reached: Prime Minister Suzuki would play down the importance of the ultimatum to give the Japanese time to hear from the Russians — but he would not reject it.

Since the newspapers had failed to carry Suzuki's message correctly, he called his own press conference at 3:00 p.m. on July 28. "The Potsdam Proclamation, in my opinion, is just a rehash of the Cairo Declaration, and the government therefore does not consider it of great importance. We must *mokusatsu* it."

According to some versions of the story, the Prime Minister went on to add that Japan would "resolutely fight for the successful conclusion of this war." According to other versions, he omitted that vain boast. In any case, the question seemed to turn on the meaning of the word *mokusatsu*. Literally, the word means "to kill with silence." The Foreign Broadcast Intelligence Service of the U. S. Federal Communications Commission translated the word as "ignore." Suzuki later told his son that he meant to have it convey the meaning of the English expression, "No comment." The headline in the *New York Times* conveyed the sense in which the American leaders chose to take the Japanese response:

JAPAN OFFICIALLY TURNS DOWN

ALLIED SURRENDER ULTIMATUM.

18
ATTLEE AND BEVIN

Clement R. Attlee, Britain's new Prime Minister, and Ernest Bevin, Britain's new foreign minister, arrived at Potsdam in the early evening on Saturday, July 28. From the moment they stepped off the plane, it was clear, as Cadogan said, that Bevin had a tendency "to take the lead over Attlee, who recedes into the background by his very insignificance...." Bevin strode toward the official greeting party and announced to Lord Ismay, "I'm not going to have Britain barged about."

Except for the absence of Eden and Churchill and Churchill's physician Moran, the British delegation had not noticeably changed. "Shortly after landing," the British interpreter Major Birse recalled, "Attlee and Bevin went to call on Stalin, taking me with them. Molotov was the only other person present at this first meeting. Stalin, I thought, eyed the two statesmen with some suspicion, and the reception lacked warmth and friendliness. It may have been natural, for although Stalin knew Attlee, the new [Foreign Minister] was an unknown factor."

Dean Acheson dealt with Bevin later on and came to know him well. "Bevin, short and stout, with broad nose and thick lips, looked more suited for the roles he had played earlier in life than for diplomacy. The child of a servant girl from western England and an unknown father, he had gone to work as a trucker after a few years of schooling. Moving on to a career as a labor leader and then to the top of the labor movement, on the way he organized the giant Transport and General Workers' Union and, with others, led the general strike of 1926." According to Acheson, Bevin was "beloved by his often formidable staff. Bevin knew his mind and his limitations. He could lead and learn at the same time, qualities much appreciated by a disciplined and professional Foreign Service. Soon he became absorbed in his work and often seemed to commune with the spirits of his predecessors with an informality that might have surprised them. One day he said to me, 'Last night I was readin' some papers of old Salisbury. 'E had a lot of sense.'"

Both Stalin and Molotov were slightly wary of this new pair of adversaries, and Molotov was especially discommoded by the results of the election. He kept saying again and again, "But you said the election would be a close thing and now you have a big majority." Yes, Attlee replied, "we could not tell what would be the result." Somehow this explanation failed to satisfy Molotov. "I am sure," Attlee wrote later, "he thought that Churchill would have 'fixed' the Election...."

Attlee and Bevin were going to take some getting used to, and it did not appear that the Russians relished the prospect. But, for that matter, Stalin and Molotov were not alone; the rest of the British delegation was not at all delighted by Attlee. "Though he proved a likeable chief," Birse said of Attlee, "patient and appreciative of his interpreter's difficulties, his manner and style were distant and cold, and I missed the Churchillian pathos, the passion which had previously communicated itself to me and had inspired some of my interpretation."

Part of Attlee's problem was that he had a difficult act to follow; part of the problem, with the British diplomats, was his social class; part of the problem was that, whatever act he may have followed and whatever his origins, he was a dreary sort of fellow. For dinner that evening he invited Gladwyn Jebb and Sir David Waley — two of the lesser lights in the British delegation — to join him, because, as

Jebb recently explained, "We were the only two people he knew well enough to do so."

At nine-fifteen that evening, Attlee and Bevin and Cadogan dropped by the Little White House for a courtesy call on Truman, Byrnes, and Leahy. "Attlee had a deep understanding of the world's problems," Truman recalled blandly, "and I knew there would be no interruption in our common efforts." Bevin, the President said, seemed "to be a tough person to deal with, but after I became better acquainted with him I found that he was a reasonable man with a good mind and a clear head." At one moment during the conversation, Bevin bounded over to a map on the wall of Truman's study to illustrate a point he wanted to make about Poland. After the British had gone, Leahy told Truman, "all that [Bevin's map lecture] illustrated was that Bevin did not know too much about Poland." The President, Leahy remembered, agreed.

At ten-fifteen that night, the new boys sat down with the old boys for a plenary session. "I want to inform you," Stalin said, "that we, the Russian delegation, have received a new proposal from Japan. " The Generalissimo assumed an injured tone: "Although we are not duly informed when a document on Japan is compiled, we believe nevertheless that we should inform each other of new proposals. " Stalin then read the request, of which the Americans already knew, from Japan's ambassador to Moscow. The ambassador's message emphasized that this peace overture "was especially charged by His Majesty the Emperor" — a signal of the seriousness and authoritativeness of the message.

"The document does not contain anything new," said Stalin coolly. "We intend to reply to them in the same spirit as the last time" — that is, in the negative.

TRUMAN: "We do not object."

ATTLEE: "We agree."

STALIN: "I have nothing more to add."

Stalin wished to return to the question of diplomatic relations with Bulgaria, Rumania, Hungary, and Finland. The Russians had understood that the heads of state had agreed on both the principles and the specific wording of a statement on the question. However, when it came to drafting an agreement, it seemed that the British were reneging. The same words were at issue: "responsible" and "recognized." It appeared further that there was some question as to whether the Big Three had agreed "to discuss" or "to examine" the matter of diplomatic recognition of these countries. "We here adopted a decision and then the Ministers got together and reversed it. That is wrong. This was agreed in principle."

TRUMAN: "I ask Mr. Byrnes to speak on this point."

Byrnes delivered a recitation of what the United States delegation had said, what he had said the President accepted, what the President had in mind, what he had told the foreign ministers that he recalled that Churchill had objected to, what Churchill had privately told him about Britain's position, what the British delegation had proposed to which the American delegation had agreed, what the Soviet delegation had proposed, and what the American delegation had accepted — "with certain amendments." ("Byrnes talks too much," Cadogan noted.)

"Unfortunately," Byrnes said, "one gets the impression that when we agree with our Soviet friends, the British delegation withholds its agreement, and when we agree with our British friends, we do not obtain the agreement of the Soviet delegation. *[Laughter.]*"

The conversation began to turn back on itself. Bevin, said Cadogan, "effaces Attlee, and... does all the talking while Attlee nods his head convulsively and smokes his pipe." Italy was mentioned again. If Italy had been recognized, why not raise the question of looking into the possibility of thinking about preparing to begin to discuss or to examine the matter of establishing diplomatic relations with the eastern European countries? Bevin dredged up the old argument: "Does not the difference lie in the fact that in respect of Italy we know what the situation there is, and we know nothing about the situation in the other countries?" Stalin chewed over his old argument: "We also knew little about Italy when we established diplomatic relations with her, possibly even less than...." No one could have been listening to the ensuing talk too carefully.

ATTLEE: "The difficulty lies in the fact that... creates the impression that...."

STALIN: "Why not put it... the three states will examine, each separately...."

ATTLEE: "One question put in Parliament..."

STALIN: "But... not concealing..."

BEVIN: "... we shall be asked... cover up... misconstrued..."

STALIN [*definitively*]: "Let's put it off."

"After Churchill left and Attlee and Bevin returned," one American diplomat recently recalled, "Stalin lost all interest. He enjoyed the give and take with Churchill across the table."

Nearly everyone at Potsdam noticed that the spark had gone out of the plenary sessions after Churchill had gone. That sense of dullness can be explained in part by Attlee's own dullness, in part by the fact that all the negotiators were weary, in part by the fact that topics of conversation had been exhausted, and that all the participants were now simply repeating themselves, in part by the fact that Stalin did not seem to want the complication of having to deal with Britain's two new faces.

It is also true that the British had been effectively shoved aside by this time, and Attlee and Bevin were unable to get back into the conversation. "It is too bad about Churchill," Truman wrote home to his mother, "but it may turn out to be all right for the world." Truman's daughter Margaret, in her biography of her father, commented, "Obviously, Dad thought he would have a better chance of reaching an agreement with Stalin without Mr. Churchill in the way."

In truth, Stalin and Truman had both lost interest in plenary sessions, for the Big Three had by this time become clearly reduced to the Big Two. (Cadogan referred to it, hopefully, as the Big Two and a Half.) And the Big Two were now doing their haggling not at the plenary sessions but behind the scenes. The time had come to hammer out a deal, and that was best done without the British, and off the record.

19
THE DEAL

SUNDAY, *July* 29

At twelve o'clock noon, on Sunday, July 29, Molotov arrived at the Little White House with his interpreter Golunsky. Generalissimo Stalin had a cold, Molotov said, and could not leave his house for any meetings—but Molotov would like to talk to the President. Truman summoned Byrnes, Leahy, and Bohlen to his study.

Whether Stain's cold was real or feigned, whether psychosomatic or diplomatic, it did permit the Russians and Americans to do some hard bargaining. At this first bargaining session, the participants were limited to six—about the right number for a poker game. Attlee was excluded, and Stalin was able to think things over before he made his plays. The arrangement was apparently comfortable to Stalin and Truman, and Attlee was given no choice.

Truman asked Byrnes to open, and the Secretary of State said that "it would be possible to consider winding up the Conference" if two questions were settled, the Polish western boundary and German reparations. Byrnes stated first that the United States would not agree to extending the Polish border all the way to the Western Neisse. Molotov answered, on cue, that Generalissimo Stalin would object. It was tedious of the Americans and Russians to keep repeating these positions, but they had to be stated this last time to establish just what was about to be traded.

On the question of reparations, Byrnes asked whether Molotov had given any thought to the American proposal "that each country looks to its own zone for reparations and then exchange reparations between zones." Molotov said that the Secretary's proposal was "acceptable in principle." With this remark, Molotov had agreed to divide Germany for the purposes of reparations.

With this remark, too, Molotov had made a substantial concession, and it was now up to the Americans to offer some concession if they were serious about making a deal. Molotov proceeded to probe immediately for the trade Byrnes was willing to make. The two foreign ministers descended together one more time into the morass of percentages and dollar amounts. According to Byrnes, 50 percent of German wealth lay in the Russian zone of occupation. If each of the occupying powers took reparations from their own zones, then Russia would be able to take 50 percent of all reparations from its own zone. Thus, if Molotov accepted the proposal to divide Germany, no other reparations were owed to Russia. According to Molotov, however, only 42 percent of German wealth lay in the Russian zone, and so the remaining 8 percent had to be made up from the other zones. He would like to have industrial equipment, he said, two billion dollars' worth from the industrialized Ruhr. In other words, his price for agreeing to the principle of a divided Germany was two billion dollars.

Unfortunately, Byrnes replied, American experts felt it was "impossible to put any specific dollar value" on potential reparations. Instead, the Americans proposed to give the Russians 25 percent of the total equipment "available for reparations" from the Ruhr. Even this 25 percent, however, would have to be exchanged for food and coal and other products from the Soviet zone. Or, Byrnes said, the Soviets could forego the 25 percent from the Ruhr alone and take *12½* percent of "equipment available for reparations" from the whole of the British, French, and American zones.

The more Molotov pressed Byrnes on reparations, the more it seemed that the Americans were talking of ever-diminishing percentages of ever more vaguely defined goods. Evidently the Americans were not going to concede any fixed dollar amount in exchange for the division of Germany; that was not the deal Byrnes had in mind. Molotov was unable to discover what Byrnes wanted to trade, and so the Russian foreign minister simply stopped probing. He would have to wait and see what Byrnes offered. However, Molotov did make it clear that percentages of unspecified amounts were not a fair trade for the concession Russia had just made.

In the meantime, Molotov changed the subject. Stalin had asked him, he said, to take up the question of "the immediate cause" of Soviet entry into the war against Japan. The Russians thought that the United States, Britain, and the other Allies should "address a formal request to the Soviet government for its entry into the war." Truman replied that he would examine Molotov's request. With that, Molotov took his leave.

What the Americans could not understand was why the Russians needed an "immediate cause" to enter the war against Japan. All Truman and his advisers could figure out was that Stalin wanted to be "begged" to join the war so that the Soviets could then appear to be the decisive element in the victory. Truman hardly wanted to beg, but neither could he quite refuse to offer an invitation that had been requested. His solution was nice. After a casual two-day delay, he wrote Stalin that it would be appropriate for the Soviet Union to join the war against Japan because the charter of the United Nations obliged all the major powers to work together to secure peace in the world. Truman did not beg; he sounded more like a teacher reminding a forgetful pupil of his chores.

Nonetheless, the invitation to Russia to join the Japanese war was only a minor distraction; the main business to be pursued was the deal in the making, and all bargaining at Potsdam now awaited Byrnes's anticipated concession.

At four-thirty that afternoon, Attlee came to call on Truman. The President later recalled that they spoke about inviting Russia into the war in the Far East; Truman did not say that they spoke about the deal in the making with the Russians, or about the offer Byrnes had made on the Ruhr — which was, not so incidentally, part of the British occupation zone. But whatever the particulars of their chat may have been, the place where the conversation occurred is significant enough. Truman did not go to Attlee; Attlee went to Truman. Nor did Truman pay a courtesy call in return. Henceforth, the President neither conferred with the Prime Minister nor sought the Prime Minister's agreement; henceforth

Britain's Prime Minister was not consulted, he was only informed. And on July 29 he was apparently informed only of the minor diplomatic ploy of the invitation for Russia to join the Far East war, not of the main business of the deal in the making that could "wind up" the conference.

MONDAY, *July* 30

On Monday, President Truman wrote a letter to Generalissimo Stalin: "I regret very much to hear of your illness. I hope it is not of a serious nature and that you will fully recover at an early date. You have my very best wishes."

At four in the afternoon, as Cadogan noted, "Jimmy Byrnes called on Bevin and we took him over afterwards to see Attlee. Mostly about reparations — a very complicated subject which I find almost unintelligible — and the Polish western frontier. Jimmy B. is a bit too active and has already gone and submitted various proposals to Molotov which go a bit beyond what we want at the moment." Cadogan had not yet caught on that it no longer mattered what the British wanted.

At four-thirty that afternoon, Byrnes met again with Molotov. According to Bohlen's minutes of the conversation, "The Secretary... said, first of all, he wished to tell Mr. Molotov that in regard to the Polish western frontier, we were prepared as a concession to... put Polish administration up to the western as against the eastern Neisse. Mr. Molotov expressed his gratification at this proposal."

Next, Byrnes said, he had "been endeavoring to find a compromise between his British and Soviet friends" on the question of diplomatic relations with Rumania, Hungary, Bulgaria, and Finland. He had found one—and never mind if it went "a bit beyond" what the British wanted. The British had objected to implying that they were prepared to give full diplomatic recognition to these countries. Very well, said Byrnes, then the Big Three could agree to examine the question of establishing diplomatic relations "to the extent possible." Perhaps the British would not grant full recognition, perhaps they would only grant partial recognition - whatever that might mean. In any case, the British would swallow the agreement if this additional vagueness were added. While the Russians had not gotten exactly what they wanted, they got something that sounded good, and it seemed somehow to dignify the governments of these eastern European countries. Molotov said he thought this proposal would be acceptable to the Soviet delegation.

Having thus given Molotov two presents, Byrnes "then said we come to the most difficult of all the questions, namely, that of reparations. " It was time for another Russian concession. Byrnes had set down his version of a percentage deal on paper, and he and Molotov spent some time haggling over the percentages. They settled nothing, and the numbers they bandied back and forth meant very little. Byrnes had already made his main point — his concession on Poland's border and his resolution of the impasse over diplomatic recognition of the eastern European countries. With these points in mind, Byrnes expected Molotov to settle for percentages of unspecified amounts of reparations. Molotov finally said that "despite the difference still existing he felt that some progress had been made in this question of reparations and he would so report to... Stalin."

At the full meeting of the foreign ministers that evening, Molotov made his last—by now quixotic—stand to have fixed dollar amounts mentioned in the reparations agreement. The Russians had begun by asking for 10 billion dollars' worth of reparations, then 8 billion. Then, once they agreed to divide Germany and take reparations from their own zone, Molotov asked for 2 billion from the Ruhr. Now he asked that a minimum dollar figure be set, and he suggested 800 million. Byrnes again said fixed dollar amounts were impossible to set.

Molotov tried a new tactic. If fixed dollar amounts could not be named, then he would try at least to be sure Russia had a voice in saying what would ultimately be "available" for reparations.

"Mr. Molotov inquired who would determine what equipment would be made available in the western zone.

"Mr. Bevin said the zone commander."

If the individual zone commanders could say what was available, then, Molotov knew, the western zone commanders could eventually say simply that nothing was available for reparations. In that way, the ultimate Russian nightmare would come true: they would be entitled to take a percentage of zero.

"Mr. Molotov suggested adding [the zone commander] *and* the [four-power] Control Council....

"Mr. Byrnes said that the thought of the United States delegation was that the Control Council should determine the matter but subject to the final determination of the zone commander.

"Mr. Molotov suggested that the Control Council should have the final decision.

"Mr. Byrnes disagreed, saying the commander in our zones and in the Soviet zone was the one who was charged with the maintaining of the economy and who had to have the final decision." Final control — in effect, veto power — had to reside in the zone commander.

The tangled business of reparations was coming clearer and clearer. Molotov must agree not only to percentages of unspecified amounts but agree, too, to let the zone commanders say what, if anything, would be available for reparations. Byrnes would not commit himself to pay 2 billion dollars or 800 million or any amount in trade for Molotov's concession. He would only agree to trade Poland. Furthermore, where previously Byrnes and Molotov had argued over percentages of 25 percent of reparations to be exchanged for goods from the Soviet zone and 15 percent of reparations to be taken with no strings attached, Byrnes was now talking of *12½* percent and 7½ percent. True enough, the first pair of percentages applied only to the single area of the Ruhr; the latter percentages applied to all three western zones. It was hardly clear, however, whether the latter deal was much of a boon; if Molotov accepted that, then the Russians would have to deal with three zone commanders, all with veto power in their own zones.

Byrnes "referred again to the proposal with regard to the Polish frontier which involved a greater concession on our part than this one from the Soviets. The paper referring to the United Nations [and recognition of the eastern European countries] involved a concession on the part of our British friends. He knew it was a concession for the Soviets to agree to percentages, but if we made concessions, the Soviets should also.

"Mr. Molotov said it was a concession to Poland and not to them.

"Mr. Byrnes said he had heard his friend, Mr. Molotov, make a plea on this matter when the Poles were present and he had made a more eloquent plea than the Poles.

Byrnes, the fixer from the Senate cloakroom, had arranged a package deal, take it or leave it. In fact, just in case Molotov missed the point, Byrnes had another meeting with him the following morning. "I told Mr. Molotov there were three outstanding issues.... I told him we would agree to all three or none and that *the President and I would leave for the United States the next day.* [Italics added.]"

Bevin did not entirely understand what Byrnes was doing. Britain's foreign minister piped up to say that it would be better to leave the reparations question and "deal with Mr. Byrnes's proposal on the western frontier of Poland." No wonder the Americans preferred to deal without the British present: Bevin was prepared to nail down an agreement on the concession *to* Russia without insisting on a concession *from* Russia.

"Mr. Byrnes replied that his proposal was a compromise proposal on three questions. He could not agree to the [separate] settlement of any one of them.... He could not agree to the other two if there were no agreement on reparations."

Molotov, slyly picking up Bevin's suggestion, "said it seemed that they could reach agreement on [the general principle of] reparations but that they had left to the Big Three the one question of an overall figure. On the rest they could reach agreement.

"Mr. Byrnes said that they might as well send the other two questions along to the Big Three for he could not agree to them unless there was an agreement on reparations."

Byrnes and Molotov had outlined a package deal as completely as they could. The deal was now kicked back up to the heads of state where Stalin would see whether he, with his bargaining powers, could squeeze out a few more concessions over reparations before the Russians accepted the package.

"I thank you for your letter of July 30," Stalin wrote in a note to Truman. "I feel better today and tomorrow, July 31, I count on taking part in the Conference."

Tuesday, July 31

Stalin was a brilliant negotiator. At the plenary session on July 31, Byrnes presented his package to the heads of state. In reply, the laconic, pipe-smoking Russian Premier opened up for the first time.

STALIN: "We have proposals on reparations.

"1. Reparations shall be levied by each Government in its own zone of occupation. They shall have two forms: lump withdrawals from the national property of Germany (equipment, materials), which shall be made during two years after surrender, and annual commodity deliveries from current production, which are to be made during 10 years after surrender.

"2. The reparations are designed to promote the earliest economic rehabilitation of the countries which have suffered from the German occupation, with an eye to the need for the utmost reduction of Germany's military potential.

"3. Over and above the reparations levied in its own zone, the U.S.S.R. is to receive additionally from the Western zones:

"a) 15 percent of the basic industrial equipment, in complete sets and good repair — primarily in the field of metallurgy, chemistry and machine-building — which, as specified by the Control Council in Germany on a report of the Reparations Commission, is subject to withdrawal in the Western zones by way of reparations; this equipment shall be handed over to the Soviet Union in exchange for an equivalent quantity of foodstuffs, coal, potassium, timber, ceramic goods and oil products in the course of five years;

"*b)* 10 percent of the basic industrial equipment levied in the Western zones by way of reparations, without any payment or exchange of any kind.

"The amount of equipment and materials subject to withdrawal in the Western zones by way of reparations is to be established not later than within three months.

"4. In addition, the U.S.S.R. is to receive by way of reparations:

"a) $500 million worth of shares in industrial and transport enterprises in the Western zones;

"b) 30 percent of German investments abroad;

"*c)* 30 percent of the German gold which the Allies have at their disposal.

"5. The U.S.S.R. undertakes to settle Poland's reparations claims from its share of the reparations. The United States and Great Britain are to do the same thing in respect of France, Yugoslavia, Czechoslovakia, Belgium, Holland and Norway.

"Now on the substance of the matter. I think we have a possibility of reaching agreement on the question of reparations from Germany. What are the main propositions of the American plan? The first is that each makes withdrawals from his own zone of occupation. We agree to this. Second: equipment is to be removed not only from the Ruhr, but from all the Western zones. We have accepted this second proposal. Third proposal: a part of the reparations taken from the Western zones is to be covered with a corresponding equivalent from the Russian zone over a period of 5 years. Then there is the fourth proposition: it is that the Control Council is to determine the volume of the withdrawals from the Western zones. That is also acceptable.

"What in that case are the differences? We are interested in the question of the time limit, the question of the final calculation of the volume of reparations. Nothing is said of this in the American draft. We should like to establish a period of three months."

Byrnes: "The question of time should be agreed."

STALIN: "It is a question of the time limit for determining the volume of reparations. Some period has to be proposed. We propose three months. Is that enough?"

TRUMAN: "I think it is."

ATTLEE: "That is a short period. I must think a little."

STALIN: "It's worth thinking about, of course. It may be three, four or five months, but some time limit should be laid down."

ATTLEE: "I propose six months."

STALIN: "Right, I agree.

"Then there is the percentage of withdrawal. Here again agreement can be reached. One per cent either way does not make much difference. I hope that in this matter of establishing the withdrawal percentage, the British and the Americans will meet us half way. We have lost a great deal of equipment in this war, a terrible quantity of it. At least one-twentieth part of it should be restored. And I expect Mr. Attlee to support our proposal."

ATTLEE: "No, I cannot do that."

STALIN: "Think a little and support us."

The British and Americans commenced to pick at Stalin's proposal. By the very fact that he had maneuvered the others into trying to hack away at his plan, Stalin had regained some initiative. He was not about to give it away easily.

Byrnes perceived the main difference to be that Stalin had suggested 15 percent and 10 percent in those areas in which the United States had proposed 12½ percent and 7½ percent.

STALIN: "Yes."

BYRNES: "But in addition you want to receive... $500 million worth of shares of industrial enterprises in the Western zones, 30 percent of Germany's investments abroad, and 30 percent of the German gold which is at the disposal of the Allies.... What do you have in mind when you speak of Germany's investments abroad?"

STALIN [without a smile]: "The investments the Germans had in other countries, including America."

BEVIN: "... Would you agree to confine yourself to the assets in neutral territories?"

STALIN: "I think that could be accepted."

BYRNES: "We cannot agree to any addition to our main proposal. I have in mind clause 4 of the Soviet proposals."

STALIN: "In that case the percentage will have to be raised...."

TRUMAN: "If you are prepared to withdraw clause 4, I am prepared to accept 15 per cent and 10 per cent."

STALIN: "Good. I withdraw it."

The deal was closed. Stalin had not been able to get much more than Molotov had obtained, but he did manage to raise the percentages somewhat and to specify a little more clearly that "basic industrial equipment in complete sets and good repair-primarily in the field of metallurgy, chemistry and machine-building..." would be available for reparations. At least if the Americans failed to make anything available for reparations, the Russians would have clear and specific grounds for complaint.

With the agreement on reparations, the questions on Poland and the eastern European governments were immediately dispatched. The Big Three agreed, too, on the political principles by which Germany was to be governed. According to these principles, Germany was to have a centralized, unified government. Thus Germany was simultaneously divided and unified; it was divided on specific economic grounds, united on vague political grounds. In the future, the Big Three would operate on the realistic grounds of their economic agreement and complain about one another on the grounds of their political agreement.

It has often been said that the Potsdam conference failed because it did not resolve Europe's most crucial postwar problem, the fate of Germany. In fact, however, the conference solved that problem most satisfactorily by dividing Germany. Without resorting to the Morgenthau plan or some other drastic measure, the Big Three reduced Germany's power severely. Few people in 1945 — few people today — could enthusiastically argue that they would like to see a fully rebuilt, economically and militarily integrated, politically unified Germany.

The Potsdam conference seemed to fail because it seemed to call for a united Germany that then seemed to fall apart because of the perfidy of the Russians or (according to revisionist historians) the perfidy of the Americans. But this is nonsense.

Reparations split Germany consciously and intentionally, realistically and definitively. The political agreements for a unified Germany were never more than high-sounding sentiments, understood as such by both Truman and Stalin, which served handily in the emerging conflict between Russia and America to provide grounds for mutual recrimination. Indeed, the agreement on a unified Germany actually served to divide the country more surely and to weld its divided halves more securely to the two opposing forces. The Americans could, and did, argue that *they* wanted a united Germany — and would have one if it weren't for the behavior of the Russians. And the Russians made the identical argument. Thus eastern and western Germany pulled apart into two hostile camps, each camp naturally aligned with its friend and bitter toward its "capitalist" or "Communist" counterpart.

Once the key problems had been resolved, the Big Three were able to run down the outstanding issues without a ripple of argument. Differences over Rumania, Hungary, and Bulgaria were reduced to the mere niceties of phraseology in the final accords. Stalin even agreed to have Truman's proposal on inland waterways referred to the Council of Foreign Ministers. When the question of the German Navy came up, Stalin suggested that it be postponed until the next day.

TRUMAN: "All right, I agree. I was going to leave tomorrow, but I could stay."

All that remained was the nit-picking. The Big Three could not quite relax; a word here or a word there could make a big enough difference later on. But even the newspaper reporters stuck back in the bars of Berlin sensed that the conference had moved into its final stages. The London *Times* noted that "unofficial reports from the Potsdam enclave tonight state that the Berlin conference is now in its 'closing hours.' Marshal Stalin has apparently recovered from the slight chill that kept him from the last meeting of the heads of government...."

20
AUGUST 1,
THE CLOSING HOURS

On Wednesday, August 1, in Washington, General Groves delivered a packet of papers to Secretary Stimson's assistant on the bomb project, George Harrison. The packet contained petitions, polls, and reports from the Metallurgical Project at the University of Chicago. At Chicago, physicist Leo Szilard had had moral qualms about the atomic bomb. Szilard was one of those who had heard Byrnes talk about the doomsday machine as a device to make Russia more manageable in Europe; with the passage of time, the physicist's reservations about the use of the bomb had become unbearably acute. Szilard finally screwed up his courage in early July and began to organize a protest among the scientists who had helped to develop the weapon. By the time Szilard's qualms and courage had joined to move him to act, he was, of course, much too late.

During the first half of July, Szilard circulated a petition among his fellow scientists, 69 of whom signed the statement that any nation that first used the atomic bomb might have "to bear the responsibility of opening the door to an era of devastation on an unimaginable scale." Szilard's petition gave rise to a flurry of argument until, at last, the director of the Metallurgical Project polled 150 of the scientists for their opinions. None of them knew the military arguments that the bomb was no longer necessary as a weapon against Japan.

In favor of using the bomb in any way to bring about Japanese surrender	15%
In favor of a military demonstration	46%
In favor of an experimental demonstration as a warning	26%
In favor of a demonstration and no threatened use	11%
In favor of no use, no demonstration, and continued secrecy	2%

Harrison looked over the packet that General Groves had delivered — at Szilard's petition, the counter-petitions, and the poll — and put all the papers away in his files.

The Big Three met in two sessions on August 1, one at three-thirty in the afternoon, and the final session of the conference at ten o'clock that night. Before the three-thirty meeting, Truman, Attlee, and Stalin posed one last time for pictures in the garden of the Cecilienhof. As the movie cameras turned, someone called out to ask that a chair be moved out of the way. Stalin stepped forward, grasped the chair, and thrust it to one side. Then, when he stood back with Truman and Attlee, his crippled left arm jerked and danced involuntarily for a moment and then subsided. Sir William Hayter, a member of the British delegation who was looking on from the sidelines, thought that "Stalin was dressed like the Emperor of Austria in a bad musical comedy; cream jacket with gold-braided collar, blue trousers with a red stripe...." Hayter put Attlee down with a passing reference to the new Prime Minister's "almost excessive modesty." Truman, Hayter felt, was "perky, precise and very definite in his manner.... He clearly had the self-confidence inspired by the immense force which he represented, a force immeasurably increased... by the [Alamogordo] explosion."

For the first of these two final sessions of the conference, the delegations had shaken down to the essential insiders. Britain was represented by Attlee, Bevin, Cadogan, and the interpreter Major Birse. Russia was represented by Stalin, Molotov, the reparations negotiator Maisky, the propagandist

Vishinsky, and the interpreter Golunsky. Truman had brought along Byrnes, Davies, and Bohlen—and one other man whom we have not noticed before, Benjamin V. Cohen.

Ben Cohen was the master wordsmith of the New Deal. A fifty-four-year-old bachelor with a receding hairline and rimless glasses, Cohen was known for his slouching posture, sloppy dress, absentminded table manners — and for a skill at drafting legislation that was generally reckoned the best in the United States. Cohen and his partner Thomas Corcoran were among the essential members of Roosevelt's "brain trust." Corcoran was the operative, the jovial, effervescent Capitol Hill salesman. Cohen was the shy counselor, student of Felix Frankfurter, and principal draftsman behind the SEC act of 1934, the Public Utility Holding Company act of 1935, plans for the TVA, RFC, the Wage and Hour Law, and, among other projects, Roosevelt's Court-packing attempt. Cohen was known to insiders as a man who could write a piece of legislation without a single loophole, and Truman took him to Potsdam to serve on the committee that drafted the Potsdam agreements. With Cohen's help, the Americans could be certain that the only loopholes in the Potsdam accords were the ones they wanted.

Jimmy Byrnes opened the discussion at the three-thirty session by harking back to Stalin's claim on "German gold, shares and assets abroad." The question was just what Stalin meant by "abroad."

STALIN: "... the Soviet delegation... will regard the whole of Western Germany as falling within your sphere, and Eastern Germany, within ours."

Stalin's remark covered Germany. Truman then extended the notion of two spheres and projected the division of Germany onto Europe as a whole by asking whether Stalin meant to establish "a line running from the Baltic to the Adriatic. " Stalin replied that he did. It was to this line that Churchill would refer when he came to make his "iron curtain" speech: "From Stettin, in the Baltic, to Trieste, in the Adriatic, an iron curtain has descended across the Continent."

"As to the German investments," Stalin said, "I should put the question this way: as to the German investments in Eastern Europe, they remain with us, and the rest, with you."

Spheres of influence were no longer a naughty secret hidden in Truman's briefing book or in private bargains struck by Stalin and Churchill. They had been openly recognized. They began with the division of Germany.

Truman proceeded to project the spheres of influence around the greater portion of the globe: "Does this apply only to German investments in Europe or in other countries as well?"

STALIN: "Let me put it more specifically: the German investments in Rumania, Bulgaria, Hungary, and Finland go to us, and all the rest to you."

BEVIN: "The German investments in other countries go to us?"

STALIN: "In all other countries, in South America, in Canada, etc., all this is yours."

BEVIN: "Consequently, all German assets in other countries lying west of the zones of occupation in Germany will belong to the United States, Great Britain and the other countries? Does this also apply to Greece?"

STALIN: "Yes."

Byrnes wished to refine the understanding even further. Say, for instance, "the head office of... an enterprise is in Berlin, " but the enterprise itself is elsewhere, "will you make any claim in respect of such enterprises?"

STALIN: "If the enterprise is in the west, we shall make no claim to it. The head office may be in Berlin, that is immaterial, the point is where the enterprise itself is located."

BYRNES: "If an enterprise is not in Eastern Europe but in Western Europe or in other parts of the world, that enterprise remains ours?"

STALIN: "In the United States, in Norway, in

Switzerland, in Sweden, in Argentina *[General laughter]*, etc. — all that is yours."

Byrnes continued to repeat and rephrase so that all details of the understanding were clear. Stalin mentioned that he laid some claim to assets in the zone occupied by the Russian Army in eastern Austria.

BEVIN: "It is clear that the assets belonging to Great Britain and the United States in that zone will not be affected."

STALIN: "Of course not. We're not fighting Great Britain or the United States."

"[General laughter.]"

An air of relaxed jollity overcame the Potsdam negotiations. Where tight bargaining positions had previously obscured unacknowledged intentions, suddenly everything seemed to have become open and aboveboard. The subject of war criminals, next on the list, was an occasion for much warm humor. The Americans did not want to list any war criminals by name. The Soviets, suspecting that the Americans wanted to keep some Nazis free to run factories in the western zone, wanted to publish a long list of Germans who would be called to trial. "Are we to take action against any German industrialists?" asked Stalin. "I think we are. We name Krupp. If Krupp will not do, let's name others."

TRUMAN: "I don't like any of them. *[Laughter.]* I think that if we mention some names and leave out others, people may think that we have no intention of putting those others on trial."

STALIN: "But these names are given here as examples. It is surprising, for instance, why Hess is still in Britain all provided for and is not being put on trial...."

BEVIN: "If there is any doubt about Hess, I will give an undertaking that Hess will be handed over, and we will also send along a bill for his keep."

Stalin at last suggested that the Big Three agree to publish a list of war criminals in one month's time, and Truman and Attlee concurred. George Kennan later commented that he would have favored directing Allied commanders to execute "forthwith" any Nazi leaders that fell into the hands of the Allies. "But to hold these Nazi leaders for public trial was another matter.... To admit to such a procedure a Soviet judge as the representative of a regime which had on its conscience... the vast cruelties of the Russian Revolution, of collectivization, and of the Russian purges of the 1930s... was to make a mockery of the only purpose the trials could conceivably serve.... The only implication this procedure could conceivably convey was, after all, that such crimes were justifiable and forgivable when committed by the leaders of one government, under one set of circumstances, but unjustifiable and unforgivable, and to be punishable by death, when committed by another set of governmental leaders, under another set of circumstances."

The last topic for the afternoon's agenda was Truman's pet project for internationalizing the inland waterways. Truman wanted to have the idea mentioned in the report on the conference. Stalin objected. "We have not discussed it," the Generalissimo said.

"I spoke thrice on the question," Truman replied sharply, "and the commission examined it for several days."

STALIN: "It was not in the list of questions, we were not prepared for the question, and had no materials; our experts on this question are in Moscow. Why such haste; why should there be such a hurry?"

Evidently Truman thought he had hold of a first-rate idea, and it may be that he only wanted to have it mentioned so that he could get a bit of historical credit for the notion. The report of the Potsdam conference was to be written in two parts: a public communiqué, and an addendum that would include some details not mentioned in the Declaration. These details were not secrets in any sense; they were merely details that no one cared to have clutter up the grandiloquent public announcement of the Big Three agreements. Truman wanted his waterways proposal mentioned in the Declaration. Stalin suggested that it be placed among the odd details of the addendum.

According to Margaret Truman Daniels's biography of her father: "Earnestly, my father looked across the table at Stalin and spoke to him in a very personal way. 'Marshal Stalin, I have accepted a number of compromises during this conference.... I make a personal request now that you yield on this point. My request is that the communique mention the fact that the waterways proposal has been referred to the Council of Foreign Ministers....' However, before the Russian interpreter could finish repeating Dad's words, Stalin broke in. 'Nyet!' he snapped. To make sure Dad knew what he was saying, he added in English [to everyone's astonishment; it was the only time Stalin spoke in English], 'No. I say no!'"

Truman pouted: "... If I have to make a statement in the Senate to the effect that the question has been referred to the Council of Foreign Ministers, shall I have the right to do so?"

STALIN [reaching for the last laugh of the afternoon's plenary session]: "No one can encroach on your rights."

During the recess that evening, Ben Cohen worked over the wording of the Potsdam Declaration,

President Truman had a quiet dinner with Charlie Ross, and the reporters in Berlin sorted through the day's news. In Berlin: "The Allied Kommandantur... announces agreement to continue the Russian policy of allowing German political parties to hold public meetings but permits must be secured from sectional authorities."

In London: "The first session of the new British Parliament is held with Winston Churchill present as the leader of the Opposition."

In Washington: "Navy Under Secretary Artemus L. Gates says the Japanese 'do not have a single battleship left in operation' and probably have only two or three carriers and cruisers still functioning."

In Guam: "Preliminary reports of the day's bag showed 114 enemy planes destroyed and 101 damaged and 41 ships sunk or damaged." In China, Lieutenant General Albert C. Wedemeyer "said after a 10-day tour of six provinces that he felt 'more optimistic about a speedy end to this war against Japan.'"

At ten-forty at night in Potsdam, the Big Three gathered for their last plenary session. Absolutely everyone showed up for this farewell meeting: for the United States, Byrnes, Leahy, Davies, Harriman, Pauley, Dunn, Matthews, Clayton, and Bohlen; for Russia, Molotov, Vishinsky, Maisky, Gromyko, and Golunsky; for the British, even Sir

William Hayter made it to the big table for this last
fling. The various items in the communiqué had,
by this time, been drafted, redrafted, amended,
modified, cut up and pasted back together,
rewritten, rearranged, retyped, and tinkered with.
The heads of state now had in their hands a mess of
papers, with dog-eared bits and scraps of different
size that had come out of different typewriters at
different times and all been stuck together in what
may have been the proper order. When Truman,
Attlee, and Stalin finished this last session, they
would all sign yet another odd scrap of paper to
be clipped onto the end of this mess — and that
would be the final form of the Potsdam accords.

The Russians had a nit to pick. "On the question
of Poland's western frontier, the second paragraph
says that the boundary line must run from the
Baltic Sea through Swinemünde, as if the line
passes through the town itself." Stalin suggested
that they say "west of" Swinemünde.

Truman, of course, wanted to know "how far
west," and Stalin suggested "immediately west of."
Evidently both Truman and Attlee were feeling
friendly; neither of them asked how immediate
was immediately; both agreed to the new wording.
A scrap of paper was returned to the typing pool.

Section by section, the heads of state and their
ministers reviewed the Declaration.

BYRNES: "Section II on the institution of the Council of Foreign Ministers. There are no differences here.

"[Section II is adopted.]"

BYRNES: "Section III—on Germany. The words 'loudly applauded' in the first paragraph ['... the German people have begun to atone for the terrible crimes committed under the leadership of those whom... they loudly applauded'] have evoked objections."

STALIN: "Let us say: 'openly approved.'"

BEVIN: "Blindly obeyed, that is obeyed in a stupid manner."

STALIN: "I propose we put it this way: 'whom in the hour of their success, they openly approved and blindly obeyed.'

"[The proposal is accepted.]"

"[Section IV, no amendments; Section V, no amendments.]"

BYRNES: "Section VI — War Criminals."

STALIN: "I think the first introductory paragraph should be..."

BEVIN: "We have already done that."

STALIN: "Good."

It was getting on toward eleven o'clock. The delegates had been haggling for more than two weeks. They were tired and, no doubt, wrinkled. Even Truman looked a bit less crisp and fresh. Some of the baggage of the American delegates had been sent ahead to be put aboard the S. S. *Augusta*. The staff back at the Little White House were carrying out suitcases and files, and the delegations' residences in Babelsberg were sliding back into the gloom of dark, empty, deserted houses. At Gatow airport, British and American planes stood ready to take Attlee and Truman out of Berlin.

Stalin, indefatigable and relentless, had something to say about Bulgaria, Rumania, Hungary, and Finland. In the first paragraph of their agreement about these countries, Stalin observed, it was said that the three governments would terminate the "present anomalous position... after the conclusion of peace treaties." But the third paragraph "provided for the possibility of establishing diplomatic relations... prior to the conclusion of peace treaties..." Stalin proposed to delete from the first paragraph the words "after the conclusion of peace treaties."

ATTLEE *[springing to attention]*: "In my opinion, that is wrong, because when we drafted the third paragraph we had in mind the establishment of diplomatic relations 'to the extent possible.' If the words 'after the conclusion of peace treaties' are excluded from the first paragraph, it will mean that we shall be going farther than we intended to."

But, said Stalin, the first paragraph "says that diplomatic relations can be re-established only after the conclusion of peace treaties, and the third paragraph says something different. This leads to a contradiction."

ATTLEE: "That is just why the British want to include these words. The first paragraph provides for mandatory action... after the conclusion of peace treaties, whereas the third paragraph proposes that an effort should be made to do this, insofar as possible, before the conclusion of peace treaties."

STALIN: "We cannot agree to that.... That changes the meaning of the whole decision. How can we agree to that?... I 'm afraid I cannot agree with this interpretation."

The Potsdam accords had not yet been signed—but it was never too soon to begin to disagree over interpretation of the provisions.

STALIN: "Nothing will come of this. Finland has much more right than Italy to the establishment of diplomatic relations."

BEVIN: "I want to reach agreement and therefore make the following proposal. I propose the following wording for the first paragraph: 'The Three Governments consider it desirable that the present anomalous position of Italy, Bulgaria, Finland, Hungary and Rumania should be terminated by the conclusion of peace treaties. They trust that the other interested Allied Governments will share these views."

STALIN: "Good."

Stalin leaned back in his chair; he had won the final point against his exhausted adversaries. Back at the Little White House, the baggage couriers could go on with their work.

STALIN: "The Soviet delegation has no more amendments."

BEVIN: "Hurrah!"

"[General laughter.]"

The last, capping nicety of the Potsdam conference was added by foreign minister Bevin. "I wish to make a small amendment," Bevin said toward the end of the session, "mainly of a psychological nature."

Bevin turned his attention to the opening paragraph of Section X: "In view of the victorious end of the war in Europe and the necessity of establishing as soon as possible the conditions of lasting peace, the Conference agreed upon the following statement of common policy...."

BEVIN: "I would phrase the introductory part of Section X as follows: 'The Conference agreed upon the following statement of common policy for establishing, as soon as possible, the conditions of lasting peace after victory in Europe.' This reads better."

STALIN: "The wording is essentially the same, there is nothing new in it."

TRUMAN: "Both are acceptable."

BEVIN: "It reads better in English. Maybe it reads worse in American?"

[Laughter.]

truman (humorlessly): "Both are acceptable."

STALIN: "... Of course, we could accept either."

BEVIN: "Suppose you prefer our wording this time."

[Laughter.]

STALIN: "If Mr. Bevin insists, I suppose we could accept his wording."

TRUMAN: "I agree."

As their final piece of business, the heads of state all signed the bit of paper that was to be attached to the ramshackle set of accords. Then they looked over a message of greetings to Eden and Churchill (to whom Attlee, ever self-effacing, referred as the "Prime Minister"). All three signed the message, and then Truman, abruptly and awkwardly, said:

"I declare the Berlin Conference adjourned. Until our next meeting, which, I hope, will be at Washington."

STALIN [*with a smile*]: "God willing."

Truman had altogether forgotten the grace notes that were called for at the end of such a conference. Attlee reminded him.

ATTLEE: "Mr. President, before we separate I should like to express our gratitude to the Generalissimo for the excellent measures taken both for our accommodation here and to provide the conditions for work, and to you, Mr. President, for so ably presiding over this conference.

"I should like to express the hope that this conference will be an important milestone on the road which our three nations are taking together towards a stable peace, and that the friendship among the three of us who have met here will be strong and enduring."

STALIN: "That is also our hope."

Truman picked up his cue dextrously, thanked the Generalissimo, and joined "Mr. Attlee in what he has said here. " Stalin in turn joined Attlee in thanking the President for presiding over the conference.

TRUMAN: "I thank you for your kind cooperation in settling all the important questions."

STALIN [*ingratiatingly*]: "I should personally like to thank Mr. Byrnes, who has helped our work very much and has promoted the achievement of our decisions."

BYRNES [*falsely modest, understanding Stalin's remark as a reference to the breakthrough of the package deal*]: "I am deeply touched by the Generalissimo's kind words, and I hope that together with my colleagues I have been of use in the work of the Conference."

Another cable was on its way from Japan to Ambassador Sato in Moscow: "The battle situation has become acute. There are only a few days left in which to make arrangements to end the war.... Efforts will be made to gather opinions from the various quarters regarding definite terms. (For this it is our intention to make the Potsdam Three-Power Proclamation the basis of the study regarding these terms.)... It is requested that further efforts be exerted to somehow make the Soviet Union enthusiastic over the special envoy.... Since the loss of one day relative to this present matter may result in a thousand years of regret, it is requested that you immediately have a talk with Molotov."

STALIN [*after a moment's silence*]: "The Conference, I believe, can be considered a success."

Another silence. Stalin's compliment to Byrnes seemed to require a return compliment.

TRUMAN: "I want to thank the other Foreign Ministers and all those who have helped us so much in our work."

ATTLEE: "I join in the expression of these feelings in respect of our Foreign Ministers."

TRUMAN *[at last]*: "I declare the Berlin Conference closed."

From the London *Times*:

POTSDAM, AUG. 2

After the concluding session of the Berlin conference, which came to an end at the Cecilienhof at 12:30 this morning, there has been a steady stream for most of the day of departing delegates and officials from Potsdam.

President Truman was the first to go, soon after 8 a. m., when he left in the presidential Skymaster.... He was followed soon afterwards by the Prime Minister; and the Foreign Secretary, who took the opportunity for a quick drive down to the Reich Chancellory, which has become the showpiece of Berlin's ruins, also left for London by air in the early afternoon. The same stringent security arrangements were made for the departures as for the arrivals.

It may be assumed, in the usual absence of any announcement, that Marshal Stalin and the principal members of his delegation have also departed, if only from the fact that correspondents, who for the past fortnight have been living on scraps from the conference table, were allowed to visit the Cecilienhof and the British and American residential areas across the lakes at Babelsberg.

The Cecilienhof, a sumptuous imitation of the English Tudor in the midst of a wooded Park by the Holy Lake, was built as recently as 1917 for the Crown Prince, and named after his wife, Princess Cecilie. Its high gables and the walls of its two floors are thickly clustered with creepers, and the whole layout of the palace round a central courtyard, in which a flower bed contained blooms in the form of the Red Star, made for a convenient division of the three delegations.

The leading delegates contrived never to drive throughthe main streets of Potsdam on their way from Babelsberg, which is a wooded suburb of *nouveau riche* villas, redeemed by their setting on the lakes.... The Prime Minister lived at 23, Ring Strasse, a pseudo-Georgian villa that is far more attractive than the heavy, gloomy house occupied by President Truman. Amid the confusion of the packing of linen and china both residences had already lost the glamour of their distinguished tenants.

21

"THE GREATEST THING IN HISTORY"

6

August

1945

0245	take-off
0300	started final loading of gun
0315	finished loading
0605	headed for Empire from Iwo
0730	red plugs in
0741	started climb. Weather report received that weather over primary and tertiary targets was good but not over secondary target
0838	leveled off at 32,700 feet
0847	electronic fuses were tested and found to be O. K.
0904	course west

0909   target Hiroshima in sight
0915½   drop bomb

—from the logbook of Captain Parsons, Weaponeer aboard aircraft Enola Gay.

President Truman sat out in the sun on the deck of the S. S. *Augusta*. The temperature was 68 degrees, the sky was clear, the sea was "moderate . . . with heavy spray because of high speed." After a concert by the ship's band, the President went into lunch with the crew. At a few minutes before noon, Captain Frank Graham, an officer in the *Augusta's* map room, handed Truman a message:

hiroshima bombed visually with one tenth [cloud] cover at 052315a [august 5, 7:15 p.m., washington time]. there was no fighter opposition and no flak. parsons reports 15 minutes after bomb as follows: 'results clear-cut successful in all respects. visible effects greater than in any test. condition normal in airplane following delivery.'

The crew members noticed that the President was mysteriously excited and pleased. Truman shook Captain Graham's hand. "This is the greatest thing in history," the President said.

The first message was followed quickly by a second, this one from Stimson.

big bomb was dropped on hiroshima august 5 at 7:15 p. m. washington time. first reports indicate complete success which was even more conspicuous than earlier test.

Truman "jumped up from his seat," according to the *Augusta's* logbook, and strode over to Jimmy Byrnes. "It's time for us to get on home!" Truman said to Byrnes. The crew, bewildered by this strange Presidential behavior, let their conversations trail off to silence as they watched the President. Truman called the stragglers to order and announced that he had just been informed that a powerful new bomb, with an explosive force of more than twenty thousand tons of TNT, had been dropped on Japan. Truman had forgotten to mention the word "atomic," but the crew cheered and applauded anyway.

With the messages clutched in his hand, the President rushed from the room, followed by Byrnes, and burst into the officers' wardroom. "Keep your seats, gentlemen," the President said. "We have just dropped a bomb on Japan which has more power than twenty thousand tons of TNT. It was an overwhelming success. We won the gamble!" The officers cheered and applauded.

Within minutes, the ship's radio began to carry news reports from Washington about the bomb, and a statement was issued in the President's name, a statement leaving no doubt that "it is an atomic bomb. It is a harnessing of the basic power of the universe. The force from which the sun draws its power has been loosed against those who brought war to the Far East." The United States would continue to drop more such bombs if the Japanese did not surrender immediately. "It was to spare the Japanese from utter destruction that the ultimatum of July 26 was issued at Potsdam. Their leaders promptly rejected that ultimatum. If they do not now accept our terms, they may expect a rain of ruin from the air, the like of which has never been seen on this earth."

That afternoon, the President and members of his party were entertained by a varied program of orchestral music and boxing on the deck of the *Augusta*. The ship's log contains the unhappy note that "the afternoon's program came to an abrupt end when the ring posts collapsed during the last boxing bout. A spectator, BM 1/C H. W. Beeman, suffered a slight head injury when hit by a falling post. He was visited in the sick bay by the President and Secretary Byrnes who wanted to be sure he was not seriously hurt."

In Japan, the nation's most distinguished nuclear physicist, Dr. Yoshio Nishina, was dispatched to Hiroshima to see whether the city had in fact been hit by an atomic bomb. Nishina surveyed the city. Later estimates would conclude that as many as 100,000 people were killed immediately by the bomb and that, while Nishina looked down from his plane, perhaps another 100,000 were dying from burns, radiation, and other injuries. On

August 7, Nishina informed Lieutenant General Seizo Arisue that Hiroshima had been hit by a uranium-type bomb.

In Moscow, Generalissimo Stalin summoned Russia's five top nuclear scientists and directed them to proceed with development of the atomic bomb without sparing the cost. They were to work with all possible speed, under the direction of Lavrenti Beria.

At last, at five in the afternoon on August 8, Japanese Ambassador Sato was received by Molotov in the Kremlin. Sato's attempt at an opening pleasantry was cut short by the Russian foreign minister. "I have here," said Molotov, "in the name of the Soviet Union, a notification to the Japanese government which I wish to communicate to you." Molotov sat at one end of a long table; Sato took his seat at the other end. Molotov read a long document reviewing the fact of the Potsdam Declaration; Russia's obligations as an ally of America, England, and China; the "proposal" by the Allies for Russia to join the war against Japan — ending with: "the Soviet government declares that from tomorrow, that is from August 9, the Soviet Union will consider herself in a state of war against Japan."

"I am grateful," Sato replied, "for the good will and hospitality of your government, which has enabled me to stay in Moscow during this difficult time. It is indeed a sad thing that we shall have to part as enemies. But this cannot be helped. At any rate, let us part with a handshake. It may be the last one. "

The S. S. *Augusta* docked at Newport News, Virginia, and the President was back at his desk in the White House on August 8. Henry Stimson showed the President a photograph of Hiroshima after the bombing. The Japanese, Stimson said, should be persuaded to surrender as soon as possible. Perhaps the Hiroshima bomb — especially now that the bomb had been followed by a Soviet declaration of war — would be sufficient to bring about Japan's surrender. Evidently, however, the President did not for a moment consider holding off on the second bomb.

In London, Lord Moran called on Churchill. "I found him sitting in his silk vest on the edge of the bed, looking at the floor. ... 'It's no use, Charles, pretending I'm not hard hit. I can't school myself to do nothing for the rest of my life. It would have been better to have been killed in an aeroplane, or to have died like Roosevelt.... I get fits of depression. You know how my days were filled; now it has all gone....'" Churchill heard a noise. "'What is that knocking? Will it go on all day? I can no longer stop it at will.... Ah, Charles, blessings become curses. You kept me alive and now—'

"He turned his back, and when he looked at me his eyes were full of tears."

The telephones and radio equipment at the Japanese embassy in Moscow had been shut down. Molotov had promised to send a message from Sato back to his government in Japan. The message was not sent. Instead, several hours after the Molotov-Sato meeting, the Soviets broadcast their declaration of war. The message was received in Tokyo shortly before dawn on August 9. At the time, the American airplane *Bock's Car* was in the air headed for Nagasaki. *Bock's Car* carried the "Fat Man," an atomic bomb named in honor of Winston Churchill.

At eleven o'clock in the morning on August 9, Prime Minister Suzuki addressed the Japanese Cabinet. "Under the present circumstances," he said, "I have concluded that our only alternative is to accept the Potsdam Proclamation and terminate the war. I would like to hear your opinions on this." One minute later, America's second atomic bomb fell on Nagasaki. Even then the Japanese militarists remained intent upon redeeming their professional reputations with the blood of their countrymen. The militarists in the Cabinet blocked all efforts to bring about surrender, until, at three in the morning on August 10, the Emperor of Japan personally ordered an end to the war. On August 14, President Truman announced that the Japanese had accepted unconditional surrender (under the condition that the Emperor of Japan be retained, subject to the command of the Supreme Allied Commander). Total dead, dying, and deformed in Nagasaki: 100,000.

Admiral Leahy concluded that the Americans "had adopted an ethical standard common to the barbarians of the Dark Ages." No one likes, or wants to confront, the fact — but it is clear from the events and conversations during the Potsdam conference that the use of the atomic bomb against Hiroshima and Nagasaki was wanton murder.

22
EPILOGUE

On August 9, as the second atomic bomb fell on the people of Nagasaki, President Truman delivered his report on the Potsdam conference to the American people. As for Bulgaria and Rumania, the President said, flatly contradicting everything he knew and had recognized to be true, "These nations are not to be spheres of influence of any one power." The United States insisted that the governments of those two nations had to be changed. Prime Minister Clement Attlee took up the refrain at once and informed Parliament that, as far as the Balkan countries were concerned, he "looked forward with hope to the emergence of democratic governments based on free elections...." Both the formal and the informal understandings reached at Potsdam were already coming apart.

On August 17, three days after the announcement of Japan's surrender, the President declared that he would ask Congress to approve a program of universal military training for all healthy young Americans. As he explained several days later, "If we are to maintain leadership among other nations, we must continue to be strong in a military way." It began to sound as though Potsdam had not ensured dependable agreements for a generation of peace.

In August of 1945, however, most Americans were implacably opposed to an internationalist foreign policy. The troops were coming home. Men who had been the most willing and eager of soldiers could not get out of the Armed Forces quickly enough. Men who had once volunteered for extra duty now besieged their superiors with requests for early discharge. The Congress understood the will of the majority of Americans — and resoundingly defeated Truman's call for universal military training. The President, it turned out, was an internationalist in a nation of people suspicious of foreign entanglements.

While the soldiers returned home, Truman's men ensnarled the United States ever more certainly in foreign problems. In September, the Council of Foreign Ministers convened for the first time in London. "Jim Byrnes had not yet gone abroad," Stimson noted in his diary before the meeting, "and I had a very good talk with him.... I found that Byrnes was very much against any attempt to cooperate with Russia. His mind is full of his problems with the coming meeting of foreign ministers and he looks to having the presence of the bomb in his pocket, so to speak, as a great weapon to get through the thing.... He also told me of a number of acts of perfidy, so to speak, of Stalin, which they had encountered at Potsdam and felt in the light of those that we could not rely upon anything in the way of promises from them."

Ernest Bevin came into the meeting with his own methods of keeping trouble stirred up. He was determined, as he told Cadogan, to "'ave it out" with Molotov. And Molotov guaranteed that the foreign ministers would keep the fight going. He opened the first meeting by presenting a memorandum on "the political situation in Greece." The Russians must insist, Molotov said — repeating almost verbatim what Truman had said about Bulgaria and Rumania — that the Greek government be entirely reorganized before "free elections" could be held.

It might seem that the Potsdam conference had not even occurred, or, if it had, that it had made no difference. On the contrary, shortly after it had adjourned, all the tedious nit-picking arguments over words assumed their greatest importance. Compromises turned out to be not compromises at all but, rather, careful constructions that permitted opposing interpretations. Where Stalin had compromised, Truman pretended that the Russians had fully accepted the American position; where Stalin had not budged, Truman pretended the Russians had come very close to accepting the American position. And Stalin did the same: where Truman had recognized a provisional border or a provisional government, Stalin pretended the Americans had fully agreed to the Soviet position. Compromise, it turned out, had not been a way to find agreement, but a way to lure an opponent that extra inch into a trap. The arguments of the Potsdam conference all surfaced again, but this time with a crucial difference: this time, because of the Potsdam agreements, each side was able to show with only a slight change in nuance that the other side had broken an agreement, was now acting in bad faith, was untrustworthy, was deviously working to undermine the generation of peace for which they had all fought and worked so hard.

At the foreign ministers' meeting, Molotov broke all the rules of diplomacy: he called a press conference. "You, as well as I myself, know well that not everybody is pleased with the existing governments in Rumania or Bulgaria, but I don't think that there are any governments with which everybody is pleased." Free elections, based on universal suffrage, had already been scheduled in these countries. One could not say the same, for example, about Greece.

Byrnes offered Molotov a deal. The United States, with its sympathetic understanding of Russia's fear of a rearmed Germany, would agree to enter into a four-power security pact against the rearming of Germany in return for having the Russians withdraw entirely from eastern Europe. The United States, that is to say, would be happy to keep its sphere of influence, and help restrain Germany from attacking Russia; all Russia had to do was utterly renounce its own sphere of influence.

Molotov was getting the worst of this exchange. On September 22, he phoned Byrnes to say that no meeting could be called that day. It had occurred to Molotov that the Americans were violating the very basis of the Council of Foreign Ministers. Byrnes had insisted that France and China take part in the drafting of peace treaties; but, at Potsdam, it had been agreed that France and China would have no part in negotiating treaties with countries with whom they had not been at war — such as, for instance, Rumania.

In effect, Molotov offered Byrnes a deal: if the Americans would withdraw their objections to the Rumanian government, Molotov would withdraw his objection to this procedural matter. Once again, Byrnes was a step ahead of Molotov. If Molotov objected to having France and China in on Council decisions, this, said Byrnes, meant the Russians wanted to settle everything only among the major powers. What, then, was to happen to the rights of the small nations of the world? Evidently, the Russians wanted to make secret deals without any regard to the rights of the little nations!

"Our attitude was a shock to them," Byrnes said — and it was no wonder, for it was Byrnes who had suggested at Potsdam that the Americans and the Russians could settle things between themselves. "Our fight to have France and China remain in the Council was generally applauded, and our fight... for the right of the smaller states to participate in the peace won for us the good opinion of those states."

Britain's Chancellor of the Exchequer asked Bevin how the conference was going. "Like the strike leader said," Bevin replied, "thank God there is no danger of a settlement."

The first meeting of the Council of Foreign Ministers broke down over Molotov's objection to procedure. The foreign ministers were not even able to agree on a communiqué recording their disagreement. "The seriousness of what happened in London cannot be underestimated," *Izvestia* reported; "... this will shake the very basis of collaboration among the three powers."

On October 27, Navy Day, President Truman spoke in New York City: "We do not seek for ourselves one inch of territory in any place in the world," he said, reassuring the anti-internationalist American people. Or, at least, the United States sought hardly an inch: "Outside of the right to establish necessary bases for our own protection, we look for nothing which belongs to any other power."

American foreign policy, the President implied, was noninterventionist, purely defensive, and motivated only by traditional American ideals: "We believe in the eventual return of sovereign rights and self-government to all peoples who have been deprived of them by force.

"We believe that all peoples who are prepared for self-government should be permitted to choose their own form of government by their own freely expressed choice, without interference from any foreign source. That is true in Europe, in Asia, in Africa, as well as in the Western Hemisphere." That is to say, American foreign policy was noninterventionist — globally.

The President elaborated his foreign policy in general words that nonetheless had specific meanings.

As far as the Russian sphere of influence was concerned: "We shall refuse to recognize any government imposed upon any nation by the force of any foreign power...."

As for his spumed proposal on internationalizing inland waterways: "We believe that all nations should have the freedom of the seas and equal rights to the navigation of boundary rivers and waterways and of rivers and waterways which pass through more than one country."

As for free trade for American businessmen and an end of the British sterling bloc: "We believe that all states which are accepted in the society of nations should have access on equal terms to the trade and the raw materials of the world."

As for an American sphere of influence: "We believe that the sovereign states of the Western Hemisphere, without interference from outside the Western Hemisphere, must work together as good neighbors in the solution of their common problems."

And, just so he did not give the impression that American interests were limited to the western hemisphere, the President said, "We believe that full economic collaboration between [sic] all nations, great and small, is essential to the improvement of living conditions all over the world, and to the establishment of freedom from fear and freedom from want."

In fact, the President's speech was a précis of all the principles on which he intended to deny the understandings just reached at Potsdam.

In conclusion, the President spoke of the atomic bomb: "In our possession of this weapon, as in our possession of other new weapons, there is no threat to any nation. The world, which has seen the United States in two great recent wars, knows that full well. The possession in our hands of this new power of destruction we regard as a sacred trust. Because of our love of peace, the thoughtful people of the world know that the trust will not be violated, that it will be faithfully executed."

Among the young thinkers in the State Department in 1945 was Louis J. Halle. In Halle's view, which can be taken to represent the State Department's non-ideological, "realist's" approach to foreign affairs, international relations deal with "such a distribution of power among a number of centers as prevents the acquisition by any one of enough power to make itself master of the rest," that is to say, with a complex balance of powers. "The American people," Halle writes, "shaped by their long tradition, could not accept considerations of power politics as reasons for going to war," either in 1945 or at any other time. Neither Halle nor any other man whose career has been devoted to international politics, would assume that the American people could possibly be right in having such noninterventionist perceptions. Thus, says Halle, since the American people would not accept what members of the State Department felt was a realist's explanation of the need for interventionism, the people had to be given some other explanation. And so, for example, the First

World War was advocated as a "war to make the world safe for democracy." There is, Halle believes, "a sort of fatality about these matters. If the American people had been told the truth in 1917, if they had fed on the reality instead of on dreams, then" — so Halle asserts — "they would not have fought, and the war would have been lost, and anarchy would have triumphed and would have prevailed over the world. So the American people were told the opposite of the truth, and they fought for it, and the war was won."

Deception, Halle believes, is not a lamentable by-product of foreign relations, but rather an essential precondition of having any foreign relations at all; only thus will an ignorant people allow their leaders a free reign to pursue "realistic" interventionist foreign policy. One might reasonably assume that State Department officers like to be interventionists because it gives them something to do; and one might assume that Presidents like to be interventionists because it provides them with a grand historical stage on which to move, increases their power, and mutes the more homely demands of citizens by uniting the people against a common external threat. Or one might even believe that interventionism — applied discreetly if not globally — is indeed a realistic approach to the world. In any case, there is a fatality to Halle's way of thought, too; having laid the foundations of foreign policy on deceptions, it is difficult — perhaps impossible — to avoid becoming the captive of a policy that is untrue and unrealistic.

Halle's basic perception of post-World War II America was nonetheless true. For whatever reasons, the President and his men in the State Department were interventionists; the rest of the country was, for the most part, anti-interventionist. The interventionists had a program in search of a salable rationale.

George F. Kennan was at that time a promising forty-one-year-old career State Department officer in Moscow. In the middle of February 1946, he had received a query from Washington. The Treasury Department wanted to know why it was so difficult to get along with the Soviets. Not everyone in Washington had yet caught on to the policy Truman was edging toward; the Treasury Department was still trying to cooperate with the Russians. The Russians, it seemed, were unwilling to go along with plans for the World Bank and International Monetary Fund. "It should be remembered," Kennan later wrote, "that nowhere in Washington had the hopes entertained for postwar collaboration with Russia been more elaborate, more naïve, or more tenaciously... pursued than in the Treasury Department...." The Treasury Department, after all, knew nothing of politics; it was interested only in postwar prosperity.

"The more I thought about this message, the more it seemed to be obvious that this was 'it.' For eighteen long months I had done little else but pluck people's sleeves, trying to make them understand the nature of the phenomenon with which we in the Moscow embassy were daily confronted.... So far as official Washington was concerned, it had been to all intents and purposes like talking to a stone."

Kennan replied to the simple little query with an eight-thousand word cable.

At the bottom of the Kremlin's neurotic view of world affairs is traditional and instinctive Russian sense of insecurity. Originally, this was insecurity of a peaceful agricultural people trying to live on vast exposed plain in neighborhood of fierce nomadic peoples.... Soviet leaders are driven by necessities of their own past and present position to put forward a dogma which pictures the outside world as evil, hostile, and menacing.... This thesis provides justification for that increase of military and political power in Russian state....

Kennan's cable sounded like an appraisal of a nation that was very dangerous indeed. Kennan also had a plan for coming to grips with the Russian threat which sounded plausible and relatively risk-free:

(One) Soviet power, unlike that of Hitlerite Germany, is neither schematic nor adventuristic.... It does not take unnecessary risks.... It is highly sensitive to logic of force. For this reason it can easily withdraw — and usually does — when strong resistance is encountered at any point. Thus, if the adversary has sufficient force and makes clear his readiness to use it, he rarely has to do so. If situations are properly handled there need be no prestige-engaging showdowns.

(Two) Gauged against Western world as a whole, Soviets are still by far the weaker force...

(Three) Success of Soviet system, as form of internal power, is not yet finally proven.... Internal soundness and permanence of movement need not be regarded as assured.

All this seemed solid enough. Then Kennan added the clincher:

In summary, we have here a political force committed fanatically to the belief that with US there can be no permanent modus vivendi, that it is desirable and necessary that the internal harmony of our society be disrupted, our traditional way of life be destroyed, the international authority of our state be broken, if Soviet power is to be secure.

This began to sound like the sort of rationale an interventionist foreign policy needed. "I read it over today with a horrified amusement," Kennan wrote in his memoirs. "Much of it reads exactly like one of those primers put out by alarmed congressional committees or by the Daughters of the American

Revolution, designed to arouse the citizenry to the dangers of the Communist conspiracy." It certainly did, and it was exactly the sort of thing Truman needed. "The effect produced in Washington," Kennan observed, "... was nothing less than sensational. The President, I believe, read it.... James Forrestal had it reproduced and evidently made it required reading for hundreds, if not thousands, of higher officers in the armed services.... My official loneliness came in fact to an end.... My reputation was made. My voice now carried."

Kennan was called to Washington where he was made the State Department's War College Deputy for Foreign Affairs and, later on, chairman of the State Department's new Policy Planning Committee, or, as he was called in the *New York Times*, "America's global planner."

Just in case anyone might be getting the idea that Truman was alone responsible for gearing up the Cold War, Stalin obliged in March of 1946 by displaying once again the way he liked to use the Russian Army. At Potsdam, we recall, the Big Three had all agreed to remove their troops from Iran. The British government announced that its forces would withdraw by the deadline of March 2, 1946. The Russians, however, did not want to withdraw before they had an agreement with the Iranians for an oil concession — and even then Stalin wanted to pull back only from central Iran and keep his forces in the northern part of the country. On March 1, the Kremlin announced that Russian troops would remain in Iran past the deadline, "pending clarification of the situation."

Ultimately, the Russian attempt to lay hold of Iranian oil fields was unsuccessful, and Russian troops were withdrawn, leaving the Americans in control of 40 percent of Iranian oil. Yet, in 1946, this new instance of Soviet readiness to use the brute force of its Army seemed very ominous indeed. Iran meant more than just Iran; it meant, too, the Middle East and the Mediterranean. Stalin threatened western Europe, and Stalin threatened the Mediterranean.

It was only eight months before that President Truman had eschewed ideology, had declined to criticize the Soviets, and had kept in check such obstreperous anti-Russians as James Forrestal and Winston Churchill. By March of 1946, however, the President had laid the groundwork of his foreign policy; he had established the essential spheres of influence at Potsdam and enunciated the principles of American foreign policy. On the basis of those principles, he was ready to cause trouble in the Soviet sphere of influence. He was ready to practice the globalism that previously had only been implied. By this time, the President's greatest problem was getting the noninterventionist American people to go along with his plans. The breakdown in talks of the Council of Foreign Ministers in London had helped to show that the Russians were aggressive and untrustworthy. Then, too, Stalin helped the President by seeking spoils, territories, secured borders, and oil and by keeping the vast Russian Army firmly planted in the positions it had achieved by the end of the war.

By March 5, 1946, the President was prepared to see whether Americans were ready for a new call to arms. And so, to deliver a speech at Fulton, Missouri, he invited — who else? — Winston Churchill, leader of the Opposition party in Great Britain.

"A shadow has fallen upon the scenes so lately lighted by the Allied victory," Churchill warned. "Nobody knows what Soviet Russia and its Communist international organization intends to do in the immediate future, or what are the limits, if any, to their expansive and proselytising tendencies.... From Stettin in the Baltic to Trieste in the Adriatic, an iron curtain has descended across the Continent. Behind that line lie all the capitals of the ancient states of Central and Eastern Europe... in what I must call the Soviet sphere, and all are subject in one form or another, not only to Soviet influence but to a very high and, in many cases, increasing measure of control from Moscow.... Whatever conclusions may be drawn from these facts — and facts they are — this is certainly not the Liberated Europe we fought to build up. Nor is it one which contains the essentials of permanent peace."

Churchill was still vainly trying to forge an Anglo-American alliance. On the train that took him to Fulton, his press aides passed out copies of his speech that carried a suggested headline: churchill proposes anglo-american alliance as russian shadow darkens over the world. But that was the last thing Truman had in mind. The President was observed enthusiastically applauding the former Prime Minister's speech, and ten days later Jimmy Byrnes found an occasion to make a speech about how the United States had no intention of entering an alliance with Britain. In Truman's scheme of things, the Fulton speech was not a call to alliance but a call to the American people to unite against a common enemy.

QUESTION: "How do you appraise Mr. Churchill's latest speech in the United States?"

STALIN: "I appraise it as a dangerous act, calculated to sow the seeds of dissension among the Allied states and impede their collaboration."

The reporter seemed to know just which question to ask.

QUESTION: "Can it be considered that Mr. Churchill's speech is prejudicial to the cause of peace and security?"

STALIN: "Yes, unquestionably. As a matter of fact, Mr. Churchill now takes the stand of the warmongers, and in this Mr. Churchill is not alone. He has friends not only in Britain but in the United States as well."

In the spring and summer of 1946, the United States presented a plan to the United Nations for the control of atomic energy. Eventually — in three years or five years or twenty years - other nations would discover how to make atomic bombs. The question over which the Americans puzzled was whether to help these other nations unravel the secrets of atomic energy — and thus gain some sort of credit and work toward some sort of mutual control of this novel force — or to keep the secrets locked up in American laboratories, let other nations shift for themselves, and build a sufficiently large stockpile of weapons to keep other nations intimidated. In the end, Truman decided to appear to want to opt for the first course while he pursued the second.

Dean Acheson and David Lilienthal prepared the first American proposal for submission to the United Nations. Acheson and Lilienthal began with several assumptions: first, that the advantage the United States then had over atomic weapons was only temporary; second, that an arms race had to be avoided; third, that America had to keep its advantage until effective controls came into being;

and finally that any broad program of international inspection was inadequate and, since it would necessitate having Americans pry into Soviet society, obviously unacceptable to the Russians.

According to Acheson and Lilienthal, the way to control atomic weapons was to control uranium and thorium deposits and place them under international ownership. These deposits, they said, were easy to find, limited in number, and simple to control. International control of these deposits would come into effect gradually, by stages; in the meantime the United States would continue to build bombs so as to retain a lead in atomic weaponry. "Should the worst happen and, during the transition period, the entire effort collapse, the United States will at all times be in a favorable position with regard to atomic weapons."

Jimmy Byrnes handed the draft report to Bernard M. Baruch. Acheson and Lilienthal were outraged; they feared Baruch would butcher their plan; as it turned out, they were right.

Baruch immediately cut the heart out of the Acheson-Lilienthal plan: international ownership of mining operations, said Baruch, would destroy or seriously damage private enterprise in the capitalist countries. Just how capitalism could be destroyed by international ownership of two raw materials, Baruch did not bother to explain. "The plan would seem to all men in the capitalistic economy as the first start to an international socialized state." In addition, Baruch fancied a broader system of inspection, because, as one of his assistants said, if the United Nations could "send fifty two-man teams all over the world, " then "it would be possible to find out what was going on in Russia."

Furthermore, said Baruch, some provision needed to be made for punishment of any who violated an agreement. The only meaningful punishment would be a declaration of war; yet, in the Security Council of the United Nations, Russia could veto any declaration of war. Therefore, the agreement on atomic weapons must specifically eliminate any United Nations veto power over the use of atomic weapons. Such a provision, Baruch informed the President, would of course constitute an "inroad on the general theory of the veto power." Obviously, too, since only the United States had nuclear weapons, only the United States could unilaterally punish violators. But, said Baruch, a treaty was useless unless it had a provision for punishment. "I quite agree with you," said Truman.

When J. Robert Oppenheimer reviewed the Baruch plan, he said that American planners should "talk about preparing the American people for a refusal by Russia." On June 14, 1946, Baruch presented his plan to the United Nations. On June 19, Andrei Gromyko declared that it was unacceptable. The fact that the Russians refused to subscribe to the Baruch plan was thereafter taken as proof that the United States favored nuclear disarmament, but that the Russians preferred a nuclear arms race. Why? Because, Baruch explained, the Russians sought "the whole control of the world."

The Russians, on the other hand, said that the United States wanted to control the whole world. As early as 1941, in the Atlantic Charter, the United States had pledged itself with Great Britain, "to further the enjoyment by all States, great or small, victor or vanquished, of access, on equal terms, to the trade and to the raw materials of the world which are needed for their economic prosperity."

In Paris, on October 10, 1946, Russian Foreign Minister Molotov addressed himself to the idea of "equal opportunity."

"The principle of so-called 'equal opportunity' has become a favorite topic of late. What, it is argued, could be better than this principle, which would establish equal opportunity for all states without discrimination?... Let us discuss the principle of equality seriously and honestly....

"Here in Paris every one of you can find a copy of the 'World Almanac, 1946.' In this book you may read the following figures: the national income of the U.S.A. in 1941 was estimated at 96, 000 million dollars, in 1942 at 122, 000 million dollars, in 1943 at 149,000 million dollars, and in 1944 at 160,000 million dollars. Thus, in four years of the war the national income of the U.S.A. rose by 64, 000 million dollars. The same book says that in 1938 the total national income of the United States was 64, 000 million dollars. Hence the mere increase in the national income of the U. S. A. during the war years was equal to its total national income in 1938. These are facts which one cannot refrain from mentioning....

"Now that you know the facts, place side by side Rumania, enfeebled by the war, or Yugoslavia, ruined by the German and Italian fascists, and the United States of America, whose wealth has grown immensely during the war, and you will clearly see what the implementation of the principle of 'equal opportunity' would mean in practice. Imagine, under these circumstances, that in this same Rumania or Yugoslavia, or in some other war-weakened state, you have this so-called 'equal opportunity' for, let us say, American capital—that is, the opportunity for it to penetrate unhindered into Rumanian industry, or Yugoslav industry and so forth: what, then, will remain of Rumania's national industry, or of Yugoslavia's national industry?

"It is surely not so difficult to understand that if American capital were given a free hand in the small states ruined and enfeebled by the war, as the advocates of the principle of 'equal opportunity' desire, American capital would buy up the local industries, appropriate the more attractive Rumanian, Yugoslav and all other enterprises, and would become the master in these small states. Given such a situation, we would probably live to see the day when in your own country, on switching on the radio, you would be hearing not so much your own language as one American gramophone record after another....

"Is it not clear that such unrestricted application of the principle of 'equal opportunity' in the given conditions would in practice mean the veritable economic enslavement of the small states and their subjugation to the rule and arbitrary will of strong and enriched foreign firms, banks and industrial companies?"

By this time, the Cold War was properly under way, and any who did not perceive that to be so were soon instructed. Secretary of Commerce Henry Wallace had suggested in the spring of 1946 that much of the difficulty America was having with the Russians could be explained by Russia's "dire economic needs and by their disturbed sense of security." He recommended "a new approach along economic and trade lines." The President ignored Wallace's suggestion. Shortly before Molotov made his speech in Paris, Henry Wallace made a speech in Madison Square Garden in New

York. It was possible to cooperate with Russia, said Wallace, once the United States had made it clear that Americans were interested in "neither saving the British Empire nor purchasing oil in the Near East with the lives of American soldiers." Wallace suggested that the Americans and Russians simply recognize one another's spheres of interests. Let them strike a bargain: America would stay out of eastern Europe if Russia would stay out of western Europe and the Americas. Four days after Wallace delivered his speech, Truman requested his resignation.

For their part, the Russians violated the Potsdam accords item by item, tightened their grip on eastern Europe, and, like the Americans, refused to agree that they had agreed on many of the Potsdam agreements. There were questions about reparations, the Polish borders, access to the Dardanelles — all of those issues laid out at Potsdam, not as bases of accord to ensure "a lasting peace," but as grounds for discord and conflict. The British, too, kept up their part in the negotiations. At one of the meetings of the Council of Foreign Ministers, Ernest Bevin "rose to his feet," Charles Bohlen recalled, "his hands knotted into fists, and started toward Molotov, saying, 'I've had enough of this, I've,' and for one glorious moment it looked as if the foreign minister of Great Britain and the foreign minister of the Soviet Union were going to exchange blows. However, security people moved in...."

The question that continues to engage the passions of historians is whether Truman and Stalin could have avoided the Cold War. If Truman had been less combative, if the United States had not exacerbated Russia's historical "paranoia," if Russia's sphere of influence had simply been recognized, would Stalin then have been less aggressive and the whole Cold War have been averted? We can only say, at best, that it might have been. Yet, the question is only meaningful if one assumes that Truman wished to avoid conflict and was searching for tactics to assure a tranquil world. In truth, very little that Truman did could be construed as part of a plan for tranquillity.

At the beginning of January 1947, the President accepted the resignation of Secretary of State Byrnes. The difficulty between the two men was not that Byrnes was insufficiently combative — he was certainly combative — but that Byrnes kept tooting off on his own without informing Truman of what he had planned. Truman was intent upon having close control of foreign policy. To replace Byrnes, the President appointed General George C. Marshall, a man distinguished in a multitude of ways, not the least of them being that he was Truman's supporter in using the atomic bomb against Japan.

Within several days of Marshall's appointment, the British government cut coal allocations to its industries by one-half. A number of factories closed altogether. On January 25, the first of a series of snowstorms struck Britain. Electricity was rationed, then food, then heat was cut off, and then came the news that the blizzards had killed the winter wheat crop. As Louis Halle observed, "Britain was like a soldier wounded in war who, now that the fighting was over, was bleeding to death."

On Friday afternoon, February 21, 1947, a member of the British embassy in Washington phoned to ask for an appointment with the Secretary of State. Marshall had already left for the weekend, but Dean Acheson, then Undersecretary of State, suggested that the British send over notes on the questions to be discussed so that the State Department could work up whatever background information Marshall might need on Monday morning. Later that afternoon, First Secretary H. M. Sichel arrived with two notes for Loy Henderson, Director of the Division of Near Eastern Affairs. "My office, in those days," recalled Louis Halle, "was around the corner from Henderson's.... I would... expect that the first thought of virtually any man in Henderson's position would be: 'There goes my weekend!'... What the two notes reported was the final end of the *Pax Britannica.*"

Until that Friday afternoon, Britain had been the primary support of the economy of Greece, and the primary underwriter of the Turkish Army.

The first note informed the State Department that Greece would need between 240 and 280 million dollars in the next several months, and that Britain could not provide it. The second note said that the British could no longer underwrite the Turkish Army. With all of the tough, shrewd, well-thought-out planning the Americans had done since the Potsdam conference, this news from Britain apparently came as a complete surprise and a shock to the State Department. The Americans had wanted to trim the British down to size, to break in on the sterling bloc, to bully the British into subservience on general foreign policy positions—but the Americans had not wanted to knock an ally out of commission. Neither Truman nor any of his advisers had believed Churchill when the former Prime Minister had whined and begged. Now, to their utter astonishment, they saw that Churchill had been telling the truth.

Henderson, Acheson, and, when he returned on Monday, Marshall, too, agreed that the United States must take up Britain's imperial role. A good many insiders had been aching to do just that in any case. As one of Baruch's aides had written Jimmy Byrnes in October 1946, "We should increase production of fissionable material, speed up the program for bases and B-36 planes, and in effect give notice that *we* are the future police force of the Security Council."

On February 27, Marshall, Acheson, and Truman met with Congressional leaders in the White House. Acheson was called upon to deliver a pitch for taking up Britain's role. In Acheson's view, the question was starkly, portentously simple: the defense of Western civilization itself was the issue, and the Undersecretary delivered a ten-minute oration — replete with references to Athens, Rome, and the great traditions and freedoms of Western civilization — which left the congressmen stunned and silent. At last, Senator Vandenberg spoke up. He had been much impressed by Acheson's speech, he said, but, if the President really wanted to sell this program to the American people, he would have to "scare hell out of the country."

On March 2, 1947, in the *New York Times*, Hanson Baldwin — having spoken with Dean Acheson — commenced to scare the hell out of the country. America, he said, "Far more than any single factor, is the key to the destiny of tomorrow; we alone may be able to avert the decline of Western civilization, and a reversion to nihilism and the Dark Ages." A good many Americans could sincerely subscribe to Baldwin's thesis; quite a few had come to the same conclusion even earlier. Those who had were singled out, encouraged, and promoted. On January 7, 1947, Truman appointed John Foster Dulles to the United States delegation to the United Nations.

On March 12, 1947, the President addressed a joint session of Congress: "The United States has received from the Greek government an urgent appeal for financial and economic assistance.... That assistance is imperative if Greece is to survive as a free nation.... The very existence of the Greek state is today threatened by the terrorist activities of several thousand armed men, led by Communists, who defy the government's authority. ... Greece must have assistance if it is to become a self-supporting and self-respecting democracy. The United States must supply that assistance....

"Greece's neighbor, Turkey, also deserves our attention. The future of Turkey as an independent and economically sound state is clearly no less important to the freedom-loving peoples of the world than the future of Greece."

So far the President's speech sounded portentous, but not scary. Then he announced what later became known as the Truman Doctrine: "At the present moment in world history nearly every nation must choose between alternate ways of life. The choice is too often not a free one.

"One way of life is based upon the will of the majority, and is distinguished by free institutions, representative government, free elections, guarantees of individual liberty, freedom of speech and religion, and freedom from political oppression.

"The second way of life is based upon the will of a minority forcibly imposed upon the majority. It relies upon terror and oppression, a controlled press and radio, fixed elections, and the suppression of personal freedoms.

"I believe that it must be the policy of the United States to support free peoples....

"If we falter in our leadership, we may endanger the peace of the world — and we shall surely endanger the welfare of our own nation."

Congressional resistance to the Truman plan was exceedingly feeble. During World War II, Congress was willing and eager to surrender its powers and prerogatives to the commander in chief — so willing that its powers had been severely diminished. Now, like an old war-horse, Congress came running to harness again when it heard the call to a new war. What shreds of power Congress had left to it at the end of World War II were almost all lost during the Cold War. Lyndon Johnson understood this phenomenon perhaps more thoroughly than anyone else. War, Johnson knew, whether hot or cold, is what enables a President to assume the maximum amount of power. Roosevelt, said Johnson, once the steam had gone out of the New Deal, "was never President ... until the war came along." Similarly, Truman was never President until he had his war.

It is absurd, in the face of all this too obvious behavior to attempt to apportion "blame" for the beginning of the Cold War, to try to say whether Truman or Stalin was the first to be distrustful or aggressive or untrustworthy or provocative. They fairly tripped over one another to be the first with a new charge against the other. They were both eager to exacerbate their difficulties. They were both quick to adopt harsh language, characterized by appeals to absolute good and absolute evil. Aboard the S. S. *Augusta*, on its return voyage to the United States, a sailor asked Truman what he thought of Stalin. "I think he's a son of a bitch," said the President — and, then, with a smile, "I guess he thinks I'm one, too."

APPENDIX I
THE POTSDAM PROCLAMATION BY THE HEADS OF GOVERNMENT, UNITED STATES, CHINA AND THE UNITED KINGDOM

1. We, the President of the United States, the President of the National Government of the Republic of China and the Prime Minister of Great Britain, representing the hundreds of millions of our countrymen, have conferred and agree that Japan shall be given an opportunity to end this war.

2. The prodigious land, sea and air forces of the United States, the British Empire and of China, many times reinforced by their armies and air fleets from the west are poised to strike the final blows upon Japan. This military power is sustained and inspired by the determination of all the Allied nations to prosecute the war against Japan until she ceases to resist.

3. The result of the futile and senseless German resistance to the might of the aroused free people of the world stands forth in awful clarity as an example to the people of Japan. The might that now converges on Japan is immeasurably greater than that which, when applied to the resisting Nazis, necessarily laid waste to the lands, the industry and the method of life of the whole German people. The full application of our military power, backed by our resolve, *will* mean the inevitable and complete destruction of the Japanese armed forces and just as inevitably the utter devastation of the Japanese homeland.

4. The time has come for Japan to decide whether she will continue to be controlled by those self-willed militaristic advisers whose unintelligent calculations have brought the Empire of Japan to the threshold of annihilation, or whether she will follow the path of reason.

5. Following are our terms. We will not deviate from them. There are no alternatives. We shall brook no delay.

6. There must be eliminated for all time the authority and influence of those who have deceived and misled the people of Japan into embarking on world conquest, for we insist that a new order of peace, security and justice will be impossible until irresponsible militarism is driven from the world.

7. Until such a new order is established and until there is convincing proof that Japan's war-making power is destroyed, points in Japanese territory to be designated by the Allies shall be occupied to secure the achievement of the basic objectives we are here setting forth.

8. The terms of the Cairo Declaration shall be carried out and Japanese sovereignty shall be limited to the islands of Honshu, Hokkaido, Kyushu, Shikoku and such minor islands as we determine.

9. The Japanese military forces, after being completely disarmed, shall be permitted to return to their homes with the opportunity to lead peaceful and productive lives.

10. We do not intend that the Japanese shall be enslaved as a race or destroyed as nation, but stern justice shall be meted out to all war criminals, including those who have visited cruelties upon our prisoners. The Japanese government shall remove all obstacles to the revival and strengthening of democratic tendencies among the Japanese people. Freedom of speech, of religion, and of thought, as well as respect for the fundamental human rights shall be established.

11. Japan shall be permitted to maintain such industries as will sustain her economy and

permit the exaction of just reparations in kind, but not those industries which would enable her to rearm for war. To this end, access to, as distinguished from control of raw materials shall be permitted. Eventual Japanese participation in world trade relations shall be permitted.

12. The occupying forces of the Allies shall be withdrawn from Japan as soon as these objectives have been accomplished and there has been established in accordance with the freely expressed will of the Japanese people a peacefully inclined and responsible government.

13. We call upon the Government of Japan to proclaim now the unconditional surrender of all the Japanese armed forces, and to provide proper and adequate assurances of their good faith in such action. The alternative for Japan is prompt and utter destruction.

POTSDAM

July 26, 1945

Harry S. Truman.

Winston S. Churchill.

Approval of President Chiang Kai-shek

obtained by radio

APPENDIX II
THE POTSDAM DECLARATION

August 2, 1945

I

On July 17, 1945, the President of the United States of America, Harry S. Truman, the Chairman of the Council of People's Commissars of the Union of Soviet Socialist Republics, Generalissimo J. V. Stalin, and the Prime Minister of Great Britain, Winston S. Churchill, together with Mr. Clement R. Attlee, met in the Tripartite Conference of Berlin. They were accompanied by the foreign secretaries of the three Governments, Mr. James F. Byrnes, Mr. V. M. Molotov, and Mr. Anthony Eden, the Chiefs of Staff, and other advisers.

There were nine meetings between July 17 and July 25. The Conference was then interrupted for two days while the results of the British general election were being declared.

On July 28 Mr. Attlee returned to the Conference as Prime Minister, accompanied by the new Secretary of State for Foreign Affairs, Mr. Ernest Bevin. Four days of further discussion then took place. During the course of the Conference there were regular meetings of the Heads of the Three Governments accompanied by the foreign secretaries, and also meetings of the Foreign Secretaries. Committees appointed by the Foreign Secretaries for preliminary consideration of questions before the Conference also met daily.

The meetings of the Conference were held at the Cecilienhof near Potsdam. The Conference ended on August 2, 1945.

Important decisions and agreements were reached. Views were exchanged on a number of other questions and consideration of these matters will be continued by the Council of Foreign Ministers established by the Conference.

President Truman, Generalissimo Stalin and Prime Minister Attlee leave this Conference, which has strengthened the ties between the three governments and extended the scope of their collaboration and understanding with renewed confidence that their governments and peoples, together with the other United Nations, will ensure the creation of a just and enduring peace.

II

Establishment of a Council of Foreign Ministers

The Conference reached an agreement for the establishment of a Council of Foreign Ministers representing the five principal Powers to continue the necessary preparatory work for the peace settlements and to take up other matters which from time to time may be referred to the Council by agreement of the Governments participating in the Council.

The text of the agreement for the establishment of the Council of Foreign Ministers is as follows:

(1) There shall be established a Council composed of the Foreign Ministers of the United Kingdom, the Union of Soviet Socialist Republics, China, France, and the United States.

(2) (i) The Council shall normally meet in London, which shall be the permanent seat of the joint Secretariat which the Council will form. Each of the Foreign Ministers will be accompanied by a high-ranking Deputy, duly authorized to carry on the work of the Council in the absence of his

Foreign Minister, and by a small staff of technical advisers.

(ii) The first meeting of the Council shall be held in London not later than September 1, 1945. Meetings may be held by common agreement in other capitals as may be agreed from time to time.

(3) (i) As its immediate important task, the Council shall be authorized to draw up, with a view to their submission to the United Nations, treaties of peace with Italy, Rumania, Bulgaria, Hungary and Finland, and to propose settlements of territorial questions outstanding on the termination of the war in Europe. The Council shall be utilized for the preparation of a peace settlement for Germany to be accepted by the Government of Germany when a government adequate for the purpose is established.

(ii) For the discharge of each of these tasks the Council will be composed of the Members representing those States which were signatory to the terms of surrender imposed upon the enemy State concerned. For the purposes of the peace settlement for Italy, France shall be regarded as a signatory to the terms of surrender for Italy. Other members will be invited to participate when matters directly concerning them are under discussion.

(iii) Other matters may from time to time come to be referred to the Council by agreement between the Member Governments.

(4) (i) Whenever the Council is considering a question of direct interest to a State not Represented thereon, such State should be invited to send representatives to participate in the discussion and study of that question.

(ii) The Council may adapt its procedure to the particular problem under consideration. In some cases it may hold its own preliminary discussions prior to the participation of other interested States. In other cases, the Council may convoke a formal conference of the State chiefly interested in seeking a solution of the particular problem.

In accordance with the decision of the Conference the three Governments have each addressed an identical invitation to the Governments of China and France to adopt this text and to join in establishing the Council.

The establishment of the Council of Foreign Ministers for the specific purpose named in the text will be without prejudice to the agreement of the Crimea Conference that there should be periodic consultation among the Foreign Secretaries of the United States, the Union of Soviet Socialist Republics and the United Kingdom.

The Conference also considered the position of the European Advisory Commission in the light of the agreement to establish the Council of Foreign

Ministers. It was noted with satisfaction that the Commission had ably discharged its principal tasks by the recommendations that it had furnished for the terms of Germany's unconditional surrender, for the zones of occupation in Germany and Austria, and for the inter-Allied control machinery in those countries. It was felt that further work of a detailed character for the coordination of Allied policy for the control of Germany and Austria would in future fall within the competence of the Allied Control Council at Berlin and the Allied Commission at Vienna. Accordingly, it was agreed to recommend that the European Advisory Commission be dissolved.

III

Germany

The Allied armies are in occupation of the whole of Germany and the German people have begun to atone for the terrible crimes committed under the leadership of those whom, in the hour of their success, they openly approved and blindly obeyed.

Agreement has been reached at this Conference on the political and economic principles of a coordinated Allied policy toward defeated Germany during the period of Allied control.

The purpose of this agreement is to carry out the Crimea declaration on Germany. German militarism and Nazism will be extirpated and the Allies will take in agreement together, now and in the future, the other measures necessary to assure that Germany never again will threaten her neighbors or the peace of the world.

It is not the intention of the Allies to destroy or enslave the German people. It; is the intention of the Allies that the German people be given the opportunity to prepare for the eventual reconstruction of their life on a democratic and peaceful basis. If their own efforts are steadily directed to this end, it will be possible for them in due course to take their place among the free and peaceful peoples of the world.

The text of the agreement is as follows:

THE POLITICAL AND ECONOMIC PRINCIPLES TO GOVERN THE TREATMENT OF GERMANY IN THE INITIAL CONTROL PERIOD

A. *Political Principles.*

1. In accordance with the Agreement on Control Machinery in Germany, supreme authority in Germany is exercised on instructions from their respective Governments, by the Commanders-in-Chief of the armed forces of the United States of America, the United Kingdom, the Union of Soviet Socialist Republics, and the French Republic, each in his own zone of occupation,

and also jointly, in matters affecting Germany as a whole, in their capacity as members of the Control Council.

2. So far as is practicable, there shall be uniformity of treatment of the German population throughout Germany.

3. The purposes of the occupation of Germany by which the Control Council shall be guided are:

(i) The complete disarmament and demilitarization of Germany and the elimination or control of all German industry that could be used for military production. To these ends:

(a) All German land, naval and air forces, the S.S., S.A., S.D., and Gestapo, with all their organizations, staffs, and institutions, including the General Staff, the Officers' Corps, Reserve Corps, military schools, war veterans' organizations and all other military and quasi-military organizations, together with all clubs and associations which serve to keep alive the military tradition in Germany, shall be completely and finally abolished in such manner as permanently to prevent the revival or reorganization of German militarism and Nazism;

 (b) All arms, ammunition and implements of war and all specialized facilities for their production shall be held at the disposal of the Allies or destroyed. The maintenance and production of all aircraft and all arms, ammunition and implements of war shall be prevented.

(ii) To convince the German people that they have suffered a total military defeat and that they cannot escape responsibility for what they have brought upon themselves, since their own ruthless warfare and the fanatical Nazi resistance have destroyed German economy and made chaos and suffering inevitable.

(iii) To destroy the National Socialist Party and its affiliated and supervised organizations, to dissolve all Nazi institutions, to ensure that they are not revived in any form, and to prevent all Nazi and militarist activity or propaganda.

(iv) To prepare for the eventual reconstruction of German political life on a democratic basis and for eventual peaceful cooperation in international life by Germany.

4. All Nazi laws which provided the basis of the Hitler regime or established discrimination on grounds of race, creed, or political opinion shall be abolished. No such discriminations, whether legal, administrative or otherwise, shall be tolerated.

5. War criminals and those who have participated in planning or carrying out Nazi enterprises involving or resulting in atrocities or war crimes shall be arrested and brought to judgment. Nazi leaders, influential Nazi supporters and high

officials of Nazi organizations and institutions and any other persons dangerous to the occupation or its objectives shall be arrested and interned.

6. All members of the Nazi Party who have been more than nominal participants in its activities and all other persons hostile to Allied purposes shall be removed from public and semi-public office, and from positions of responsibility in important private undertakings. Such persons shall be replaced by persons who, by their political and moral qualities, are deemed capable of assisting in developing genuine democratic institutions in Germany.

7. German education shall be so controlled as completely to eliminate Nazi and militarist doctrines and to make possible the successful development of democratic ideas.

8. The judicial system will be reorganized in accordance with the principles of democracy, of justice under law, and of equal rights for all citizens without distinction of race, nationality or religion.

9. The administration of affairs in Germany should be directed towards the decentralization of the political structure and the development of local responsibility. To this end:

(i) local self-government shall be restored throughout Germany on democratic principles and in particular through elective councils as rapidly as is consistent with military security and the purposes of military occupation;

(ii) all democratic political parties with rights of assembly and of public discussion shall be allowed and encouraged throughout Germany;

(iii) representative and elective principles shall be introduced into regional, provincial and state (Land) administration as rapidly as may be justified by the successful application of these principles in local self-government;

(iv) for the time being no central German government shall be established. Notwithstanding this, however, certain essential central German administrative departments, headed by State Secretaries, shall be established, particularly in the fields of finance, transport, communications, foreign trade, and industry. Such departments will act under the direction of the Control Council.

10. Subject to the necessity for maintaining military security, freedom of speech, press and religion shall be permitted, and religious institutions shall be respected. Subject likewise to the maintenance of military security, the formation of free trade unions shall be permitted.

B. *Economic Principles.*

11. In order to eliminate Germany's war potential, the production of arms, ammunition and

implements of war as well as all types of aircraft and sea-going ships shall be prohibited and prevented. Production of metals, chemicals, machinery and other items that are directly necessary to a war economy shall be rigidly controlled and restricted to Germany's approved postwar peacetime needs to meet the objectives stated in Paragraph 15. Productive capacity not needed for permitted production shall be removed in accordance with the reparations plan recommended by the Allied Commission on Reparations and approved by the Governments concerned or if not removed shall be destroyed.

12. At the earliest practicable date, the German economy shall be decentralized for the purpose of eliminating the present excessive concentration of economic power as exemplified in particular by cartels, syndicates, trusts and other monopolistic arrangements.

13. In organizing the German economy, primary emphasis shall be given to the development of agricultural and peaceful domestic industries.

14. During the period of occupation Germany shall be treated as a single economic unit. To this end common policies shall be established in regard to:

(a) mining and industrial production and allocation;

(b) agriculture, forestry and fishing;

(c) wages, prices and rationing;

(d) import and export programs for Germany as a whole;

(e) currency and banking, central taxation and customs;

(f) reparation and removal of industrial war potential;

(g) transportation and communications.

In applying these policies account shall be taken, where appropriate, of varying local conditions.

15. Allied controls shall be imposed upon the German economy but only to the extent necessary:

(a) to carry out programs of industrial disarmament and demilitarization, of reparations, and of approved exports and imports.

(b) to assure the production and maintenance of goods and services required to meet the needs of the occupying forces and displaced persons in Germany and essential to maintain in Germany average living standards not exceeding the average of the standards of living in European countries. (European countries means all European countries excluding the United Kingdom and the Union of Soviet Socialist Republics.)

(c) to ensure in the manner determined by the Control Council the equitable distribution of essential commodities between the several zones so as to produce a balanced economy throughout Germany and reduce the need for imports.

(d) to control German industry and all economic and financial international transactions, including exports and imports, with the aim of preventing Germany from developing a war potential and achieving the other objectives named herein.

(e) to control all German public or private scientific bodies, research and experimental institutions, laboratories, et cetera, connected with economic activities.

16. In the imposition and maintenance of economic controls established by the Control Council, German administrative machinery shall be created and the German authorities shall be required to the fullest extent practicable to proclaim and assume administration of such controls. Thus it should be brought home to the German people that the responsibility for the administration of such controls and any breakdown in these controls will rest with themselves. Any German controls which may run counter to the objectives of occupation will be prohibited.

17. Measures shall be promptly taken:

(a) to effect essential repair of transport;

(b) to enlarge coal production;

(c) to maximize agricultural output; and

(d) to effect emergency repair of housing and essential utilities.

18. Appropriate steps shall be taken by the Control Council to exercise control and the power of disposition over German owned external assets not already under the control of the United Nations which have taken part in the war against Germany.

19. Payment of reparations should leave enough resources to enable the German people to subsist without external assistance. In working out the economic balance of Germany the necessary means must be provided to pay for imports approved by the Control Council in Germany. The proceeds of exports from current production and stocks shall be available in the first place for payment for such imports.

The above clause will not apply to the equipment and products referred to in paragraphs 4(a) and 4(b) of the Reparations Agreement.

IV

Reparations from Germany

In accordance with the Crimea decision that Germany be compelled to compensate to the greatest possible extent for the loss and suffering that she has caused to the United Nations and for which the German people cannot escape responsibility, the following agreement on reparations was reached:

1. Reparation claims of the U.S.S.R. shall be met by removal from the zone of Germany occupied by the U.S.S.R., and from appropriate German external assets.

2. The U.S.S.R. undertakes to settle the reparations claims of Poland from its own share of reparations.

3. The reparation claims of the United States, the United Kingdom and other countries entitled to reparations shall be met from the Western Zones and from appropriate German external assets.

4. In addition to the reparations to be taken by the U.S.S.R. from its own zone of occupation, the U.S.S.R. shall receive additionally from the Western Zones:

(a) 15 percent of such usable and complete industrial capital equipment, in the first place from the metallurgical, chemical and machine manufacturing industries, as is unnecessary for the German peace economy and should be removed from the Western Zones of Germany, in exchange for an equivalent value of food, coal, potash, zinc, timber, clay products, petroleum products, and such other commodities as may be agreed upon.

(b) 10 percent of such industrial capital equipment

as is unnecessary for the German peace economy and should be removed from the Western Zones to be transferred to the Soviet Government on reparations account without payment or exchange of any kind in return.

Removals of equipment as provided in (a) and (b) above shall be made simultaneously.

5. The amount of equipment to be removed from the Western Zones on account of reparations must be determined within six months from now at the latest.

6. Removals of industrial capital equipment shall begin as soon as possible and shall be completed within two years from the determination specified in paragraph 5. The delivery of products covered by 4(a) above shall begin as soon as possible and shall be made by the U.S.S.R. in agreed installments within five years of the date hereof. The determination of the amount and character of the industrial capital equipment unnecessary for the German peace economy and therefore available for reparations shall be made by the Control Council under policies fixed by the Allied Commission on Reparations, with the participation of France, subject to the final approval of the Zone Commander in the Zone from which the equipment is to be removed.

7. Prior to the fixing of the total amount of equipment subject to removal, advance deliveries

shall be made in respect of such equipment as will be determined to be eligible for delivery in accordance with the procedure set forth in the last sentence of paragraph 6.

8. The Soviet Government renounces all claims in respect of reparations to shares of German enterprises which are located in the Western Zones of occupation in Germany as well as to German foreign assets in all countries except those specified in paragraph 9 below.

9. The Governments of the United Kingdom and the United States of America renounce their claims in respect of reparations to shares of German enterprises which are located in the Eastern Zone of occupation in Germany, as well as to German foreign assets in Bulgaria, Finland, Hungary, Rumania and Eastern Austria.

10. The Soviet Government makes no claims to gold captured by the Allied troops in Germany.

V

Disposition of German Navy and Merchant Ships

The Conference agreed in principle upon arrangements for the use and disposal of the surrendered German Fleet and merchant ships. It was decided that the Three Governments would appoint experts to work out together detailed plans to give effect to the agreed principles. A further joint statement will be published simultaneously by the Three Governments in due course.

VI

City of Konigsberg and the Adjacent Area

The Conference examined a proposal by the Soviet Government that pending the final determination of territorial questions at the peace settlement, the section of the western frontier of the Union of Soviet Socialist Republics which is adjacent to the Baltic Sea should pass from a point on the eastern shore of the Bay of Danzig to the east, north of Braunsberg-Goldep, to the meeting point of the frontiers of Lithuania, the Polish Republic and East Prussia.

The Conference has agreed in principle to the proposal of the Soviet Government concerning the ultimate transfer to the Soviet Union of the City of Konigsberg and the area adjacent to it as described above subject to expert examination of the actual frontier.

The President of the United States and the British Prime Minister have declared that they will support the proposal of the Conference at the forthcoming peace settlement.

VII

War Criminals

The Three Governments have taken note of the discussions which have been proceeding in recent weeks in London between British, United States, Soviet and French representatives with a view to reaching agreement on the methods of trial of those major war criminals whose crimes under the Moscow Declaration of October, 1943, have no particular geographical localization. The Three Governments reaffirm their intention to bring those criminals to swift and sure justice. They hope that the negotiations in London will result in speedy agreement being reached for this purpose, and they regard it as a matter of great importance that the trial of those major criminals should begin at the earliest possible date. The first list of defendants will be published before September 1.

VIII

Austria

The Conference examined a proposal by the Soviet Government on the extension of the authority of the Austrian Provisional Government to all of Austria.

The Three Governments agreed that they were prepared to examine this question after the entry

of the British and American forces into the city
of Vienna.

IX

Poland

The Conference considered questions relating to
the Polish Provisional Government and the western
boundary of Poland. On the Polish Provisional
Government of National Unity they defined their
attitude in the following statement.

We have taken note with pleasure of the agreement
reached among representative Poles from Poland
and abroad which has made possible the formation,
in accordance with the decisions reached at
the Crimea Conference, of a Polish Provisional
Government of National Unity recognized by the
Three Powers. The establishment by the British
and United States Government of diplomatic
relations with the Polish Provisional Government
has resulted in the withdrawal of their recognition
from the former Polish Government in London,
which no longer exists.

The British and United States Government have
taken measures to protect the interest of the
Polish Provisional Government as the recognized
government of the Polish State in the Property
belonging to the Polish State located in their
territories and under their control, whatever the

form of this property may be. They have further taken measures to prevent alienation to third parties of such property. All proper facilities will be given to the Polish Provisional Government for the exercise of the ordinary legal remedies for the recovery of any property belonging to the Polish State which may have been wrongfully alienated.

The three Powers are anxious to assist the Polish Provisional Government in facilitating the return to Poland as soon as practicable of all Poles abroad who, wish to go, including members of the Polish Armed Forces and the Merchant Marine. They expect that those Poles who return home shall be accorded personal and property rights on the same basis as all Polish citizens.

The three Powers note that the Polish Provisional Government in accordance with the decisions of the Crimea Conference has agreed to the holding of free and unfettered elections as soon as possible on the basis of universal suffrage and secret ballot in which all democratic and anti-Nazi parties shall have the right to take part and to put forward candidates, and that representatives of the Allied press shall enjoy full freedom to report to the world upon developments in Poland before and during the elections.

The following agreement was reached:

On the western boundary of Poland; in conformity

with the agreement on Poland reached at the Crimea Conference the three Heads of Government have sought the opinion of the Polish Provisional Government of National Unity in regard to the accession of territory in the north and west which Poland should receive. The President of the National Council of Poland and members of the Polish Provisional Government of National Unity have been received at the Conference and have fully presented their views. The three Heads of Government reaffirm their opinion that the final limitation of the western frontier of Poland should await the peace settlement.

The three Heads of Government agree that, pending the final determination of Poland's western frontier, the former German territories east of a line running from the Baltic Sea immediately west of Swinemunde, and thence along the Oder River to the confluence of the western Neisse River and along the western Neisse to the Czechoslovak frontier, including that portion of East Prussia not placed under the administration of the Union of Soviet Socialist Republics in accordance with the understanding reached at this conference and including the area of the former free city of Danzig, shall be under the administration of the Polish State and for such purposes should not be considered as part of the Soviet zone of occupation in Germany.

X

Conclusion of Peace Treaties and Admission to the United Nations Organization

The Conference agreed upon the following statement of common policy for establishing as soon as possible the condition of lasting peace after victory in Europe.

The Three Governments consider it desirable that the present anomalous position of Italy, Bulgaria, Finland, Hungary and Rumania should be terminated by the conclusion of Peace Treaties. They trust that the other interested Allied Governments will share these views.

For their part the Three Governments have included the preparation of a Peace Treaty for Italy as the first among the immediate important tasks to be undertaken by the new Council of Foreign Ministers. Italy was the first of the Axis Powers to break with Germany, to whose defeat she has made a material contribution, and has now joined with the Allies in the struggle against Japan. Italy has freed herself from the Fascist regime and is making good progress towards the reestablishment of a democratic government and institutions. The conclusion of such a Peace Treaty with a recognized and democratic Italian

Government will make it possible for the Three Governments to fulfill their desire to support an application from Italy for membership of the United Nations.

The Three Governments have also charged the Council of Foreign Ministers with the task of preparing Peace Treaties for Bulgaria, Finland, Hungary and Rumania. The conclusion of Peace Treaties with recognized democratic Governments in these States will also enable the Three Governments to support applications from them for membership of the United Nations. The Three Governments agree to examine each separately in the near future, in the light of the conditions then prevailing, the establishment of diplomatic relations with Finland, Rumania, Bulgaria, and Hungary to the extent possible prior to the conclusion of peace treaties with those Countries.

The Three Governments have no doubt that in view of the changed conditions resulting from the termination of the war in Europe, representatives of the Allied press will enjoy full freedom to report to the world upon developments in Rumania, Bulgaria, Hungary and Finland.

As regards the admission of other states into the United Nations Organization, Article 4 of the Charter of the United Nations declared that:

1. Membership in the United Nations is open to all other peace-loving States who accept the obligations contained in the present Charter, and, in the judgment of the organization, are able and willing to carry out these obligations;

2. the admission of any such State to membership in the United Nations will be effected by a decision of the General Assembly upon the recommendation of the Security Council.

The Three Governments, so far as they are concerned, will support applications for membership from those States which have remained neutral during the war and which fulfill the qualifications set out above.

The Three Governments feel bound however to make it clear that they for their part would not favor any application for membership put forward by the present Spanish Government, which, having been founded with the support of the Axis Powers, does not, in view of its origins, its nature, its record and its close association with the aggressor States, possess the qualifications necessary to justify such membership.

XI

Territorial Trusteeships

The Conference examined a proposal by the Soviet Government concerning trusteeship territories as defined in the decision of the Crimea Conference and in the Charter of the United Nations Organization.

After an exchange of views on this question it was decided that the disposition of any former Italian territories was one to be decided in connection with the preparation of a peace treaty for Italy and that the question of Italian territory would be considered by the September Council of Ministers of Foreign Affairs.

XII

Revised Allied Control Commission Procedure in Rumania, Bulgaria, and Hungary

The Three Governments took note that the Soviet Representatives on the Allied Control Commissions in Rumania, Bulgaria and Hungary, have communicated to their United Kingdom and United States colleagues proposals for improving the work of the Control Commission, now that hostilities in Europe have ceased.

The Three Governments agreed that the revision of the procedures of the Allied Control Commissions in these countries would now be undertaken, taking into account the interests and responsibilities of the Three Governments which together presented the terms of armistice to the respective countries, and accepting as a basis the agreed proposals.

XIII

Orderly Transfers of German Populations

The Conference reached the following agreement on the removal of Germans from Poland, Czechoslovakia and Hungary:

The Three Governments, having considered the question in all its aspects; recognize that the transfer to Germany of German populations, or elements thereof, remaining in Poland, Czechoslovakia and Hungary, will have to be undertaken. They agree that any transfers that take place should be effected in an orderly and humane manner.

Since the influx of a large number of Germans into Germany would increase the burden already resting on the occupying authorities, they consider that the Allied Control Council in Germany should in the first instance examine the problem with special regard to the question of the equitable distribution of those Germans among the several zones of occupation. They are accordingly instructing their respective representatives on the Control Council to report to their Governments as soon as possible the extent to which such persons have already entered Germany from Poland, Czechoslovakia and Hungary, and to submit an estimate of the time and rate at which further transfers could be carried out, having regard to the present situation in Germany.

The Czechoslovak Government, The Polish Provisional Government and the Control Council in Hungary are at the same time being informed of the above, and are being requested meanwhile to suspend further expulsions pending the examination by the Governments concerned of the report from their representatives on the Control Council.

XIV

Military Talks

During the Conference there were meetings between the Chiefs of Staffs of the three Governments on military matters of common interest,

Approved:

J. V. Stalin

Harry S. Truman

C. R. *Attlee*

A NOTE ON SOURCES

The essential sources consulted for this book were the transcripts of the Potsdam conference. The Russian transcripts were published in *The Tehran, Yalta & Potsdam Conferences, Documents*, by Progress Publishers, Moscow, 1969; the British transcripts reside in the Foreign Office archives (Reference: CAB 99-38-8461); the American transcripts are published in *Foreign Relations of the United States, Diplomatic Papers, The Conference of Berlin*, 1945, two volumes, United States Government Printing Office, Washington, 1960. The American volumes include, in addition to transcripts of the plenary sessions of the conference, a good many additional papers and notes of the meetings of the foreign ministers and subcommittees at

Potsdam. The collection as a whole is referred to in the notes that follow as the "Potsdam Papers." While all these documents have been checked against each other for accuracy, I have in general relied on the Russian transcripts for the plenary sessions, since the Russian notes are the most detailed record of the conversations; the Russian transcripts do not disagree in any important respect with the British or American transcripts. For other conference sessions, there are no Russian notes, and I have relied on the American records; the American records do not disagree with the British in any important respect.

On January 21, 1972, the State Department declassified all its diplomatic documents for 1945, so that additional material related to Potsdam is now available in the National Archives. The 740 Decimal Files are the most pertinent to the Potsdam conference. In addition, several collections of papers are of interest, including the Henry L. Stimson papers at Yale, the William D. Leahy papers in the Library of Congress, and the James F. Byrnes papers at Clemson University. The Harry S. Truman Library in Independence, Missouri, contains the *Log of the President's Trip to the Berlin Conference* (referred to in the notes below as the "Log"). The Log was written and compiled by Lieutenant William M. Rigdon, U. S. N., and is kept among the papers of James H. Foskett at the Truman Library. The Library also contains the papers of Samuel I. Rosenman, Will Clayton, and, of course, Truman's own papers.

The acknowledgments at the front of the book mention a number of people who were kind enough to submit to questioning by the author or his assistant, Sarah Waters, and it is to those "conversations" that some of the notes below refer.

In addition to these primary sources, I should like to acknowledge several secondary works that I consulted most frequently as I wrote this book: *Atomic Diplomacy: Hiroshima and Potsdam*, by Gar Alperovitz, Vintage Books, New York, 1967; two books by Herbert Feis, who comes as close as anyone to writing the "official State Department history" of Potsdam — *The Atomic Bomb and the End of World War II*, Princeton University Press, Princeton, New Jersey, 1966, and *Between War and Peace, The Potsdam Conference*, Princeton University Press, Princeton, New Jersey, 1960; *Architects of Illusion, Men and Ideas in American Foreign Policy*, 1941-1949, by Lloyd C. Gardner, Quadrangle Books, Chicago, 1972; *The Cold War as History*, by Louis J. Halle, Harper and Row, New York, 1967; and *The Politics of War, The World and United States Foreign Policy*, 1943-1945, by Gabriel Kolko, Random House, New York, 1968.

For President Truman, I relied heavily on his own memoirs, *Years of Decision*, Doubleday and Company, Inc., Garden City, New York, 1955, and on the Log. For information on Stalin, I am particularly indebted to the definitive biography by Adam B. Ulam, *Stalin, The Man and His Era,* the Viking Press, New York, 1973; and, of course, to *Conversations with Stalin* by Milovan Djilas, Harcourt, Brace and World, Inc., New York, 1962. For Churchill I read his own memoirs, *The Second World War,* Houghton Mifflin Company, Boston, 1953; and quoted liberally from *The Diaries of Sir Alexander Cadogan,* O. M., 1938-1945, edited by David Dilks, Cassell, London, 1971; and *Churchill, Taken from the Diaries of Lord Moran, The Struggle for Survival, 1940-1965,* Houghton Mifflin Company, Boston, 1966.

CHAPTER 1

Truman's letter to his mother is quoted in Margaret Truman Daniels's *Harry S. Truman* (page 265), published by William Morrow and Company, New York, 1972. The details of Truman's boarding of the *Augusta* are taken from the logbook in the Truman Library. (References to the logbook, as well as to diaries, can be located under the appropriate date.) The personal notes on James F. Byrnes come from *Current Biography,* the annual edition of 1941. Acheson's comments on Byrnes are on page 136 of *Present at the Creation,* by Dean Acheson, W. W. Norton and Company, New York, 1969. No one has yet written a good, or even adequate, biography of Truman. Jules Abels has made an attempt at muckraking in *The Truman Scandals,* Henry Regnery Company, Chicago, 1956, and Jonathan Daniels has written a laudatory book in *The Man of Independence,* J. B. Lippincott Company, Philadelphia, 1950. The story of Truman's nomination for the Vice-Presidency appears in Daniels. Leahy's background is given in *Current Biography* for 1941. The notes on Vaughan come from Abels (the material on Albert Verley and Company comes from pages 43ff.), and from Daniels (the story of how Vaughan was chosen for the campaign appears on page 200; the "cherchez le Vaughan" story appears on page 267).

The background material on Charles Bohlen is taken from his own memoirs, *Witness to History* 1929-1969, W. W. Norton and Company, New York, 1973; and from *Current Biography* for 1948. The background material on Truman and Pendergast appears in Daniels, and the quote comparing Pendergast to Stalin is on page 23 in Daniels. That Truman played poker so often aboard the *Augusta* was confirmed in the author's interview with Charles Bohlen, as was the nature of the daily briefing sessions. The intensity of these briefing sessions was noted by Byrnes in his memoirs *Speaking Frankly,* published by Harper and Brothers, New York, in 1947, and by Leahy in *I Was There,* published in 1950. (Byrnes's other book, *All in One Lifetime,* was not as useful as *Speaking Frankly* for the purposes of this book on the Potsdam conference.)

Davies's memo to Byrnes appears in the Potsdam Papers (Document Number 221). I am indebted to Louis Halle, *The Cold War as History,* Harper and Row, Evanston, 1967, for inspiring some of the general thoughts on Americans' traditional view of foreign affairs, as well as to another excellent book, *Power and Impotence,* by Edmund Stillman and William Pfaff, Random House, New York, 1966, and to Walter LaFeber, *America, Russia, and the Cold War,* 1945-1971, John Wiley and Sons, New York, 1972. The notes on the United Nations owe a good deal to Gabriel Kolko. (For a critique of the revisionist historians, see the essays in Robert James Maddox, *The New Left and the Origins of the Cold War,* Princeton University Press, Princeton, 1973.) Bohlen's conversation with Leahy is recounted in *Witness to History.* The activities in Japan during this period are written about in fascinating detail by John Toland in *The Rising Sun,* volume 2, Random House, New York, 1970; and the events at Alamogordo are reported by Lansing Lamont in *Day of Trinity,* Atheneum, New York, 1965.

Truman's knowledge and intentions are best seen in the preconference material in the Documents in the Potsdam Papers and, especially, in the Briefing Book—consisting of five volumes in the National Archives under the single file number 740.00119 (Potsdam)/5-2446. The history of changing ideas about the treatment of postwar Germany is given succinctly in a memo in the Truman Papers

(Potsdam Papers, Document Number 300) from
G. M. Elsey to Truman.

One Briefing Book Paper (Document 224)
is especially interesting for the candid
acknowledgment that "eastern Europe is, in fact,
a Soviet sphere of influence" and further that
"spheres of influence do in fact exist." This paper
also documents Truman's disingenuousness about
a "full peace conference" by saying that "a proposal
has also been made for the creation of a Council
of Foreign Ministers of the Big Five which would
settle on an *ad hoc* basis particular problems
growing out of the war and which would replace
a formal peace conference." This intention about
the peace conference is recorded in several other
places, among them a telegram from Stettinius
to Grew (740.00119 E W/6-1945: Telegram), in
which it is said, "It seems clear that it would be
desirable to avoid the convocation of a full-fledged
peace conference. ... It is therefore suggested that
the problems concerned be dealt with on an *ad hoc*
basis by a council of Foreign Ministers...." Thus, too,
the Briefing Book Paper (Document 228), which
states that "the experience at Versailles following
the last war does not encourage the belief that a
full, formal peace conference is the best procedure."

That Stalin nonetheless thought there was to be a
full peace conference is documented in a telegram
of May 30, 1945, from Hopkins to Truman (Leahy

Papers), in which Hopkins says, "Stalin on two occasions has emphasized the importance of planning at once for the organization of the peace conference...."

CHAPTER 2

Churchill has been written about by many able biographers. I have relied, for general information, on a biography I edited, *Churchill, The Life Triumphant*, published by American Heritage Publishing Company, Inc., New York, 1965. The details of, and the quotations from, Churchill's stay at Hendaye are taken from Lord Moran's diary. The quotation from Kolko appears on page 490 of Kolko's *The Politics of War*. The report of Joseph Davies's visit with Churchill can be found in the Potsdam Papers (pages 63ff.). Churchill's memo to Truman is reprinted on pages 578 through 582, volume VI, of Churchill's memoirs. The information on preparations for the conference came principally from *The Inner Circle* by Joan Bright Astley, Hutchinson, London, 1971, and from a conversation the author had with Lady Astley. The remark about Amazonian Russian women was made by George Mallaby in *From My Level* (page 130), Hutchinson, London, 1965. The quotations from Sir Alexander Cadogan can be found, here as well as subsequently, under the appropriate dates in his diaries. Background information on Cadogan, Eden, and Attlee is taken from *Current Biography*.

Acheson's remarks on Attlee appear in Acheson's *Present at the Creation*. Eden's *The Reckoning* was published by Cassell and Company Ltd., London, in 1965. Attlee's memoirs, *As It Happened,* were published by William Heinemann Ltd., London, 1956. Churchill's "iron curtain" cable is in the Leahy Papers. The American understanding of Churchill's intentions and of the British desire to establish a western European bloc is given in a Briefing Book Paper (Document 224). For a caustic appraisal of Britain's declining powers, see another Briefing Book Paper (Document 223), in which it is said that "Mr. Churchill often offends the susceptibilities of the Dominions by forgetting that the British Empire has changed since Kipling's day."

CHAPTER 3

For Stalin, I have relied most heavily on Adam Ulam and, as noted in the text, on Milovan Djilas. I have quoted Djilas at some length, too, on the other figures in the Kremlin. I also consulted *Current Biography* for contemporary comments on Stalin's associates, and *Stalin & Co.* by Walter Duranty, William Sloane Associates, Inc., New York, 1949. Acheson's remark on Vishinsky appears on page 294 of his *Present at the Creation*. Walter Lippmann's great set of essays on this period of foreign policy is, of course, *The Cold War,* Harper and Brothers, New York, 1947. Hopkins's reports on his conversations with Stalin are under file number 740.00119 (Potsdam)/6-645

(Document 24). Harriman's report to Truman has the file number 711. 61/6-1145: Telegram (Document 30). Bohlen's notes of the Hopkins-Stalin conversation are part of the Hopkins reports. The cables between Stalin and Truman on Finland appear in *Correspondence Between the Chairman of the Council of Ministers of the U.S.S.R. and the President of the U.S.A. and the Prime Ministers of Great Britain During the Great Patriotic War of 1941-1945,* published in Moscow by the Foreign Languages Publishing House in 1957.

CHAPTER 4

Truman's early morning activities are given in the Log. The cables from Japan to the Japanese ambassador in Moscow (which begin on July 11 and continue throughout the conference) are all filed under 761. 94/7-2145: Telegram. That these cables were being passed up the line to Truman is evident from Stimson's diary entry for July 16 ("... I also received important paper *in re* Japanese maneuverings for peace....") and Truman's own remarks to Department of State historians in a conference on January 24, 1956, in which he said he was familiar with the Togo-Sato cable #893 before he was informed of it by Stalin. (See also Walter Millis, *The Forrestal Diaries,* pages 74 to 76.)

The meeting of the President with the Joint Chiefs of Staff is summarized in a memo by the secretary of the J.C.S., McFarland (Document 598, from the

J.C.S. Files). King's remark about not begging the Russians to join the Japanese war was made in a meeting on June 18 at the White House (J.C.S. Files, Document 608).

King's judgments on the Japanese war and the atomic bomb can be found in *Fleet Admiral King: A Naval Record*, by King and Walter Muir Whitehall, W. W. Norton and Company, Inc., New York, 1952. The newspaper accounts of the events of the Japanese war are taken from *Facts on File* for the appropriate days. The countdown on the bomb is reported by Lansing Lamont, as well as by General Groves himself in *Now It Can Be Told*, by General Leslie R. Groves, Harper and Brothers, New York, 1962. A detailed account of the development of the bomb is also given in *The New World, 1939-1946*, Volume I of A *History of the United States Atomic Energy Commission* by Richard G. Hewlett and Oscar E. Anderson, Jr., Pennsylvania State University Press, University Park, Pennsylvania, 1962. Leahy's assessment of the "political" nature of the decision to use the bomb is quoted in the transcripts of the combined chiefs of staff meeting (C. C. S. 193rd meeting, J. C. S. Files). The observations on Berlin's ruins come from *Memoirs of an Interpreter,* by A. H. Birse, Coward-McCann, Inc., New York, 1967. It was George Mallaby who noticed the *boîtes de nuit.* The London *Times* reported on Churchill's visit to Berlin in dispatches from Reuters as well as from the *Times's* special correspondent. Ismay's observations

The Deal: Churchill, Truman, and Stalin Remake the World

were published in *The Memoirs of General the Lord Ismay* by Heinemann, London, 1960. It was Field Marshal Sir Alan Brooke (Viscount Alanbrooke) who got the German decoration still in its box, as recorded in *Triumph in the West 1943-1946,* an account by Arthur Bryant based on Alanbrooke's diaries and published by Collins, London, 1959. Mallaby took the "trumpery medals."

CHAPTER 5

Stimson's activities are related in Hewlett and Anderson's *The New World,* and his sense of the conference is given in *On Active Service in Peace and War* by Henry L. Stimson and McGeorge Bundy, Octagon Books, New York, 1971. His conversation with Churchill appears in his diary for July 17. Stalin's visit was recorded in penciled notes by Bohlen (740.00119 Potsdam/7-1745) and is remarked on in both Bymes's and Bohlen's memoirs. That Byrnes, too, hoped to avoid having the Russians take part in the Japanese war is confirmed in the entry for July 16, as well as subsequent entries, in "W. B.'s book," Folder 602, Byrnes Papers; that Byrnes knew the Russians could not really be kept out of the war is documented in a note he wrote some days later in his own hand ("Forrestal thought it would take an army to keep Stalin out of the war and I agreed with him") in Folder 636 of the Byrnes Papers. The arrivals of Churchill and Truman for the plenary session were described by Mallaby. The conversations at the plenary session on this and subsequent days can be found under the appropriate dates in the Russian and American transcripts and may be compared to the British transcripts (CAB 99 38 8461, pages 89ff.).

Observations on the smoke in the room and similar anecdotal details come from the author's conversations with Robert Murphy and Charles Bohlen. Leahy's admiring remark about Truman is from his *I Was There*. The Englishman in the second row who described Stalin was Walter Monckton, whose autobiography containing the description was published by Weidenfeld and Nicolson, London, 1969. Churchill, who was proud of his little jest about his cigar, reported it to Moran, in whose diary the story appears.

Notes on Truman's dinner party that night come from the Log, and from the author's conversation with Eugene List.

The cables from Washington about the atomic bomb are from Department of the Army files (Documents 1303 and 1304).

CHAPTER 6

The Churchill-Truman meeting is reported by Churchill in his memoirs, Volume VI, pages 631 to 634, and by Moran in his diary entry for this day.

Churchill informed the British War Cabinet of his meeting with Truman in a note dated July 18.

CHAPTER 7

The Truman-Stalin meeting was recorded by Bohlen in notes that are printed in the Potsdam Papers, pages 86 to 87. That Stalin was prepared to stay with the unconditional surrender formula is attested to in the entry for July 18 in "W. B. 's book," Folder 602, Byrnes Papers.

CHAPTER 8

The Churchill-Stalin dinner is again reported by Churchill in his memoirs and by Moran in his diary.

CHAPTER 9

The foreign ministers' meetings for these days are recorded in the British Foreign Office Archives (CAB 99 38 8461, pages 93 to 98, 106 to 110, 122 to 128). I have relied, however, on the American notes — the Thompson Minutes, from the Truman Papers, for the meetings of July 18 and 19; and the Department of State Minutes, from the Truman Papers, for July 20. The meeting of the economic subcommittee on July 20 was reported in a memo by Murphy (Frankfurt USPolAd Files —500 Potsdam Conference). On the subject of trusteeships for Russia, Gromyko presented Byrnes on July 20 with an exchange of correspondence Gromyko had had with Stettinius (Document 734). Truman's position on Italy, to which Byrnes refers on July 20, is outlined in Document 1089. A United States Delegation Memorandum, from the Truman Papers, summarizing the July 19 ministers' meeting, contains an interesting hint of Truman's tactics in the pairing of issues. In the margin of this paper, which lists the topics discussed by the ministers, Truman wrote such notes as "agreed to" and "tomorrow." Next to two items — a Russian proposal on the Franco government, and the American position on the implementation of the Yalta Declaration on Liberated Europe — Truman wrote "postpone" and "postponed," quite probably with the thought of effecting a trade later on.

CHAPTER 10

Churchill's apparent inability to hear was noted by Sir William Hayter in a conversation with Sarah Waters. The quotations from the plenary sessions are taken, as noted above, from the Russian transcripts. They may be compared with the British transcripts (CAB 99 38 8461, pages 99 to 105, 111 to 122, 129 to 137), and with the American minutes in the Potsdam Papers. Churchill's warning about Communist fifth-column movements in Europe echoed a report on the subject given to the President by Grew on June 27 (811.00b/6-245,

Document 226). For a fuller understanding of the American position on Spain, see Documents 1175 through 1179. Two Briefing Book papers (Documents 464 and 473) give a concise summary of American preconference positions. Churchill's speech on Italy repeated to a great extent a rather pained aide-mémoire sent by the British embassy to the Department of State on July 16 (740.00119 P.W./7-1645, Documents 722 and 1088).

CHAPTER 11

Stimson's activities are reported in Hewlett and Anderson's *The New World* (page 388ff.) and in Stimson's *On Active Service in War and Peace*. The reports on the bomb are in Document 1305 from the Department of the Army Files. Stimson's remarks on his reading of the report are in his diary for July 21. At one point in the report, Groves wrote, "Dr. Kistiakowsky, the impulsive Russian, threw his arms around Dr. Oppenheimer and embraced him with shouts of glee." Groves reread his report and, after his reference to Kistiakowsky, inserted: "An American and Harvard professor for many years." The conversations at the plenary session are taken from the Russian transcripts and may be compared to the American notes in the Potsdam Papers and to the British version (CAB 99 38 8461, pages 144-153). Truman's letter home is quoted by Margaret Truman Daniels, pages 279 to 280.

CHAPTER 12

The plenary sessions, once again, are narrated from the Russian transcripts. The American notes are in the Potsdam Papers; the British record for July 22 through 24 can be found in CAB 99 38 8461, pages 163 to 174, 182 to 191, 200 to 209. In *I Was There*, page 408, Admiral Leahy maintains that it was during the discussion of Poland on July 22 that Churchill spoke of the rights of Catholics in Poland, and Stalin made his famous reply: "How many divisions has the Pope?" The remark, as fine as it is, appears to be apocryphal; the same comeback was attributed to Stalin at the Teheran conference; but neither Russian nor British nor American transcripts record the quip at either Teheran or Potsdam.

Churchill's special request for cold ham, the activities of the Russian and British guards just before the dinner party, and the awkward moment after the "second to none" toast were all reported in *The War and Colonel Warden,* by Gerald Pawle, based on the recollections of Commander C. R. Thompson, George G. Harrap and Company, Ltd., London, 1963. Pawle also gives the menu, seating arrangements, and program of dinner music for the evening. Truman asked Bohlen to write a memo preserving the toasts at the dinner party; Bohlen's memo to the President bears the file number 811. 001 Truman, H.S. /7-2445. The autograph session and Truman's "Ah, my boy..." remark appear in Birse. The foreign ministers' meeting with the Poles is documented in Annex 1 of the American transcripts of the foreign ministers' meeting for July 24. Truman's meeting with Bierut was documented in a memo by Harriman (740.00119 Potsdam/7-2445); Churchill's meeting with the Poles is in Churchill's *Triumph and Tragedy*, pages 661 to 667.

For a bitter recollection of the treatment accorded Poland at the end of the war, see *The Rape of Poland: Pattern of Soviet Aggression,* by Stanislaw Mikolajczyk, Greenwood Press, Westport, Connecticut, 1972.

CHAPTER 13

The principal texts on the treatment of Germany and reparations are the Briefing Book papers (Document 327 with appendix and supplement, Document 328, 330, 331, 356, 358, 363, 366, 367). Pauley's letter to Maisky appears as Appendix L to 740.00119 E.W./7-1445 (Document 376). The Bohlen Minutes of the Bymes-Molotov meeting can be found under the appropriate date in the Potsdam Papers.

CHAPTER 14

For Kennan's full remarks about Konigsberg and other territorial issues, see page 263 and following of his *Memoirs:* 1925-1950, Little, Brown and Company, Boston, 1967. Bohlen's vague comment on Truman's proposal to internationalize the waterways was made in conversation with the author. The background notes on Allen and Dunn come from *Current Biography.* The whispered message is documented in a letter worth looking at for curiosity's sake; it is in file No. 740.00119 (Potsdam) /8-1845, and is a letter from Allen to Minister George Wadsworth at Bierut. The figures on the location of oil resources in the world are in Document 181 from the Truman Papers. Eugene List's recollection of Churchill's manner of speaking was mentioned in a conversation with the author. The order to drop the bomb is reproduced in Groves's *Now It Can Be Told.* Other information about these several hours of Stimson's activities are reported in Hewlett and Anderson's *The New World.* Viscount Alanbrooke's words about Churchill can be found on page 478 of Bryant's *Triumph in the West.*

CHAPTER 15

Stimson's early morning activities are described in *The New World* by Hewlett and Anderson. The readiness of the bomb was reported to Stimson in a cable from Harrison (Document 1312). The rumors that circulated about the reasons Truman kept his advisers from so much in formation were recalled by Robert Murphy in a conversation with the author. The Byrnes-Molotov conversation can be found in the Potsdam Papers. That the British chiefs filched books from the Cecilienhof is recalled on page 647 of A *Sailor's Odyssey,* the autobiography of Admiral of the Fleet Viscount Cunningham of Hyndhope, Hutchinson, London, 1951. Mallaby reported on who fell asleep in *From My Level.* The official statements of the chiefs are to be found in the Potsdam Papers. Truman's account of the way he informed Stalin of the atomic bomb appears on page 416 of his first volume of memoirs; Byrnes's account is on page 263 of *Speaking Frankly;* Leahy's is on page 429 of his *I Was There;* Churchill's is on pages 669 to 670 of volume VI of his memoirs; Bohlen's is on page 237 of his *Witness to History.* Zhukov's version appears on pages 674 to 675 of *The Memoirs of Marshal Zhukov,* Delacorte Press, New York, 1971.

CHAPTER 16

Churchill's dream was reported in Moran's diary. Among the Truman Papers is a United States Delegation Working Paper prepared for the July 25 plenary session; four items were typed out on the paper, and written in (in Truman's hand) is the fifth item, "waterways. " Truman's full statement on the constitutional authority of the President is from the Truman Papers (Document 744); the typescript itself bears a marginal note in Bymes's handwriting: "For consideration & possible use before adjournment, — for the record." The British transcripts of the plenary session appear in CAB 99 38 8461, pages 210 to 213. The two closing paragraphs of the chapter are based on Robin Maugham's memory of the evening as he told it to Harold Nicolson.

CHAPTER 17

For the events on the American side, see Feis's *The Atomic Bomb and the End of World War II* (pages 103 to 108). For a revisionist interpretation, see Gar Alperovitz (pages 177 to 182). The Truman quote that his decision was not one to worry about appears on page 179 in Alperovitz. For the events in Japan, see John Toland's *The Rising Sun.* For the last-minute American considerations on use of the bomb, see also "The Decision to Use the Atomic Bomb" by Louis Morton, pages 512ff., in *Command Decisions,* edited by Kent Roberts Greenfield, Washington: Office of the Chief of Military History, Department of the Army, 1960; and for the military operations see *The Army Air Forces in World War II,* Volume V, *The Pacific: Matterhorn to Nagasaki,* University of Chicago Press, Chicago, 1953. For the events at Tinian, see pages 198 to 202 of William L. Laurence's *Dawn Over Zero: The Story of the Atomic Bomb,* and, of course, Groves's *Now It Can Be Told.* Henry Stimson reviewed the whole decision in "The Decision to Use the Atomic Bomb," in *Harper's*

Magazine, February 1947. See also "A Personal History of the Atomic Bomb," by Leo Szilard, University of Chicago *Roundtable*, September 25, 1949, pages 14 to 15. Truman's luncheon menu was recorded in the Log in the Truman Library. Churchill's conclusions about the usefulness of the bomb appear on page 646 of volume VI of his memoirs.

CHAPTER 18

Bevin's opening remark is quoted on page 403 of Ismay's memoirs. Birse's recollections are on pages 210 and 211 of his memoirs. Acheson is quoted from pages 270 and 271 of his memoirs. And Attlee's exchange with Molotov is on page 149 of Attlee's memoirs. The story about Attlee's dinner invitation to Waley and Jebb was recounted by Jebb in a conversation with Sarah Waters. Leahy's remarks come from his *I Was There*. The British transcripts of the plenary session can be found under CAB 99 38 8461, pages 224 to 228. That the spark left the negotiations with the arrival of Bevin and Attlee has been mentioned in several sets of memoirs and in the author's conversations with Murphy and Bohlen.

CHAPTER 19

The conversation on Sunday at noon was recorded by Charles Bohlen, whose Minutes are among the Truman Papers. The exchanges about Stalin's indisposition are in 740.00119 (Potsdam)/7-2945; and on page 257, Volume II of *Correspondence Between the Chairman of the Council of Ministers of the U.S.S.R....* Truman's hesitations about formally asking Russia to join the Japanese war are reported in Hewlett and Anderson's *The New World,* where it is also noted that Benjamin Cohen came up with the idea Truman ultimately used to answer Molotov's request. The Attlee-Truman meeting is recalled on page 402 of Truman's *Year of Decision.* The Monday conversation between Molotov and Byrnes is also taken from the Bohlen Minutes in the Truman Papers. Byrnes's veiled threat to leave the conference is reported on page 85 of his *Speaking Frankly.* The British transcript of the Tuesday plenary session can be found under CAB 99 38 8461, pages 241 to 253.

CHAPTER 20

The Szilard material resides in Box 1 of the Truman Papers, under a memo of September 6, 1945, from, Matthew Connelly. The observation about the bizarre movement of Stalin's left arm comes from *The Rise and Fall of Stalin* by Robert Payne (page 624). The background information on Benjamin Cohen comes from *Current Biography.* For an intriguing — and significant — detail of these final sessions of worrying over word changes, see Walter Brown's diary for August 1, and his memo of the same date to Byrnes and Truman (740.00119

Potsdam/8-145). Truman had said that the most important task before him at Potsdam was to ensure Russian entry into the Japanese war. When it came to drafting the communiqué, however, the Americans did not want to mention the Japanese war at all. The American draft of the communiqué said that Russian, British, and American military men had conferred on military matters "of common interest affecting Europe." The Russians wanted to delete "affecting Europe" in order to imply that the Japanese war had also been discussed. After a day's intermission, the Russians wanted to return to the phrasing of this one paragraph that limited military discussions to Europe — evidently with the thought of writing in an entirely separate paragraph addressed to the Japanese war. The question was passed by the drafting committee back up to the Big Three, and, in the final plenary session, Stalin said he did not insist that the reference be restricted to Europe — that is to say, he wanted the communique to imply that the talks *did* go beyond Europe, but he had dropped the thought of a separate paragraph on the Japanese war. Truman consented. Thus, again, though Truman maintained he had wanted to be certain to clinch Russian participation in the Japanese war — and that that was his primary goal at Potsdam — it was Stalin who had to ensure that the communiqué did not explicitly say that military talks had been restricted to European matters.

CHAPTER 21

The Parsons log is printed on page 318 of Groves's *Now It Can Be Told.* The events on board the *Augusta* are recorded in the Log in the Truman Library. See also "W.B.'s book" in Folder 602 of the Byrnes Papers. Truman's cheerful mood was reported in the *U.S.S. Augusta Evening Press* for August 6, which is in the Rosenman Papers under "Material Relating to Potsdam." The last days in the Japanese Cabinet are reported in Toland's *The Rising Sun* and in *Command Decisions.* The Nishina episode and the Sato mission are in *The Rising Sun* by Toland.

CHAPTER 22

The Origins of the Cold War, 1941-1947, A *Historical Problem with Interpretations and Documents,* edited by Walter LaFeber, John Wiley and Sons, Inc., New York, 1971, provides the texts for Truman's first speech, the Navy Day speech, Churchill's "iron curtain" speech, Stalin's interview, Molotov's Paris speech, and Truman's address to the joint session of Congress. The observations on the London foreign ministers' conference come from Andre Fontaine, *History of the Cold War,* Vintage Books, New York, 1970 (pages 297 to 299), and, as noted in the text, from Stimson's diaries. Bevin's intentions were reported in Cadogan's diaries. Louis Halle's remarks are taken from his

The Cold War as History. Kennan's cable is given in his *Memoirs 1925-1950.* Russian activities in Iran are mentioned by Fontaine (pages 283 to 285). The Baruch plan is given a lucid treatment by Lloyd Gardner in *Architects of Illusion* (pages 174 to 176 and 191 to 195). The collapse of Great Britain in Greece is treated by Gardner (pages 217ff.) and Fontaine (page 292), and the Truman Doctrine is spoken of by Gardner (pages 221ff.) and Fontaine (page 293). The "S.O.B." remark is recorded in "W.B.'s book," under August 3, 1945, Byrnes Papers, Folder 602.

BIBLIOGRAPHY

POTSDAM CONFERENCE TRANSCRIPTS

BRITISH FOREIGN OFFICE ARCHIVES, Reference CAB 99-38-8461.

The Tehran, Yalta & Potsdam Conferences, Documents, Moscow, 1969. u.s. DEPARTMENT OF STATE, *Foreign Relations of the United States, Diplomatic Papers, The Conference of Berlin, 1945,* Washington, D. C., 1960.

PUBLISHED GOVERNMENT SOURCES

Correspondence Between the Chairman of the

Council of Ministers of the U.S.S.R. and the President of the U.S.A. and the Prime Ministers of Great Britain During the Great Patriotic War of 1941-1945, Moscow, 1957.

EHRMAN, J., *GRAND Strategy, October 1944-August* 1945, Volume VI of *History of the Second World War,* United Kingdom Series, London, 1956.

GREENFIELD, KENT ROBERTS, ed., *Command Decisions,* U. S. Department of the Army, Washington, D. C., 1960.

TRUMAN, HARRY S., *Public Papers of the Presidents of the United States, April 12 to December* 31, 1945, Washington, D. C., 1961.

U. S. DEPARTMENT OF STATE, *Foreign Relations of the United States, Diplomatic Papers, The Conferences at Malta and Yalta, 1945,* Washington, D. C., 1955.

–––, *Postwar Foreign Policy Preparation:* 1939-45, Washington, D. C., 1950.

UNITED STATES STRATEGIC BOMBING SURVEY, *Japan's Struggle to End the War,* Washington, D. C., July 1, 1946.

PUBLISHED SOURCES

ABELS, JULES, *The Truman Scandals,* Chicago, 1956.

ACHESON, DEAN, *Power and Diplomacy*, Cambridge, Mass., 1958.

–––, *Present at the Creation: My Years in the State Department*, New York, 1969.

ALPEROVITZ, GAR, *Atomic Diplomacy: Hiroshima and Potsdam*, New York, 1967.

AMERICAN HERITAGE MAGAZINE and UNITED PRESS INTERNATIONAL, *Churchill, The Life Triumphant*, New York, 1965.

ANDERSON, PATRICK, *The President's Men*, Garden City, 1968.

ASTLEY, JOAN BRIGHT, *The Inner Circle*, London, 1971.

ATTLEE, CLEMENT, *As It Happened*, London, 1956.

BIRKENHEAD, LORD, *Walter Monckton: The Life of Viscount Monckton of Brenchley*, London, 1969.

BIRSE, A. H., *Memoirs of an Interpreter*, New York, 1967.

BLACKETT, P. M. S., *Fear, War, and the Bomb: Military and Political Consequences of Atomic Energy*, New York, 1948, 1949.

BOHLEN, CHARLES E., *Witness to History*, 1929-1969, New York, 1973.

BROAD, LEWIS, *Winston Churchill,* Volume II: *The Years of Achievement,* New York, 1963.

BRYANT, ARTHUR, *Triumph in the West: A History of the War Years Based on the Diaries of Field-Marshall Lord Alanbrooke, Chief of the Imperial General Staff,* Garden City and London, 1959.

BUTOW, ROBERT J., *Japan's Decision to Surrender,* Stanford, 1954.

BYRNES, JAMES F., *All in One Lifetime,* New York, 1958.

---, *Speaking Frankly,* New York and London, 1947.

CHURCHILL, SIR WINSTON S., *The Second World War,* Volume VI: *Triumph and Tragedy,* Boston, 1953.

CLAY, LUCIUS D., *Decision in Germany,* New York and London, 1950.

COCHRAN, BERT, *Harry Truman and the Crisis Presidency,* New York, 1973.

COMPTON, ARTHUR HOLLY, *Atomic Quest: A Personal Narrative,* New York, 1956.

CRAVEN, WESLEY FRANK, and CATE, JAMES LEA, eds., *The Army Air Forces in World War II,* Volume V: *The Pacific: Matterhorn to Nagasaki, June 1944 to August 194s,* Chicago, 1953.

CUNNINGHAM OF HYNDHOPE, Admiral of the Fleet Viscount, A *Sailor's Odyssey,* London, 1951.

Current Biography: Who's News and Why, Volumes II-XI, New York, 1941-1950.

DANIELS, JONATHAN, *The Man of Independence,* Philadelphia, 1950.

DAVIS, NUEL PHARR, *Lawrence and Oppenheimer,* New York, 1968.

DEANE, JOHN R., *The Strange Alliance: The Story of Our Efforts at Wartime Co-operation with Russia,* New York, 1947.

DEUTSCHER, ISAAC, *Stalin: A Political Biography,* New York and London, 1949.

DILKS, DAVID, ed., *The Diaries of Sir Alexander Cadogan, O. M., 1938-1945, London, 1971.*

DJILAS, MILOVAN, Conversations with Stalin, New York, 1962.

DURANTY, WALTER, Stalin & Co., New York, 1949.

EDEN, ANTHONY, Earl of Avon, *The Eden Memoirs: Facing the Dictators, 1923-1938,* Boston, 1962, and *The Reckoning,* London, 1965.

Facts on File, Person's Index of World Events, Volumes I-V, New York, 1941-1945.

FEIS, HERBERT, *The Atomic Bomb and the End of World War II,* Princeton, 1966.

–––, *Between War and Peace: The Potsdam Conference,* Princeton, 1960.

–––, *Churchill, Roosevelt, Stalin: The War They Waged and the Peace They Sought,* Princeton, 1957.

–––, *From Trust to Terror: The Onset of the Cold War,* 1945-1950, New York, 1970.

–––, *Japan Subdued: The Atomic Bomb and the End of the War in the Pacific,* Princeton, 1961.

FISCHER, LOUIS, *The Road to Yalta: Soviet Foreign Relations 1941-1945, New York, 1972.*

FLEMING, DENNA FRANK, *The Cold War and Its Origins, 1917-1960, 2 volumes, Garden City, 1961.*

FONTAINE, ANDRE, *History of the Cold War, 2 volumes, New York, 1970.*

GADDIS, JOHN LEWIS, *The United States and the Origins of the Cold War,* 1941-1947, New York, 1972.

GARDNER, LLOYD C., *Architects of Illusion, Men and Ideas in American Foreign Policy, 1941-1949,* Chicago, 1972.

GREW, JOSEPH C., *Turbulent Era, A Diplomatic*

Record of Forty Years, 1904-1945, 2 volumes, Boston, 1952.

GRODZINS, MORTON, and RABINOWITCH, EUGENE, eds., *The Atomic Age: Scientists in National and World Affairs,* New York, 1963.

GROUEFF, STEPHANE, *Manhattan Project: The Untold Story of the Making of the Atomic Bomb,* Boston, 1967.

GROVES, LESLIE R., *Now It Can Be Told: The Story of the Manhattan Project,* New York, 1962.

HALLE, LOUIS J., *The Cold War as History,* New York, 1967.

HARRIMAN, W. AVERELL, *Peace with Russia?,* New York, 1959.

HEWLETT, RICHARD G., and ANDERSON, OSCAR E., JR., *The New World,* 1939-1946, Volume I of A *History of the United States Atomic Energy Commission,* University Park, Pa., 1962.

HULL, CORDELL, *Memoirs,* 2 volumes, New York, 1948.

HYDE, H. MONTGOMERY, *Stalin: The History of a Dictator,* New York, 1971.

ISMAY, HASTINGS, *The Memoirs of General the Lord Ismay,* London, 1960.

JONES, F. C., BORTON, HUGH, and PEARN, B. R., *Survey of International Affairs,* 1939-1946: *The Far East, 1942-1946,* London, 1955.

JUNGK, ROBERT, *Brighter Than a Thousand Suns: A Personal History of the Atomic Scientists,* New York, 1958.

KENNAN, GEORGE F., *American Diplomacy,* 1900-1950, Chicago, 1951.

–––, *Memoirs:* 1925-1950, Boston, 1967.

–––, *Russia and the West Under Lenin and Stalin,* Boston, 1960, 1961.

KING, ERNEST J., and WHITEHILL, WALTER MUIR, *Fleet Admiral King: A Naval Record,* New York, 1952.

KOLKO, GABRIEL, *The Politics of War: The World and United States Foreign Policy, 1943-1945,* New York, 1968.

LAFEBER, WALTER, *America, Russia, and the Cold War,* 1945-1971, New York, 1972.

–––, ed., *The Origins of the Cold War, 1941-1947, A Historical Problem with Interpretations and Documents,* New York, 1971.

LAMONT, LANSING, *Day of Trinity,* New York, 1965.

LANE, ARTHUR B., *I Saw Poland Betrayed,*

Indianapolis, 1948.

LAURENCE, WILLIAM L., *Dawn Over Zero: The Story of the Atomic Bomb*, New York, 1960.

LEAHY, WILLIAM D., *I Was There: The Personal Story of the Chief of Staff to Presidents Roosevelt and Truman, Based on his Notes and Diaries Made at the Time*, New York, 1950.

LIPPMANN, WALTER, *The Cold War: A Study in U. S. Foreign Policy*, New York, 1947.

MADDOX, ROBERT JAMES, *The New Left and the Origins of the Cold War*, Princeton, 1973.

MALLABY, GEORGE, *From My Level*, London, 1965.

MCNEIL, WILLIAM H., *Survey of International Affairs, 1939-1946: America, Britain and Russia: Their Co-operation and Conflict, 1941-1946*, London, 1953.

MIKOLAJCZYK, STANISLAW, *The Rape of Poland: Pattern of Soviet Aggression*, Westport, Conn., 1972.

MILLIS, WALTER, ed., *The Forrestal Diaries*, New York, 1951.

MONTGOMERY OF ALAMEIN, Field Marshal the Viscount, *The Memoirs of Field-Marshal the Viscount Montgomery of Alamein, K. G.*, Cleveland and New York, 1958.

MORAN, LORD, *Churchill: Taken from the Diaries of Lord Moran, The Struggle for Survival, 1940-1965,* Boston, 1966.

MORISON, ELTING E., *Turmoil and Tradition: A Study of the Life and Times of Henry L. Stimson,* Boston, 1960.

MURPHY, ROBERT D., *Diplomat Among Warriors,* New York, 1964.

PAWLE, GERALD, *The War and Colonel Warden,* London, 1963.

PAYNE, ROBERT, *The Rise and Fall of Stalin,* New York, 1965.

ROSE, LISLE A., *Dubious Victory: The United States and the End of World War II,* Kent, Ohio, 1973.

ROZEK, EDWARD J., *Allied Wartime Diplomacy: A Pattern in Poland,* New York and London, 1958.

RUSSELL, RUTH B., A *History of the United Nations Charter, The Role of the United States, 1940-1945,* Washington, D. C., 1958.

RYAN, CORNELIUS, *The Last Battle,* New York, 1966.

SMITH, ALICE KIMBALL, "Behind the Decision to Use the Atomic Bomb: Chicago 1944-45," *Bulletin of the Atomic Scientists* (October, 1958).

SMITH, W. BEDELL, *My Three Years in Moscow*, Philadelphia and New York, 1949, 1950.

SMYTH, HENRY DEWOLF, *Atomic Energy for Military Purposes: The Official Report on the Development of the Atomic Bomb under the Auspices of the United States Government, 1940-1945*, Princeton, 1945.

STILLMAN, EDMUND, and PFAFF, WILLIAM, *The New Politics: America and the End of the Postwar World*, New York and London, 1961.

–––, *Power and Impotence*, New York, 1966.

STIMSON, HENRY L., "The Decision to Use the Atomic Bomb," *Harper's Magazine* (February, 1947).

–––, and BUNDY, MCGEORGE, *On Active Service in Peace and War*, New York, 1947, 1948, 1971.

STRANG, WILLIAM, LORD STRANG, *Home and Abroad*, London, 1956.

SZILARD, LEO, "A Personal History of the Atomic Bomb," *University of Chicago Roundtable* (September 25, 1949).

TOLAND, JOHN, *The Rising Sun: The Decline and Fall of the Japanese Empire, 1936-1945*, 2 volumes, New York, 1970.

TRUMAN, HARRY S., *Memoirs, Volume II: Year of Decisions*, Garden City, 1955.

———, Mr. *Citizen,* New York, 1960.

———, *Truman Speaks,* New York, 1960.

TRUMAN, MARGARET, *Harry S. Truman,* New York, 1972.

ULAM, ADAM B., *Stalin, The Man and His Era,* New York, 1973.

ZHUKOV, G. K., *The Memoirs of Marshal Zhukov,* New York, 1971.

UNPUBLISHED SOURCES

BYRNES, JAMES F., Papers, Clemson University, Clemson, South Carolina.

CLAYTON, WILLIAM L., Papers, Harry S. Truman Library, Independence, Missouri.

GREW, JOSEPH C., Papers, Houghton Library, Harvard University, Cambridge, Massachusetts.

LEAHY, WILLIAM D., Diary, 1945, Library of Congress, Washington, D. C.

RIGDON, LT. WILLIAM M., U. S. N., Log of the President's Trip to the Berlin Conference, Harry S. Truman Library, Independence, Missouri.

ROSENMAN, SAMUEL I., Papers, Harry S. Truman Library, Independence, Missouri.

STIMSON, HENRY L., Diary, Yale University Library, New Haven, Connecticut.

TRUMAN, HARRY S., Papers, Harry S. Truman Library, Independence, Missouri.

U.S. DEPARTMENT OF STATE, Briefing Book, 5 volumes, file number 740.00119 (Potsdam)/5-2446, National Archives, Washington, D. C.

U.S. DEPARTMENT OF STATE, Diplomatic Documents for 1945 (740 Decimal Files in particular), National Archives, Washington, D. C.

Printed in Great Britain
by Amazon